未来
全球金融治理

[新加坡] 尚达曼 朱民 等著
朱隽 等译

中信出版集团｜北京

图书在版编目（CIP）数据

未来全球金融治理 /（新加坡）尚达曼等著；朱隽
等译 . -- 北京：中信出版社，2020.11
ISBN 978-7-5217-1941-3

Ⅰ.①未… Ⅱ.①尚…②朱… Ⅲ.①国际金融管理
—研究 Ⅳ.① F831.2

中国版本图书馆 CIP 数据核字 (2020) 第 096542 号

未来全球金融治理

著　　者：［新加坡］尚达曼　朱民　等
译　　者：朱隽　等
出版发行：中信出版集团股份有限公司
　　　　　（北京市朝阳区惠新东街甲 4 号富盛大厦 2 座　邮编　100029）
承 印 者：北京楠萍印刷有限公司

开　　本：880mm×1230mm　1/32　　印　　张：10.75　　字　　数：197 千字
版　　次：2020 年 11 月第 1 版　　　　印　　次：2020 年 11 月第 1 次印刷
书　　号：ISBN 978-7-5217-1941-3
定　　价：59.00 元

版权所有·侵权必究
如有印刷、装订问题，本公司负责调换。
服务热线：400-600-8099
投稿邮箱：author@citicpub.com

目 录

中文版序一　尚达曼 / *003*

中文版序二　朱　民 / *007*

前　言　为什么需要改革 / *015*

核心观点 / *019*

第一章　概　览 / 001

第二章　加大跨系统合作：实现更强有力的全球
　　　　发展效应 / 031

第三章　强化增强全球金融韧性的改革：确保
　　　　日益关联的全球金融市场服务全球 / 065

第四章　提升 G20 和国际金融机构的领导作用：
　　　　维护系统整体有效运行 / 091

附　录 / 109

缩略语 / 127

关于 G20 "全球金融治理名人小组" / 131

G20 全球金融治理名人小组职责 / 135

鸣　谢 / 137

未来全球金融治理

CONTENTS

PREFACE / 145

FOREWORD WHY THE NEED FOR REFORM? / 149
ACKNOWLEDGEMENTS / 155
KEY THRUSTS / 157
OVERVIEW / 161

01 ACHIEVING GREATER DEVELOPMENT IMPACT: COLLABORATING ACROSS THE SYSTEM / 193

02 SECURING THE BENEFITS OF INTERCONNECTED FINANCIAL MARKETS: REFORMS FOR GLOBAL FINANCIAL RESILIENCE / 231

03 THE G20 AND THE IFIs: MAKING THE SYSTEM WORK AS A SYSTEM / 259

ANNEXES / 279

ABBREVIATIONS / 301

ABOUT THE G20 EMINENT PERSONS GROUP ON GLOBAL FINANCIAL GOVERNANCE / 305

TERMS OF REFERENCE G20 EMINENT PERSONS GROUP ON GLOBAL FINANCIAL GOVERNANCE / 309

LIST OF CONTRIBUTIONS / 311

中文版序一

全球发展和经济增长面临的挑战从未像现在这样艰巨、复杂而紧迫。毫不夸张地说，一些人口众多的地区正面临着发生经济和社会灾难的风险。

二十国集团（G20）全球金融治理名人小组（EPG，以下简称名人小组）于2018年10月就全球金融架构和国际金融机构体系的改革提出了政策建议。2020年，全球发生了新冠肺炎疫情大流行，疫情加剧了全球发展中已有的问题，一些发展中国家近几十年来所取得的成就面临被疫情吞噬的风险，并使得未来十年实现包容性和可持续增长的挑战成倍增加。

我们需要更加强有力的全球行动以重启面向未来的增长。但是，我们的财政资源因为新冠疫情而变得更加紧张，债务水平比十年前要高得多。

因此，名人小组的建议比以往任何时候都更加重要。在落实其中一些建议方面，名人小组已经取得了可喜的进展，尤其是建立国家发展平台框架的建议已获得G20财长和中央银行行长的支持。这个国家发展平台可以将各种发展伙伴聚集在一起，并在动员私人投资的过程中努力保持各方的一致性。多边投资担保机构（MIGA）也已着手建立伙伴关系，向世界银行集团以外的多边发展机构提供政治风险保险和其他产品，从而分散并降低风险。为了应对当前的新冠疫情，国际货币基金组织（IMF）还引入了短期流动性额度，为各国受到全球冲击时提供流动性支持。

我们必须保持这一势头。我们必须利用当前危机的紧迫性，在解决我们今天面临的直接威胁的同时，着手解决国际金融体系中长期存在的遗留问题。我们推迟解决这些问题的时间已经太久，拖延的时间越长，挑战就越大，最终的成本就越高，而失败的风险也会越大。

名人小组这份报告的核心是呼吁建立新的国际合作秩序。但是，在新冠疫情下，国际治理与合作被进一步削弱了。我们看到了更多的保护主义、"本国优先"措施以及不断升级的地缘政治紧张局势。然而，疫情也格外凸显了各国在国际合作方面的共同利益，包括确保关键医疗产品和服务的广泛和公平分配，刺激全球增长以及加快实施可持续发展的实践。

新冠肺炎不会是世界经历的最后一场危机。我们必须增强发展中国家应对危机的韧性。我们可以并且必须改善国际金融体系，以应对资本流动的波动和跨境溢出效应。我们必须加强国际货币基金组织的作用，将全球金融安全网的各个层次结合起来，并加强全球金融监督，以便提早发现脆弱点。

我要感谢朱民博士和中国人民银行的同事将这份报告翻译成中文，这是一项意义重大的工作。

名人小组对有关问题进行了广泛的咨询和深入的讨论，并提出了我们认为在未来几年内切实可行的建议。建议的落实需要各国共同下定决心,并达成一个简单却强有力的共识,即我们在全球增长、稳定和维护全球公共资源方面具有共同利益,并且希望造福于所有的国家。

新加坡内阁资政、二十国集团全球金融治理名人小组主席
尚达曼
2020 年 10 月

中文版序二

2017年4月，鉴于全球经济金融治理改革的重要性和各方认知的不同，当年的G20主席国德国倡议建立一个G20全球金融治理名人小组，邀请全球知名经济和金融专家就全球金融治理方面的问题开展研究、提出独立的政策建议，并在2018年秋季的国际货币基金组织与世界银行年会期间提交最终政策报告。随后，在华盛顿举办的G20财长和央行行长会议通过了德国的倡议，全球金融治理名人小组成立。名人小组由时任新加坡副总理尚达曼担任主席，包括16位来自不同国家的专家，我也荣幸地受邀参加。之后的18个月内，名人小组展开了一系列高强度的调研、分析、辩论和起草活动。名人小组在伦敦、华盛顿、法兰克福、旧金山、巴黎和达沃斯等地先后召开了八次全体会议和数次研讨会。在非会议期间，成员之间通过大量的邮件往来进行沟通，对议题进行了深入和充分的讨论。名人小组还与一些国家的政府机构、国际金融机构、社会团体、智库、学术界和慈善界的思想领袖以及私人部门专家进行了广泛的交流。

名人小组的任务是思考开放、竞争的国际秩序将何去何从。过去70多年中，开放、竞争的国际秩序为前所未有的全球和平和增长奠定了基础。然而，当前的国际形势已经发生了根本性的变化。一方面，大多数发达国家内部的经济、社会分化和政治分歧进一步扩大，长久以来的社会契约关系遭到损害，削弱了公众对国际合作和开放世界秩序的支持。另一方面，全球走向多极化的进程不可逆转，国际经济决策中的参与者越来越多，贸易、资本和思想的自由流动把全世界紧密地联系在一起。

名人小组成员充分地认识到任务的重要性和紧迫性。但一开始，我们在报告的主旨上就遇到意见不统一的问题。我从中国改革开放40年的实践和在国际货币基金组织工作期间对全球观察出发，提出开放、多极、合作和共享的新全球化是人类共同的未来。经过激烈、认真和理性的辩论，名人小组提出了"世界已经多极化，决策更加去中心化，联系却更加紧密了。面对这些不可逆转的变化，我们的核心挑战是创造一个合作性的国际秩序"这一基本观点，并得出"开放的世界秩序对每个国家的未来都至关重要，然而作为其支撑的国际治理和合作体系正摇摇欲坠。如果放任不管，我们很可能会陷入一个分割的世界，如果各国和各地区的政策不是相互促进，而是相互冲突，则最终每个国家都是输家"这一论断，改革迫在眉睫。名人小组聚焦于系统性改革，围绕发展、金融和全球治理三大支柱提出了22条既有宏观视野，又有微观意义的建议。

名人小组的报告和提出的建议得到了G20的认可，继德国任G20主席国的阿根廷和日本都对名人小组的报告和建议予以肯定和支持，并把报告的主要思想写入当年的联合公报，强调要予以贯彻落实。名人小组的报告也在国际金融机构、国际监管机构、G20成员国、社会团体、智库、学术界引起了认真的思考和讨论，考虑如何真正贯彻与落实名人小组提出的建议。市场和一些商业机构也就名人小组提出的建议进行了具体落地的尝试。在华盛顿的"全球发展研究中心"还拉起了一个名为"名人小组的朋友"的圈子，有各方的学者、智库、社会团体参加。每年利用国际货币基金组织年会和世界银行年会期间在华盛顿举办有关名人小组建议的研讨，平时就在网上交流。当然，落实名人小组的各项建议，还需要国际社会的长时间、持续和共同的努力。

名人小组的成员来自不同的国家和行业，有不同的学术背景和国际经验，但都有丰富的经济金融理论的基础和国际经济金融治理实践的经验，也大都在国际经济金融组织或政府中担任过要职。我和名人小组的成员大都是多年相熟的朋友或同事，其中还有我的学术前辈。我们都曾在不同的场景下，无论是学术讨论或是国际政策制定，还是在监管政策研讨或金融市场分析的过程中，有过交流、辩论、合作甚至分歧。这次深度合作给了我一次极其深刻和鲜活的学习机会。

斯特恩勋爵是伦敦政治经济学院教授，曾任英国首相的气候变化特别顾问和世界银行首席经济学家。他是国际著名的公共政策专家、气候变化专家，多年关注可持续发展问题。他的《发展中国家公共财政政策》(*The Theory of Taxation for Developing Countries*)是我20世纪90年代初在世界银行工作时做国别财政研究的案头书。进入21世纪，他的气候变化对策以及气候变化和科技创新下的增长模式相关观点也是我特别关注的。他是一位关注世界经济金融治理改革的大家，当年我得以进入国际货币基金组织任总裁特别顾问也有他的推动作用。我们相识多年，每次国际货币基金组织年会和达沃斯会议期间我们都相约交流对世界经济金融大趋势的观察，我每每受益于他对世界经济金融表象底下的根本动因的洞察力。恩戈齐·奥孔乔-伊韦拉是全球疫苗免疫联盟（GAVI）董事会主席，曾任尼日利亚财长兼经济统筹部长和世界银行常务副行长。她对非洲一往情深，对帮助非洲发展坚持不懈。这次的专题合作中，他们对可持续发展的坚持，对开放的国际经济金融秩序的热忱令我非常感动。我们合作推动形成了关于开放、合作和发展的全球秩序的基本观点。

约翰·B.泰勒教授是著名的经济学家，他是斯坦福大学的经济学教授、斯坦福大学胡佛研究所高级经济学研究员，曾任美国财政部副部长。他的理论功底深厚，政策实践丰富，对货币政策从理论到实践都有权威的观点。以他名字命名的泰勒公式是宏观经济学的必学内容，我在普林斯顿大学读书时就花了很长时间琢磨泰勒公式。但是由于经历和背景不一，我们的观点也常常不一样。在资本开放和对全球资本流动管理方面，他有完整的理论体系，而我有新兴经济体的实践和国际货币基金组织的全球实践的背景，我们常常各不相让。此外，我还邀请了其他几位专家参加我们的讨论。雅各布·弗兰克是摩根大通国际董事长，曾任以色列央行行长和国际货币基金组织首席经济学家和研究部主任。他在国际金融方面集理论、政策和市场实践于一身，他的从市场看政策的角度，既独特又丰富。他也是我多年的好朋友，对我总是爱护有加，每有见解，总愿意先和我分享。让－克劳德·特里谢是三边委员会欧元区集团主席，曾任欧洲央行行长和法国央行行长，是一位我特别尊重的名副其实的老前辈。他亲历了欧元危机，对资本流动的因果、规模和速度都有极其深切的体会。他的欧洲视角具有全球意义。安德烈斯·贝拉斯科是伦敦政治经济学院公共政策系主任，曾任智利财长，既聪明又机智，他的拉美经验是全球资本流动和资本流动管理的经典案例。他们既是权威也都是很好的倾听者，我们做了很认真和严肃的辩论，我从与他们的讨论中也学到了很多东西，对货币理论、政策和市场实践的整体架构有了更深刻的理解。我们最终达成了一致的观点。

尚达曼时任新加坡副总理兼财政部长，曾经担任新加坡货币监管机构的主席，又刚卸任国际货币基金组织的国际货币与金融委员会（IMFC）主席，对财政政策、货币政策和监管政策，以及全球经济金融治理都有深厚的理论功底和丰富的实践经验。他是优秀的领导者，视野开阔，坚持从全球的立场提出和讨论问题，不轻易放弃，直到找到全球方案。他也是一位天生的优秀的政治家，他总是认真倾听大家的意见，归纳分析共同点，讨论分歧，直到大家达成一致意见。他工作极其勤奋，常常亲自动笔起草和修改文稿，我常常在新加坡时间凌晨三四点时收到他的电子邮件。正是因为有他担任小组主席，我们才能完成这个极其具有挑战性的任务。我对尚达曼的领导力深深佩服。

为支持名人小组的工作，尚达曼还牵头建立了名人小组秘书处，以国际货币基金组织战略、政策与审核局原局长悉达多·蒂瓦里为首，欧洲复兴开发银行（EBRD）原首席经济学家、现任伦敦政治经济学院全球事务研究所所长埃里克·伯格洛夫，国际货币基金组织前首席风险官大卫·马斯顿和世界银行运营部高级副行长凯尔·彼得斯担任秘书。这真是一个超强的秘书班子。他们为讨论提供理论背景和案例介绍，组织会议时，总把方方面面考虑得周周全全，细节完美，对名人小组的工作起了强有力的协调和支持作用。我和他们都共事多年，此次和他们又一次合作，真是非常顺畅和愉快。

名人小组成员的工作不领取任何薪酬，是对建立未来新国际经济金融治理机制的奉献。感谢时任中国人民银行行长周小川的信任和推荐，使我有幸参与这项工作，在离开国际货币基金组织后又一次回到国际经济金融的政策舞台。能和15位极其出色的国际专家成员共商未来国际经济金融治理机制的改革和架构，真是我极大的荣幸。18个月内，在和小组成员的讨论和密切合作中，我对国际经济金融从理论到实践都有了新的体会，从他们身上学到了很多东西，对国际经济金融治理改革更有信心。我对小组成员对推进国际经济金融治理改革的满腔热忱和义不容辞的责任感非常感动，他们真是杰出的世界公民。

从我们接受任务到完成报告，世界经济金融和政治局势进一步动荡和分化。全球化和反全球化的争议变得更为尖锐，全球面临的共同挑战，例如经济可持续发展、人口老龄化和人口非平衡分布、气候变化、大规模流行传染疾病和突发公共卫生事件、金融市场脆弱等，都变得更为紧迫。科技创新层出不穷，全球科技治理远远落后。这一切都在要求更全球化、更公平和更有效率的全球经济金融治理机制的构建。

展望未来，全球经济发展、金融稳定仍然面临重重挑战，然而目前支撑国际秩序的国际治理和合作体系摇摇欲坠，缺乏一致性、协同能力和有效性，不足以支持全球发展和金融稳定的最根本目标。因此，必须使这一体系与时俱进，符合新时代的现实情况，为多极化的世界实现共赢而建立一个适合21世纪的合作性国际秩序。

今天，中国正在世界经济金融舞台上发挥更大的作用。2017年初我在瑞士达沃斯聆听了习近平主席的主旨演讲，习主席的演讲坚持世界整体利益，坚持全球化，坚持世界公平和包容。他强调了中国坚持对外开放发展、推动经济全球化进程的承诺，并把中国的承诺放入构建人类命运共同体之中。这赢得了世界舆论普遍和高度的赞扬。把本报告翻译成中文并出版，也许对中国参加全球经济金融治理改革的讨论不无裨益。

感谢中国人民银行国际司朱隽司长在繁忙的工作之余牵头本报告的翻译工作，多年来她一直参与国际经济金融治理改革的讨论，熟悉内容，译来顺手。

清华大学国家金融研究院院长
朱　民
2020年6月

前言

为什么需要改革

2017年4月,G20成员国财长和央行行长要求成立全球金融治理名人小组并就全球金融架构和国际金融机构(IFIs)[①]体系的治理提出改革建议,以便在新的全球时代促进经济稳定和可持续增长,并考虑G20如何更好地发挥持续领导作用,为实现这些目标提供支持。[②]

我们接受了这个任务,考虑的核心问题是为新的开放、竞争的世界秩序构建未来金融治理架构。过去70多年中,得益于开放、竞争的世界秩序,大量人口脱贫,各国生活水平普遍提高。这一秩序为前所未有的世界和平奠定了基础。开放的世界秩序对每个国家的未来都至关重要,然而作为其支撑的国际治理和合作体系正摇摇欲坠。如果放任不管,我们很可能会陷入一个分割的

[①] 这些国际金融机构指国际货币基金组织和多边开发银行(MDBs),包括非洲开发银行(AfDB)、亚洲开发银行(ADB)、亚洲基础设施投资银行(AIIB)、欧洲复兴开发银行、欧洲投资银行(EIB)、泛美开发银行(IDB)、伊斯兰开发银行(IsDB)、新开发银行(NDB)和世界银行集团。

[②] 关于G20全球金融治理名人小组的信息及其职责范围,请见本书文末。

世界，如果世界各国和各地区的政策不是相互促进，而是相互冲突，则最终每个国家都是输家。

我们无法回到过去，现在面临的核心挑战是为已经发生的不可逆的变化的世界创建合作的国际新秩序。世界已经表现为多极化，在决策上更加去中心化，各国之间联系也更加紧密。相比过去几十年来我们所经历的，未来的挑战只会更加严峻和紧迫。

为实现包容性增长和共同繁荣，关键是各国要采取正确的国内政策，国际政策倡议也应当相互促进，为所有人创造更美好的未来。开放、竞争和协调良好的国际秩序将为所有国家创造共赢的结果。若这一秩序被削弱，全球增长和新的就业机会将被逐步侵蚀，金融稳定和全球共同目标将会更加脆弱，最终导致满盘皆输。同样，合作性的国际主义只有促进更多国家实现包容性增长，才能长存不衰。

名人小组将最终的改革建议形成了这份报告，本报告提出的改革建议旨在加强全球金融治理并使其更具韧性，从而促进这一新的、合作性的国际秩序。当前体系缺乏一致性、协同能力和有效性，不足以支持全球发展和金融稳定中的最根本目标。我们必须使这一体系与时俱进，符合新时代的实际。

我们提出的这些改革建议是我们力所能及的，并且我们要通过坚定地落实改革的措施来实现金融治理体系整体更加有效运行。

我们提出的改革建议并不需要设立新的国际机构。我们只需要采取大胆和明确的步骤，确保现有的机构——无论是全球、区

前　言

域还是双边机构——能够作为一个整体运行。为此，我们需要在这些不同的机构间建立信任并提高透明度，利用它们共同的力量，让整个体系产生更强大和更持续性的发展效应，降低危机的频率和危害。

我们的建议本身建立在国际金融机构现行改革的基础之上，并力图使之更进一步。在改革过程中，各利益相关方都必须具有紧迫感，提高对统一认识和加强合作的认知，才会有利于各方。

为确保下个十年所必需的增长、就业机会和可持续性，我们的改革步伐和规模需要更上层楼。失败将不仅仅影响经济领域。为避免大规模的系统性危机，使发展中国家能为目前发展阶段所必需的可持续经常账户赤字进行融资，同时避免出现不稳定和低增长的恶性循环，我们需要坚定地推进改革。

名人小组的任务是为所需要的变革提供一份独立的报告。我们聚焦于系统性改革，而非单个机构的改革。我们未探讨国际金融机构资本及股权结构这一重要问题，因为 G20 和国际金融机构正在对此进行审议。

我们秉持实事求是的指导原则，希望我们提出的建议能够得到 G20 和国际金融机构以及国际货币与金融体系内的其他相关机构的真正贯彻与落实。为此，除了借助小组成员在政策制定方面的集体经验外，我们还与一些国家的政府机构、国际金融机构、社会团体、智库、学术界和慈善界的思想领袖，以及私人部门的专家进行了磋商。广泛的交流互动帮助我们提炼了报告中的建议，希望这些建议可以在合理的时间框架内得以实施，并产生变革性的影响。

这是一份有雄心的报告,需要实干和落实。一些改革可以通过国际协调在短期内获得成效。如果能集中精力全力落实,大部分改革可以在几年内看到效果。还有一些改革则无须立即实施,我们敦促各方以开放的心态对待这些改革,并在必要时予以调整,以确保其落实。

本小组深入的研究和讨论[①],得到了以悉达多·蒂瓦里为首的秘书处提供的有力支持。感谢 G20 给我们机会来研究这些重大事项。在提交这份报告时,我们既清醒地认识到国际社会面临的重重挑战,同时也对国际社会的共同信念满怀希望。愿这些信念能使我们步入相互合作的国际主义新时代,这将使所有人受益。

Tharman Shanmugaratnam (Chair)	Jacob A. Frenkel	Ngozi Okonjo-Iweala	John B. Taylor
Sufian Ahmed	Otmar Issing	Raghuram Rajan	Jean-Claude Trichet
Ali Babacan	Takatoshi Ito	Fabrizio Saccomanni	Andrés Velasco
Marek Belka	Nora Lustig	Nicholas Stern	Zhu Min

---

① 在 15 个月的时间里,小组召开了八次全会,并在其间进行了长时间的交流。

核心观点

一、加大跨系统合作：实现更强有力的全球发展效应

下一个十年至关重要。

我们需要大力促进发展，帮助各国实现可持续发展和包容性增长，并应对全球公共领域所面临的不断增长的压力。但当前改革的步伐尚不足以帮助我们实现目标。我们需要更加大胆的改革，增强发展体系内在的互补性和协同效应。

- ◎ 国际金融机构应该重新聚焦于帮助各国加强治理能力及人力资本，为建设有吸引力的投资环境、创造就业及实现社会稳定打下基础。
- ◎ 需要激活国际金融机构之间以及它们和其他发展伙伴之间尚未开发的巨大合作潜力，使其整体贡献最大化，并向一系列核心标准趋同。
- ◎ 推动系统性的保险，使风险分散化，建立一个大规模的新资产类别，大幅提高私人部门参与程度。
- ◎ 提高合作能力，应对全球公共领域面临的挑战。

我们还应更积极地调动非政府部门的力量，包括非政府组织和慈善机构。

二、强化增强全球金融韧性的改革：确保日益关联的全球金融市场服务全球

国际金融危机十年后，我们仍需要进一步改革，以减少金融不稳定和经济低增长的恶性循环的频率，各国要继续走开放之路，以避免另一场大规模危机。

第一，为充分获得跨境资本流动的收益，给各国提供更多支持，各国需要提高国内金融市场的深度，并制定和发展一套政策指导框架，以确保以下两点。

◎ 各国既受益于国际资本流动又避免市场过度波动。
◎ 资本流出国既实现国内目标又避免重大溢出效应。

第二，通过全面系统性考量各方观点，为当前复杂、紧密相连的全球金融体系建立更加稳健、一体化的风险监督体系。

第三，通过将现有割裂的各公共金融环节连接在一起，建立更强劲可靠的全球金融安全网（GFSN）。

三、提升 G20 和国际金融机构的领导作用：维护系统整体有效运行

需要重新定位 G20 在全球金融架构中的角色的重要性。G20 应致力于在关键战略性问题和危机应对方面凝聚政治共识，为此，G20 需要从目前过于饱和的议程中释放空间，将有些工作下放给国际金融机构。

为保证系统整体有效运行，G20 需要建立如下治理结构。

◎ 重新确定发展融资的方向。G20 应建立工作组，纳入重要的非 G20 利益相关方，在未来 3 年为这一改革把握方向，之后将协调工作交给国际金融机构，在多个（多边、区域和双边）机构间实现互补，建立一个清晰的指标体系，以计量发展效应及资金利用效率。

◎ 提前预见发展的挑战。在现有国际金融机构对话和磋商的基础上，建立两年一度的战略对话，以便所有国际金融机构和其他重要利益相关方能够在潜在发展风险未造成持续损害前对其予以认定，并评估集体应对措施是否充分。

◎ 国际货币基金组织应在促进全球金融抗风险能力的治理改革中发挥关键性作用，并与其他机构通力合作，定期向国际货币与金融委员会报告。

在治理改革中，国际金融机构应减少执行董事会与管理层之间现存的严重职能重复，应使执行董事会更加关注战略性重点，赋予管理层更多的权力并向其问责。

第一章
概 览[1]

---

[1] 本概览提供了大背景和报告所提建议背后的逻辑,并且还提供了这些建议的摘要。

第一章 概 览

一、建立新时代合作性国际秩序

我们正处在关键的历史时期。我们面临的根本挑战是为多极化的世界实现共赢而建立一个适合 21 世纪的合作性国际秩序。这也是我们必须做到的。否则，世界将四分五裂，我们未来应对更严峻挑战的能力也会被削弱。

与布雷顿森林体系设立时期相比，当今现实已经完全不同，世界秩序发生了巨大变化。

第一，大多数发达国家内部的经济、社会分化和政治分歧进一步扩大，长久以来的社会契约关系遭到损害。技术进步和国际贸易中总有赢家和输家。增长放慢加剧了这些鸿沟和分歧，相当多的国家从来未曾有效应对这些鸿沟和分歧，这破坏了社会对政府及政府机构的信任，并削弱了公众对国际合作和开放世界秩序的支持。

第二，世界稳步进入多极化的进程不可逆转。这是成功市场化和开放带来的必然结果，它们不仅促进了全球增长，而且推动了各国生产率和生活标准的趋同。一些新兴市场国家在过去 30 年以非凡速度成长并赶超上来。因此，出现了新的全球增长支柱，国际经济决策中出现了更多的平等参与者，去中心化趋势更加明显。

第三，未来十年，我们面临的挑战在规模、紧迫性和复杂性方面都将是前所未有的，特别是在创造就业、环保和金融可持续性方面。即将进入劳动力市场的年轻人口规模将显著超越过去几十年，其中许多年轻人生活在脆弱国家。同时，环境恶化、传染病风险上升和全球公共领域面临的其他问题交织在一起,多重危险叠加也将加剧这一挑战。①此外,由于公共和私人债务大幅增长,一大批发达国家和发展中国家都面临着前所未有的融资可持续性挑战。

第四,由于资本和思想的自由流动,全世界被紧密地联系在一起。资本、思想和贸易成为世界各地增长的强劲引擎。然而,金融市场的复杂性和相互关联性给金融市场的稳定带来的挑战是单个国家无法独立应对的。

当今世界,决策更加分散化,但又更加相互关联,未来面临重重挑战。为此,我们需要建立起具有一定公信力、协调顺畅的全球金融架构,以满足当今世界的需求。

我们无法回到旧的多边主义。由一个乐团指挥引领的时代已经过去了。现在的世界已经由多个乐队演奏,我们需要新的和谐乐章。

新的多边主义必须使去中心化的世界体系更有韧性,作为一个整体更加坚强。我们必须系统性地发动体系内多边、区域和双边机构以及其他关键利益相关方的力量,在众多参与者之间建立信任,提高透明度。这个合作性的新国际秩序应当帮助各国实现更具包容性和可持续性的增长,帮助我们有效应对共同的挑战。

实现包容性社会和共同繁荣,关键在于各国要实施正确的

---

① 可持续发展目标(SDGs)和全球社会联合实施的 2030 年议程,旨在解决这些增长和发展领域的多项挑战。

第一章 概览

政策。最根本的是，随着数字经济的不断壮大，机器学习的进步和大数据的发展加速，政府应帮助公民通过教育和终身学习来适应未来的工作。我们急需为培训发展中国家的大量年轻人口而投资，避免新技术给就业和增长带来破坏性影响。

然而，国际和国内倡议之间的相互作用，对于为所有人创造更好的未来至关重要。为此，国际货币和金融体系的合作以及国际金融机构可以发挥如下核心作用。

◎ **使各国的政策能够相互支持并使负面溢出效应最小化。** 旨在促进增长和维护金融稳定的政策，若能够广泛实施或在全球范围内加以协调，将成为最有效的国内政策。[①] 然而，由于各国市场高度关联，部分经济体的政策可能对其他经济体产生负面溢出效应，或缩小后者的政策空间。因此，需要一个协调机制来尽可能地减少溢出及其影响。国际承诺也有助于避免"以邻为壑"的政策，这一政策仅对一国有利但损害他国利益。

◎ **充分利用国际金融机构作为发展放大器的独特作用——** 特别是在制度建设，传播政策知识，帮助政府改善投资环境以及降低风险以促进私人部门投资等方面。

◎ 共同增强能力建设并协调行动，**避免系统性金融危机，**

[①] 例如，2008年国际金融危机期间在宏观经济政策方面开展的更紧密的国际合作就是相互增强的。历史上也是如此，国内生产率的创新和进步可以互相促进，从而实现常和而非零和博弈。

应对全球公共领域日益面临的挑战。

因此，为促进增长和维护金融稳定，我们不需要在合作的国际主义和各国的国家战略之间二选一。开放、竞争和协调良好的国际秩序将帮助所有国家实现共赢。削弱这一国际秩序则会导致满盘皆输：全球增长和新工作机会逐渐流失，金融稳定和全球公共领域变得更加脆弱。同样，合作型国际主义只有在最大范围内帮助各个国家实现包容增长，才能继续存在。

世界已经更加去中心化，挑战日益严峻，需要合作型的国际秩序。报告中的改革建议可以增强全球金融治理的抗风险能力，以推动合作型国际秩序。改革旨在：产生更为显著的可持续和包容的发展效应；帮助各国维护金融稳定，以获得金融市场互联互通的益处；使治理聚焦于使国际体系整体有效运行，而非仅仅一些各自为政的机构。我们还建议重新定义 G20 在国际货币和金融体系中的作用，释放议题空间，使部长们专注于就当今的关键性战略问题和危机应对达成政治共识。

二、加强国际体系内全方位合作，以实现更显著的发展效应

为在未来十年大幅提振增长、就业并实现可持续发展，我们迫切需要大胆改革发展政策和发展融资政策。当前改革的速度无法实现上述目标。

第一章 概览

各种挑战交织在一起，错综复杂。冲突和安全环境恶化，人力资本和基础设施投资不足，就业和收入增长乏力，这些因素彼此加强。如果再不妥善应对环境问题和传染性疾病的威胁，大量人口将陷入赤贫或被迫移民。未来15年，为满足经济和就业增长的需要，全球基础设施应当增加一倍，因而基础设施将长期面临难以为继的风险。由于世界已经紧密联系在一起，一个地方能否实现可持续性发展，将对其他地区的发展前景产生深刻影响。

同时，我们也看到了诸多积极因素。创业和创新浪潮席卷发展中国家，并进入低收入国家。移动技术、云计算和电子商务给世界各地的小企业打开了市场，提高了劳动生产率，促进了普惠金融。若全球范围内的医疗研发得以持续，将有潜力解决疟疾和其他重大疾病问题，创造重要的经济和社会红利。随着城市管理技术的发展，交通、公用事业和其他服务将更加以人为本。

每个大洲都需要改革，以应对这些挑战并使技术和市场的潜力得到最大化发展。要改写历史，我们必须在非洲取得成功，这里的贫困、人口和环境挑战是最为严峻的，促进世界经济增长和维护全球公共领域的机会也是最大的。失败的后果，将远不止于经济层面。

发展面临资金方面的巨大挑战，需要从所有途径获取比以往更多的资源，包括国内存款和公共收入以及外部的私人、官方和慈善资金。根据保守预测，仅基础设施融资缺口每年就远超1万亿美元。因此，必须堵住融资缺口，这对于确保未来十年的经济和社会基础设施投资的质量和规模非常关键。

然而，大幅增加发展融资的战略必须考虑这样的现实情况：很多发展中国家的公共部门债务（含或有债务）正在接近不可持续的水平。实现发展目标不能仅依靠主权贷款，金融体系必须保持稳定，2030年发展议程才能实现。

因此，需要更优先考虑两个关键战略。一是加强对公共财政和国内资源的动员。在中央和地方政府层面，有很大潜力加强税收征管，降低腐败和浪费引起的税收流失。这些公共资源能够支持人力资本开发并改善投资环境，并且与建立本币市场和刺激国内储蓄的努力相结合，提高国内金融体系的抗风险能力，这正是长期投资所需要的。国际社会必须通过打击避税和洗钱，支持上述国家政府部门的努力。

二是大规模刺激私人投资，使之远远超过历史最高水平。鉴于很多国家的负债率显著增加，未来更应该强调股权融资。然而，迄今为止，发展中国家基础设施私人投资的潜力只开发了一小部分。就当前倡议的政策和市场环境而言，虽然私人资金在全球的供应非常充裕，但很难大规模提升。除了那些最为专业的投资者之外，投资者面临的现实和潜在的投资风险仍然非常高，所要求的回报率可能超过各国的承受能力。基础设施投资的市场过于碎片化，实现项目和国别风险多样化的工具也十分有限。

因此，我们必须以新的方式来组织世界的多边开发能力和资源，以应对上述挑战，实现更显著和持久的发展效应。我们需要将国际体系作为一个整体而非单独的机构来进行治理，以释放更大的潜力。

第一章 概览

鉴于对私人投资，特别是股权融资的需求巨大，促进发展融资的战略应以防风险为核心。国际金融机构必须将它们在缓解和管理风险方面的独特能力发挥到极致。

◎ 帮助各国**化解整体投资环境的风险**（不仅通过单个降风险项目）。国际金融机构必须加强合作，帮助各国利用好治理和监管方面的最佳做法，并坚持改革。

◎ 在低收入和脆弱国家的能源基础设施等关键领域先降低**已有共识的现存风险**，为私人投资铺路。

◎ 通过一级损失担保和联合投资等工具**降低风险**，带动私人投资。重要的是，国际金融机构应使用风险缓释工具，**充分开发低收入国家私人投资的潜力**，不应仅在混合融资已高度集中的中等收入国家开展工作。

◎ 利用大部分未开发的潜力，在发展融资体系中实施风险多元化，为私人投资者创造新的资产类别。

由于基础设施融资需求巨大而又迫切，**整个发展融资系统需要为此转型**。需要系统和根本的措施来提高发展效应。

建议1：应更加关注治理能力和人力资本，以此作为改善投资环境的基础。

◎ **更加关注治理能力以及开发人力资本**。过去数十年的经验已经证明，支持各国开展上述工作将为改善投资环境、创造就业、提高经济活力和社会稳定打下基础。
- ◆ 治理改革只有从内部开始才能持续下去。国际金融机构作为采纳最佳做法和制度性创新的可信伙伴，应与各国的其他发展伙伴加强合作，支持长期治理改革。
- ◆ 国际金融机构还必须支持各国政府，广泛地开发人力资本，为所有人提供公平机会，无论其性别、种族或社会背景为何。

建议2：建立有效的国家发展合作平台，动员所有发展伙伴启动投资，使发展伙伴整体贡献最大化，并向一系列核心标准趋同。

◎ 将国际金融机构以及其他发展伙伴的各项工作结合起来，增强发展效应。

- ◆ **建立国家层面的发展合作平台可以带来变革性的影响。有效的国家平台可以使各种发展伙伴的贡献作为一个整体最大化，通过核心标准的趋同扩大私人投资的规模。**①

---

① 对于脆弱国家，应有一套数量为5~6个、顺序合理的核心发展标准，包括债务可持续性，环境、社会和治理标准（ESG），一致定价政策，地方能力建设，采购以及透明度和反腐标准。作为符合当下情况的第一步，国际金融机构应在同一平台内同意使用彼此的标准，这有助于尽早开展标准实施并促进共识。核心标准的趋同应通过与股东紧密合作来实现。

第一章　概　览

» 国家发展合作平台应为政府所有，鼓励竞争并保留政府与最合适伙伴合作的灵活度。平台内部的透明度对于防止由补贴或低标准等导致的零和竞争至关重要。
» 各个发展伙伴之间连续而互补的合作将有助于扩大私人部门投资的规模。采纳核心标准也会降低私人部门与一系列伙伴开展合作的成本。
» 在脆弱国家的首要工作应是与联合国机构和其他伙伴合作，将安全、人道主义和发展工作整合起来。
» 国家发展合作平台内部的合作有助于对危机的快速响应。
» 国际发展合作平台应支持国家层面的合作，国际金融机构特别要在可持续的基础设施等专题问题上进行合作。

建议3：落实区域发展合作平台，以促进重大跨境投资和互联互通。

◆ 落实区域平台，便利重大跨境基础设施项目，实现地区内的互联互通并开辟新的供应链和市场。

建议4：建立系统性的降低和分散风险的发展融资框架，更多动员私人投资，包括基于投资组合的基础设施融资。

建议4a：多边开发银行的基本运作模式由直接贷款转向提供以调动私人资本为目的的风险缓释工具。

建议4b：系统地开发政治风险保险工具，并加大利用私人再保险市场。

建议4c：开发一种发展中国家基础设施投资新资产类别，使其规模和多元化水平足以吸引机构投资者。

◎ 通过**系统性建立发展融资**的保险和证券化体系，成倍地提升私人资本的投入。迄今为止，参与发展中国家的基础设施开发的私人机构投资者凤毛麟角，需要开发一种标准化的大规模的能在发展融资体系之间化解风险的新资产类别，将有利于启动这个尚未被动用的巨大投资池。

建议5：在考虑既有经验的基础上，使多边开发银行和其他基础设施投资者的资本金要求更加合理。

建议5a：为多边开发银行量身设定资本和流动性框架。

建议5b：重新审议机构投资者基础设施投资的监管待遇。

◎ 基于**多边开发银行以及基础设施**[①]**机构投资者**的既往经验，重新评估对其监管资本要求和其他审慎规范指引。

建议6：提高联合应对全球公共领域所面临挑战的能力。

建议6a：将支持全球公共领域服务纳入国际金融机构的核心业务，并融入国家发展合作平台内部的协调。

---

① 目前，在基础设施投资方面，机构投资者面临一些监管负面激励措施。

建议 6b：建立全球平台，由联合国的相关机构及世界银行在支持全球公共领域的各项工作中进行协调并发动关键参与方。

◎ **全球发展合作平台将各领域的参与者联合起来，加强合作能力，应对全球公共领域的挑战**——由指定的联合国负责机构以及世界银行进行协调，后者与多边开发机构的联系最为广泛。为实现具体的共同目标，地区开发银行和能力卓越的其他利益相关方应发挥关键作用。

建议 7：信托基金活动融入多边开发银行的核心业务，避免其碎片化。

◎ **国际金融机构将支持全球共同目标作为其核心国别工作的主流。**信托基金活动应融入多边开发银行的战略和业务，避免重复工作降低效率并削弱影响力。

建议 8：填补数据和研究缺口，有效支持科学和实践的政策制定，尤其是在发展中国家。

◎ **在数据和研究方面进行投资**，支持以实证为基础的稳健政策。很多发展中国家缺乏基础数据。数据和研究属于公共产品。国际货币基金组织和世界银行应与联合国机构以及区域开发银行合作，加强这些领域的工作。

建议 9：系统性地利用企业联盟、非政府组织和慈善机构的观点和运营网络。

◎ 与企业联盟、非政府组织以及慈善机构形成更为强大的合力，从它们来自实地工作的观点、创新和执行能力中获益。国际金融机构应与政府合作，与上述各方开展系统性合作，识别关键需求，按需提供政策空间和联合融资，使其充分发挥作用。

这种系统性转变能够满足国际社会未来显著增加的发展需求。系统性转变可以发动私人资本和发挥私人资本改变发展融资格局的潜力。不过，若要发动私人资本的大规模参与，国际金融机构也应积极参与项目发起、共担风险，并与政府在改革上保持合作。

虽然名人小组的职责不包括为强化国际金融机构资本提出建议，但我们认为，在发展、增长和稳定日益面临挑战的背景下，各国政府作为股东应定期评估增资的必要性，确保国际金融机构能充分实现其潜力。在评估资本的同时，对国际金融机构进行改革，使其有效发挥私人资本催化剂和发展放大器的作用。为有效发挥国际金融机构的作用，也必须定期对其股权结构进行更新，以反映不断演变的世界经济格局。

三、强化增强全球金融韧性的改革：确保日益关联的全球金融市场服务全球

国际货币金融体系治理最根本的核心目标是使各国充分实现增长发展潜力，避免国际金融危机带来的损失。

国际金融危机之后，通过实施更严格的审慎监管和标准，国际货币金融体系已在诸多方面得到加强。然而，国际货币金融体系的一些特点仍可能导致危机频繁爆发，并通过传染导致在单个国家、在一些情况类似国家，或在全球范围内发生危机。需要通过改革，使发展中国家能为其在发展阶段所必需的、可持续的经常账户赤字进行融资，同时避免出现不稳定和低增长的恶性循环。国际货币体系的改革应支持各国自身努力，为长期可靠的资本流动创造环境。

为实现国际货币金融体系的根本目标，必须修复并加强体系内三个相互依赖的支柱。

（一）从国际资本流动中获益，防范市场过度波动的风险

国内金融市场和跨境投资给全球带来了巨大益处。然而，发展中国家还未能充分利用它们为投资和经济增长提供资金。

为了能从开放的国际资本流动中获益，一国需要具备稳健的宏观经济政策、可靠的法治以及有深度的国内金融市场。然而，在全球金融市场高度关联的今天，即使是运行良好的经济

体也受发达国家政策以及全球风险情绪转变的外溢影响。过度波动会减少政策斡旋的空间,应对波动的措施可能会影响其国内和部分地区的经济增长。经验表明,只有当一国有能力应对资本流动和汇率的过度波动并维护国内金融稳定时,才能实现可持续开放。

这历来是国际货币金融体系的难题。往常对此的决策思路通常取决于一国是资本流出国还是流入国。我们必须超越这一思维方式。应利用已有的还在不断发展的实践基础,建立一个基于规则的国际框架来提供政策建议,使各国避免出台有较大溢出效应的政策,发展有韧性的金融市场,从资本流动中获益,同时管理好金融波动风险。

为推动各国将开放作为长期目标,管理好开放的速度和顺序,同时维护金融稳定至关重要,我们提出以下几点建议。

建议 10:各国际金融机构应强化并加速努力,帮助各国发展有深度、有韧性和有包容性的国内金融市场。

◎ **深化国内金融市场。**国际货币基金组织、世界银行和地区开发银行应加强并协调其技术援助工作,加强与各国政府的伙伴关系。应以政策框架为重点,包括法律和监管基础设施,促进发展稳健的银行业、资本市场和国内机构投资者基础、宏观金融和普惠金融。

第一章 概 览

建议11：国际货币基金组织的政策指导框架应帮助各国逐步迈向资本流动开放的长期目标，并更好地管理金融波动风险。

建议11a：制定基于实证的政策选项，使各国从资本流动中获益，同时维护金融稳定，并向市场保证所采取的措施是恰当的。

建议11b：为使资本输出国既实现国内目标，又能避免大的负面国际溢出效应，要加强对政策选项的研究和宣传。

◎ **国际货币基金组织应发展并扩展其机构观点，使成员国从资本流动中获益，并管理好金融波动风险。** 基金组织应评估资本流入国的资本流动和宏观金融波动风险，评估流出国资本流动的"推动因素"以及流动出现逆转的可能。应汲取各种工具的有效经验，特别是宏观审慎政策的作用。应在成员国采取符合资本流动管理框架的政策组合时，为市场提供保证。

◎ **国际货币基金组织还应为资本流出国开发政策框架**，支持其国内目标，避免大规模国际溢出效应。尽管这并非易事，但为使开放的国际体系继续获得支持，为使资本流入国继续放松管制，这一框架至关重要。[1] 该框架需吸纳各国政府和国际清算银行（BIS）的意见，应建立

---

[1] 在金融稳定理事会（FSB）的推动下，各国接受了审慎标准并推动其不断演变，这是国际社会一致达成政策框架的成功范例。在该框架下，各国自愿使用巴塞尔银行监管委员会、国际保险监督官协会和国际证监会组织的标准评估本国金融机构的风险缓冲是否充足。

在国际货币基金组织溢出效应工作的基础上，并纳入关键系统性重要国家的第四条款磋商[①]中。

◎ 为支持全球金融架构，**国际货币基金组织还需要通过其常备便利工具来提供临时流动性支持**，作为支持成员国从资本流动开放中获益的一揽子措施的一部分。常备便利工具应支持成员国制定良好政策，只在出现全球流动性冲击或传染引发冲击时使用。[②]

（二）加强风险监督，避免再次发生重大危机

每一场金融危机都能造成持久的损失。危机破坏了未来的投资计划，对贫困人口的伤害最大，后果可影响一代人甚至更久。

我们无法预测下一次危机何时爆发。但是，如果我们毫无准备，它必然会是一场全面危机，会产生广泛的全球性的破坏影响。因此，必须加强风险早期识别能力，预判风险如何通过复杂的、高度互相关联的全球金融系统传导，及时遏制风险升级。

建议 12：整合国际货币基金组织、金融稳定理事会和国际清算银行的监督工作，构建具有一致性的全球风险地图，同时保

[①] 第四条款磋商是指，根据《国际货币基金组织协定》第四条款，国际货币基金组织派工作人员访问成员国，搜集经济和金融信息并与该国官员讨论经济发展情况和政策，并最终形成一份报告。——编者注

[②] 见建议 15。

第一章 概　览

持各机构观点的独立性。

建议 12a：系统性地纳入非官方部门和反对观点，提高风险监督的稳健性。

官方机构并未预测到 2008 年全球金融危机的爆发。十几年后的今天，风险监督虽有所完善，但依然过于分散。为避免下一场金融危机，我们任重道远。风险监督体系应该更加一体化，将国际货币基金组织、金融稳定理事会和国际清算银行不同的监督视角综合在一起，构建并不断更新涵盖金融联系和脆弱性的全球风险地图。[①]一体化的风险评估仍要保持三家机构观点的独立性，避免趋同于削弱的共识。同时，要定期向中央银行和监管当局寻求意见，并将包括非官方部门在内的反对观点纳入考虑。

建议 13：以国际货币基金组织和金融稳定理事会早期预警演练为基础，在政策上跟进处理全球风险地图识别的风险。

应利用这张全球风险地图来定期讨论政策行动，达到预防危机的目的。应当延伸国际货币基金组织和金融稳定理事会早期预警演练（EWE），确保对已识别风险的跟进处理。

[①] 一个综合监测系统应当保持三家机构各自的比较优势，即：国际货币基金组织尤其要关注经济和宏观金融风险以及主权脆弱性；金融稳定理事会关注金融系统的脆弱性；国际清算银行关注全球资本流动和市场基础设施风险。

（三）将碎片化的全球金融安全网联合在一起

建议 14：将全球金融安全网的各个层面联结在一起，提高规模和可预见性。

我们需要有效的全球金融安全网，维护市场开放，支持全球增长。过去十年间，一个涵盖全球、区域和双边安排的去中心化、多层次的金融安全架构逐渐成形，但规模和区域覆盖面并不均衡，主要组成部分基本未经历危机考验，缺乏协调机制。因此，它缺乏可预见性，这恰恰是有效的金融安全网所不可或缺的。因此，各国仍倾向于为自我保险而积累储备，发展中国家仍倾向于避免或者降低经常账户逆差，尽管经常账户逆差有助于发展中国家发挥全部的增长潜力。

在下一场危机发生前，建成可靠的全球金融安全网至关重要。第一，必须及时完成国际货币基金组织份额检查，确保国际货币基金组织全球金融安全网的资源充足。[①] 第二，国际货币基金组织应与区域金融安排（RFAs）合作，实现在危机中的一致行动，达到所需的规模和全球影响。全球金融安全网应设计合理，具有可预见性，方能防止道德风险，降低国家之间的传染，并促进开放与增长。

建议 15：国际货币基金组织建立常备流动性便利工具，在

[①] 国际货币与金融委员会号召国际货币基金组织执行董事会在 2019 年春季会议之前尽快完成第 15 次份额总检查，最晚不超过 2019 年年会。

第一章 概览

全球流动性冲击时为各国提供及时的临时性支持。

建议15a：在启动区域金融安排支持时，以一国能够获得国际货币基金组织流动性便利工具为前提条件。

第三，设置常备全球流动性便利工具[1]，充分利用国际货币基金组织永久资源，加强各国抵御全球流动性冲击、防止深层次危机的能力。可靠的流动性便利工具能够帮助各国在放开资本流动的同时不必积累过多的储备，避免阻碍经济增长。流动性便利工具应针对有合理政策的国家，并在使用过程中尽量减少污名化。

建议16：允许国际货币基金组织在发生大规模及严重全球危机时迅速调动额外资源。

在未来发生大规模的严重危机时，必须满足全球金融安全网的规模需求。现有国际货币基金组织的永久资源无力满足这一需求。上次危机使用的解决方案，特别是几家中央银行之间的大规模流动性互换协议，未来未必能够再次使用。[2] 必须探索用临时

---

[1] 应符合国际货币基金组织正常的贷款政策，并且是短期的。
[2] 在上一次国际金融危机中，美联储与几家中央银行开展了约5 000亿美元的流动性互换，确保了全球美元支付系统完整性，并稳定了全球市场。不过，多数新兴市场经济并未直接受益。未来，未必能继续实施此种行动。此外，为临时增加国际货币基金组织的资源，一些国家响应国际货币与金融委员会和G20的联合号召，在危机中承诺提供4 500亿美元的流动性。并非所有国家都参加了这一行动。以双边贷款应对未来重大危机的方案，需要快速调集资金。

机制调动一定规模的资源,在系统性"尾部风险"事件中确保全球稳定。因为存在不同观点,现有的解决方案面临治理和政策上的挑战。需要建立共识予以解决。名人小组在目前阶段尚未能提出一个待认可的解决方案。

四、G20 和国际金融机构:确保系统整体运行

G20 是国际经济治理机制改革的强大推动者。在以共识为基础的框架下,各成员地位平等,这使 G20 在多极世界里更有公信力。它在全球危机之后利用这些优势推动了多项倡议,通过金融稳定理事会加强了金融监管,通过经济合作与发展组织(OECD)实现税收透明。

然而,G20 不是各国普遍参与的组织。它也不是以条约为基础的组织,不具备实施决策的法律框架。它必须与国际金融机构和其他国际组织协调合作,方能实现目标。因此,G20 和国际金融机构之间的治理关系是实现有效全球金融治理的关键所在。

大家都认识到,G20 内部的诸多倡议和会议可能使之无法聚焦需要提供战略性指导和建立政治共识的议题。G20 议程和各种活动不断增加,已经与国际金融机构和其他国际组织的治理和职能出现了重叠。

在与有关利益相关方讨论后,我们提出了三个建议。一是 G20 应在全球金融治理和危机应对的前瞻性研究中发挥作用。二是将国际金融机构作为一个整体来治理,使其集体发挥的力量

第一章 概 览

大于个体贡献的总和。三是简化国际金融机构执行董事会和管理层的职责，增强有效性，实现成果驱动型的监督。

建议17：G20应重新聚焦长期战略性议程，工作流程应更加合理，把更多工作移交给国际金融机构。

G20的重点应回归到在全球战略性目标上构建共识、大幅精简议程和利用国际金融机构和其他国际组织上来。正常情况下，G20财金渠道部长级会议应每年召开1~2次，关注需要国际协调的战略性问题和新威胁，解决系统内的治理障碍。副手会议一年举行2次，支持和跟进部长会议的议程。G20的双层架构能够实现其大多数目的，目前工作组的大多数工作均可交给国际金融机构和其他有能力的组织。若G20建立工作组来推动重大的系统性倡议，运行期限最好不超过3年。

为实现更大规模的发展效应，在国际金融机构的系统治理方面，需要两大巨变：一是确保在多样化的、去中心化的世界里实现协同和互补效应；二是在系统内实现经营模式的转变，有效地动员私人投资。

建议18：G20小组（包含来自非G20和国际金融机构的成员）在未来三年中指导发展融资重新定位，之后将此协调职能交给国际金融机构。应在各发展伙伴间建立互补性，构建一个清晰的指标体系，持续衡量发展效应和资金利用率。

为实现发展融资的重新定位，需要一个有效的论坛。现在尚无一个全球普遍参与、职责涵盖整个系统的有效论坛，发挥引导转变的作用，以确保国际金融机构之间以及与其他开发伙伴之间的一致性和互补性。需要在国际金融机构已有倡议的基础上，专门进行3年持续的引导，以形成新的格局。应建立一个清晰的指标体系，持续衡量影响效应和资金利用效率，并确保该阶段完成之后改革的连贯性。在未来3年内，由G20副手小组会同来自非G20核心选区和国际金融机构的代表[①]，定期向部长们汇报，应是填补论坛缺位的最有效方法。此后，可将此协调职能移交给国际金融机构负责人。[②]

我们必须加强系统合作，应对重大挑战，预判发展中的风险，避免风险造成长期破坏性影响，或在多个国家间传播蔓延。从过去几十年的实践来看，我们经常做不到这一点。

建议19：国际货币与金融委员会和发展委员会召开两年一度的战略论坛，识别潜在风险以及需要何种集体应对措施。

---

① 除了国际货币基金组织和世界银行之外，还应有来自区域开发银行的代表。也应考虑将国际发展金融俱乐部主席纳入进来，该俱乐部由几个主要的开发性金融机构（DFIs）组成。
② G20领导的小组聚焦于就目标、里程碑事件和相关的全系统测算指标达成一致，评估在国际金融机构之间和与发展伙伴之间实现一致性和互补性的进展，以及引入私人部门参与的进展。这个小组应帮助消除治理障碍，促进进步，同时其运行不应破坏每家机构治理架构。

第一章 概览

极为重要的是，财政部长们应参与风险应对。全球风险地图对话应该每两年举行一次，国际货币与金融委员会和发展委员会①的成员国参加（共代表25个选区），国际金融机构、联合国开发计划署、主要民间团体、慈善机构和私人部门的代表也应参加。全球风险地图有助于利益相关方评估应对措施是否充分以及未来的共同行动。②

为培育全球金融抗风险能力，改革国际货币与金融体系治理。上文已经列出了三个相互关联领域的改革，主报告中将详细探讨。为方便参考，总结如下。

◎ **资本流动**。首先，国际货币基金组织、世界银行和区域开发银行帮助各国加快建立**有深度、有韧性和有包容性的国内金融市场**。其次，国际货币基金组织开发政策指导框架，帮助各国迈向资本流动开放的长期目标，开放的速度和顺序能够维护金融稳定，并妥善管理过度波动。为此，需要：（1）发展和延伸国际货币基金组织的机构观点，作为流入国制定政策方案的基础；（2）国际货币基金组织建立一个政策框架，支持**资本输出国实现国内目标，并避免发生大的负面国际溢出效应**，要有国家政

---

① 国际货币与金融委员会是为国际货币基金组织的工作和政策制定提供战略方向的核心部级论坛。发展委员会是世界银行集团和国际货币基金组织在发展问题上建立政府间共识的部级论坛。
② 世界银行和国际货币基金组织可为绘制全球风险地图提供秘书处服务。

府和国际清算银行的投入。最后，需要就建立国际货币基金组织常备流动性便利工具达成共识。

◎ **关于风险监督。国际货币基金组织、金融稳定理事会和国际清算银行整合风险监督工作，形成连贯的全球风险地图，同时保持各机构观点的独立性。三家机构组成联合小组，吸收各种官方信息，例如位于金融中心的中央银行，吸纳非官方渠道信息。国际货币基金组织和金融稳定理事会早期预警演练应为政策讨论和风险跟进提供基础。**

◎ **全球金融安全网。**为确保全球金融安全网在全球层面上资源充足，必须及时完成国际货币基金组织份额检查。此外，**国际货币基金组织和区域金融安排**应为联合行动**确立清晰的职责分工和程序**，建立更加强大和可靠的全球金融安全网。这应包括在调整案例中讨论事后条款是否一致、确定流动性需求、国际货币基金组织流动性便利的信号作用。国际货币基金组织也应探索建立并利用**临时机制，在未来发生大规模、系统性危机时**迅速调动所需规模的资源来确保全球稳定。

鉴于这三组改革的重要性和国际货币基金组织在实施过程中的关键作用，应定期向国际货币与金融委员会报告实施情况和面临的挑战。

建议 20：国际金融机构执行董事会应聚焦于本机构的战略

优先事项，推进实现系统性目标。

建议 21：国际金融机构应采用切实可行、基于风险的方法，将更多责任下放管理层，并对管理层问责。

国际金融机构自身的治理应当与时俱进，以应对战略挑战的复杂性和新时代多边开发银行经营模式的转变。每个国际金融机构应建立框架，以精简执行董事会和管理层的职责，避免相互重合，确保权责分明。董事会应重点关注战略问题和方向，避免过于关注操作决策和交易功能。应当给管理层赋权并对其问责，确保国际金融机构和系统战略重点有效地转化为政策、行动和激励措施。

为实现目标，应考虑让国际货币基金组织、世界银行和其他多边开发银行必要时修订其协议或章程，适当将决策责任下放至各机构的管理层。应当采用切实可行的、基于风险的方法为这种职责下放奠定基础。

建议 22：各机构执行董事会和管理层应拥有多样化技能，更好地适应经营模式的转变和日益复杂的挑战。

为更好发挥职能，执行董事会需要有正确的技能、多样性和专业知识。选区遴选执行董事时，执行董事会应当明确执行董事所需的技能要求，并指导管理层的遴选过程。执行董事会应邀请外部专家在专门委员会任职（例如审计、风险评估及催化促私有投资的战略等）。

角色和职责重新明确后，股东们应考虑国际金融机构执行董事会的不同模式，评估其有效性、成本结构和会议频率。

为确保国际金融机构的持续合法性和有效性，国际金融机构负责人遴选应公开、透明、择优。

五、结论

以上提出的这些改革整体服务于共同的主题：促进各国未来创造就业，实现可持续、包容增长，消除极端贫困，支持年轻人实现理想，避免金融危机及其持久危害，应对全球公共领域面临的紧迫挑战，因为这些挑战影响全球。

目前，国际货币金融体系缺乏支持这些目标的一致性、合作能力和有效性。必须使之适应新时代的现实。为此，应实施大胆改革，使国际货币金融体系整体有效运行。这些改革在我们的能力范围之内。

不需要设立新的国际机构。但要采取大胆、明确的措施，促进现有的全球、区域及双边机构作为一个整体有效运行。需要在各个机构间建立信任和透明度，充分利用其所有长处。为应对未来十年的发展挑战，帮助各国阻止危机并促进改革和经济增长，上述改革极其重要。

这份报告的建议以各个国际金融机构已有的改革为基础，但更进一步。各国际机构的成员国应有更强的紧迫感，深化对加强

第一章 概览

国际金融机构以及各利益相关方之间一致性和合作的认识，才能推动整个进程。

有雄心还需要实干。有些改革措施可以成为早期收获。大多数改革措施需要多方合作，方可在几年内完成。也有一些改革措施目前暂未列入考虑，我们呼吁以开放的思维对待这些改革，若有需要则进一步设计并调整方案，确保其顺利实施。

上述改革措施的实现，有助于达成一个使每个国家都受益的目标。我们将为新的多极化时代建立合作性的国际秩序，使所有国家都能实现人民的理想，并服务于全球福祉。

第二章

加大跨系统合作：实现更强有力的全球发展效应

第二章 加大跨系统合作：实现更强有力的全球发展效应

下一个十年至关重要。

我们需要大幅提升发展的整体效应，帮助各国实现可持续发展和包容性增长，应对全球公共领域所承受的日益增长的压力。当前变革的步伐无法帮助我们实现这些目标。

我们需要大胆改革，实现发展的互补性和协同效应。

◎ 国际金融机构重新聚焦于加强各国的治理能力和人力资本，为改善投资环境、创造就业及保持社会稳定打下基础。

◎ 促进国际金融机构间及其与发展伙伴间的合作，使尚未开发的潜力得以发挥，使这些机构作为一个整体的贡献最大化，并向一系列核心标准趋同。

◎ 系统推进保险和风险分散化，创建一个大规模的新资产类别，显著提高私人部门参与度。

◎ 加强合作能力，应对全球公共领域面临的挑战。

此外，必须更积极地调动非政府部门的力量，包括非政府组织和慈善家。

为在未来十年提高全球增长、促进就业和可持续发展，发展政策和融资急需大胆改革。

每个大洲都必须实现更强的发展整体效应，特别是非洲，这是实现可持续发展目标不可或缺的部分。未来几十年中，非洲有能力为全球增长做出重大贡献。然而，非洲也需要应对贫穷、人口、就业和环境等前所未有的挑战（详情见专栏1）。失败的后果将不仅仅局限于经济层面。

为应对这些挑战，实现更强大持久的发展整体效应，全球的多边发展能力和资源需要新的组织方式。国际机构作为促进发展的放大器，有得天独厚的能力来支持各国采取稳健政策、改进制度、促进创新、实现项目的规模效应并调动私人部门投资。对国际金融机构实施系统性治理，而非仅着眼于单个机构，将释放更大的潜力。

鉴于吸引私人风险资本的迫切性，特别是股本融资，必须最大限度地发挥国际金融机构的独特能力，促进降低风险，通过以下方式吸引私人投资。

◎ 降低各国**整体投资环境的风险**（包括实施化解风险的项目）。国际金融机构要通力合作，帮助各国受益于治理和监管最佳实践。

◎ 在**低收入国家及脆弱国家和地区**，在能源基础设施等关键领域**进行开拓性投资**，降低投资者对风险的感受，为私人投资铺路。

◎ 通过初始损失担保和联合投资等工具**降低风险**，促进私人投资。

◎ 利用发展融资体系巨大的未开发潜力，构建风险池并分散风险，为私人投资者创造新的资产类别。

为实现目标，国际金融机构的治理必须严格强调其附加值，即确保担保和优惠资源在吸引私人资本和解决市场失灵方面发挥

第二章 加大跨系统合作：实现更强有力的全球发展效应

最大的催化作用。重要的是，混合融资目前高度集中在中等收入国家，国际金融机构必须在最不发达国家使用风险缓解工具，吸引私人投资进入最不发达的国家。

专栏 1 非洲的机会和挑战

过去十年，非洲发展良好，平均增长率超过 4%。但是，非洲大陆依旧面临重大挑战，且其中一些地区还出现了倒退，急需克服。

未来几十年，非洲面临巨大机遇。通过在治理、人力资本和投资环境方面的强劲改革，可以打造出有利于为迅速增长的非洲青年人口创造就业并促进可持续和包容性增长的环境。

然而，贫困和环境挑战仍然严峻，如果不通过持续改革和投资来创造就业机会，如果不未雨绸缪应对气候变化对粮食安全和疾病传播的影响，这些问题将会进一步恶化。

非洲年轻的工作年龄人口将以史无前例的速度增长。非洲中产阶级预计增加 1 亿人，可为全球商品和服务提供重要市场。

从现在到 2030 年，非洲工作适龄人口将经历增长最快时期（见图 2.1）。2030 年，非洲在全球最贫困人口中的占比预计将达到 90%。

但是，在当前的经济增长速度下，就业增长仍显不足，这意味着减少极端贫困将长期面临困难。到 2030 年，预计非洲在世界贫困人口中的占比将达 90%（见图 2.2）。未有效就业的年轻人口可能成为不稳定的根源。

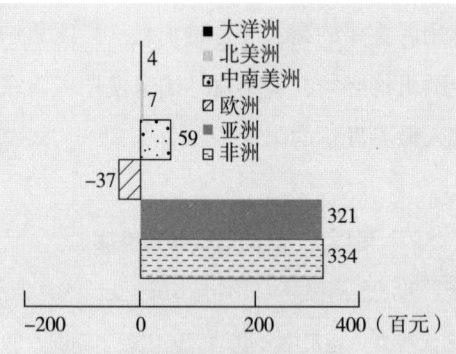

图 2.1　2030 年全球适龄工作人口增长

资料来源：联合国经济和社会事务司人口处，2017 年修订。

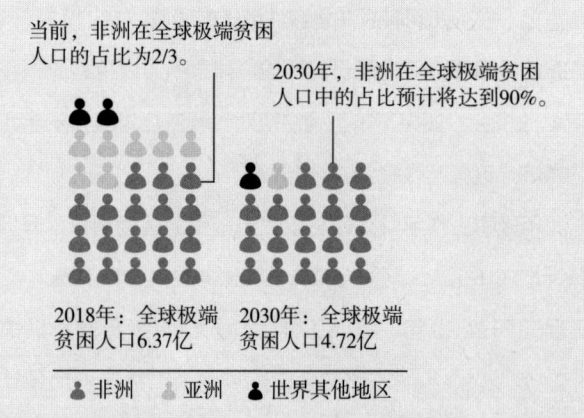

图 2.2　2018 年和 2030 年全球极端贫困人口分布对比

资料来源：世界贫困钟。

非洲拥有广阔的可耕地，农业增长潜力巨大，但实现这些潜力要靠技术升级、商业化以及优化水资源利用。非洲各国在发展数字化经济和资源型制造业以提高国内附加值方面，也有巨大机遇。

第二章 加大跨系统合作：实现更强有力的全球发展效应

> 调动私人部门投资对实现这些目标来说至关重要。欣欣向荣的非洲经济若与全球市场互联互通，可成为增长的新引擎，并有助于应对全球公共领域面临的挑战。

相关需求规模大且很紧迫，需要举全系统之力予以应对。我们认为，以下措施可显著加强发展效应。

◎ **重新关注各国治理能力和人力资本的改善，为这两项至关重要的工作提供支持**。几十年的发展经验表明，治理能力和人力资本的改善是**建设有吸引力的投资环境**、创造就业和提高经济活力的关键基础。
  - ◆ 治理改革只有从内部推进才能持久。国际金融机构在推广最佳实践和制度创新方面是各国的可靠伙伴。各机构要加强合作，与各国其他发展伙伴一道，支持改革持久推进。
  - ◆ 国际金融机构还须支持各国政府确保全面发展人力资本：为所有人提供平等机会，不论其性别、种族和社会背景如何。

◎ **国际金融机构**及其他发展伙伴在运营等方面加强合作，从而增强发展效应。
  - ◆ 建立有效的国别发展合作平台，以动员所有发展伙伴促进投资，通过向核心标准趋同等方式，使各方贡献最大化。

» 该平台必须为政府所有，鼓励竞争，并保持政府与其最佳合作伙伴接洽时的灵活性。但是，必须维护平台内部的透明度，从而避免通过补贴或降低标准等手段进行零和竞争。
» 发展伙伴间的业务协调和互补将有助于扩大私人部门投资。采用核心标准可以降低私人部门与一系列发展伙伴合作的成本。
» 必须优先考虑整合脆弱国家的安全、人道主义和促发展工作，并与联合国机构和其他伙伴开展合作。
» 国别发展合作平台间的合作将有助于在危机时期迅速反应。
» 国家层面的合作还应得到国际金融机构全球发展合作平台的支持，以便在可持续性基础设施等关键议题上开展合作。

◆ **实施区域发展合作平台，推进有助于实现区域互联互通、开辟新供应链和市场的重大跨境基础设施项目。**

◎ **系统性地**开发对发展融资的保险和证券化方法，以吸引**私人资本倍增**。迄今为止，机构投资者对发展中国家基础设施的参与微乎其微。开发一个标准化的、大规模的新资产类别，建立风险池，分散和多元化整个发展融资系统的风险，将有助于调动这一巨大的、尚未开发的投资资源。

◎ **以违约实证为基础**，重新评估多边开发银行和基础设施机构投资者的监管资本要求和其他审慎准则指引。[1]

◎ 各领域不同组织建立**更紧密、有效的协作机制**，加强联

---

[1] 机构投资者目前在投资基础设施方面面临一些不利于金融活动的监管政策。

第二章 加大跨系统合作：实现更强有力的全球发展效应

手应对全球共同领域的挑战，从而提高应对能力，并确保资金充足。

◎ **国际金融机构还须将支持全球公共领域的活动纳入其核心国别业务的主流**。还应将信托基金活动与多边开发银行的战略和业务相整合，避免平行结构对其效率和发展效应的不利影响。

◎ **投资于数据和研究**，支持以实证为基础的稳健决策。许多发展中国家的基础数据仍不足。数据本身是公共品，国际货币基金组织和世界银行应与联合国机构和区域开发银行合作，加强这一领域的工作。

◎ **加强与商会、非政府组织和慈善机构的合作**，从它们的实践经验、创新能力和执行能力中获益。国际金融机构要在与各国政府合作的同时，更系统地与商会、非政府组织和慈善机构等合作，共同确定关键需求，在需要时提供空间和联合融资，充分发挥其力量。

建议1：应更加关注治理能力和人力资本，以此作为改善投资环境的基础。

加强治理能力和开发人力资本是过去半个世纪成功发展的核心经验所在。

只有各国充分发挥主动性才能成功推进上述目标。国际金融机构，无论是单个机构还是整体而言，都应再次聚焦于帮助各国加强治理能力，更快地传播最佳实践经验，促进新技术应用，提高生产率，使教育和医疗惠及更广泛人群。

无论在地方还是在国家层面，加强治理能力对于调动国内金融资源和创造有吸引力的投资环境来说都是必不可少的，还要采纳如下措施。

- ◎ 改善国内税收管理，减少税收流失。
- ◎ 减少腐败，腐败是制约经济发展的主要因素。
- ◎ 发展国内金融体系，特别是**深化本币资本市场的发展**。
- ◎ 加强法治，增加监管的确定性，从而提振长期投资者的信心。

国际金融机构还可有效强化各国政府对一项尚未完成的人力资本开发关键任务的认识：无论性别、种族和社会背景，都必须实现人人机会平等。[1] 国际金融机构还应鼓励各国政府调动非官方部门积极性，广泛地传播机遇。非官方部门包括非政府组织、慈善机构和私人部门。

不过，治理能力建设和人力资本开发非一日之功，要特别关注具有重大脆弱性因素的国家，帮助改革派政府在创造就业机会并向更广泛人群提供服务方面取得进展，促使公众支持改革的持续推进。若民众福利没有明显改善，治理改革很可能受阻。

---

[1] 世界银行最近编制的综合人力资本指数将为各国制定政策提供基准，并衡量其进展情况。

第二章　加大跨系统合作：实现更强有力的全球发展效应

建议2：建立有效的国家发展合作平台，动员所有发展伙伴启动投资，使发展伙伴整体贡献最大化，并向一系列核心标准趋同。

由各国政府主导的国家发展合作平台将强化包括私人部门在内的所有发展伙伴的贡献。国别平台可对发展产生变革性影响。

◎ 发挥一国各发展伙伴之间的互补性——包括国际金融机构、联合国机构、双边官方机构，在某些情况下还有慈善机构和非政府组织——以汇集各机构的力量和知识。
◎ 使发展伙伴能够为政策和制度的改革提供更加一致、更加协调的支持。
◎ 各发展伙伴之间协调互补，扩大私人部门投资。
◎ 推动采用共同的核心标准，以确保产生可持续的发展效应，并降低与众多伙伴分别合作的成本。
◎ 强化危机应对能力，国家发展合作平台也能提供即刻响应的协调机制。

重要的是，国家发展合作平台不能成为政府或发展伙伴的束缚。

◎ 为取得成效，国家发展合作平台须由**本国政府**主导，保持政府与有适当实力的合作伙伴接触的灵活性。不同国家的平台发展方式不尽相同，在一定程度上取决于各国政府的规划能力。
◎ 然而，国家发展合作平台也有潜力帮助各国政府为公共资产的整个生命周期提供规划，并加强政府内部机构间协调，财政部门通常在其中发挥协调作用。
◎ 对于发展伙伴来说，平台内部的透明度和向核心标准趋同将会鼓励围绕创新、效率和市场化速度而展开健康竞争，并改善投资环境。

到目前为止，国家发展合作平台的应用是不全面和选择性的。[①]现有平台或主要用于冲突后重建，或仅在行业层面应用（各种形式平台的情况，详见附录1）。现有平台尚未实现透明度，有待向共同发展标准趋同，也未采纳标准化做法，而这恰是大幅促进私人部门投资所需要的。因此，为发展国家发展合作平台，发展共同体需大幅转变运作方式。

有效的国家发展合作平台需要高度透明，确保所有伙伴都能得到并共享信息，合作伙伴需要采纳一套商定的核心标准，以确保可持续性，避免补贴等零和竞争。[②]采用共同核心标准，将便利私人部门与不同发展伙伴之间的合作（详情见专栏2）。

---

① 卢旺达已经建立运转良好的捐助者协调机制，具备了有效国家平台的诸多关键属性。其他一些机制也具备了名人小组所建议的各种关键要素，如巴西多个行业的私人部门参与平台、哥伦比亚4G（第四代公路网）机制以及印度尼西亚的国家贫民窟改造升级项目（详见附录1）。
② 作为务实的第一步，国际金融机构应同意在一个平台内使用彼此的标准，这将促进早期实施和达成共识。

第二章 加大跨系统合作：实现更强有力的全球发展效应

> **专栏2 核心标准**
>
> 核心标准旨在促使发展融资的众多参与者协同一致，使其专注于发挥系统的协同效应。核心标准还能降低政府和私人部门与各种发展伙伴合作的成本，并且更有效。
>
> 为此，要在体系内商定一系列、五六个核心发展标准，并为具有脆弱性的国家提出适当的优先顺序，可包括以下六点。
>
> 1. 债务可持续性
> 2. 环境、社会和治理标准
> 3. 一致的定价政策
> 4. 本地能力建设
> 5. 采购
> 6. 透明度和反腐败
>
> 目前，国际金融机构广泛遵循核心标准的主要组成部分。**核心标准的制定和趋同必须与成员国密切合作。某些标准（例如透明度和反腐败、债务可持续性和一致的定价政策）的趋同要加快进程。其他标准的趋同可基于等效法，就原则和结果达成一致。**从而使各国采用不同方法，实现在当下以及未来保护本国公民的共同目标，并逐渐实现趋同。

重要的是，向核心标准趋同，可为引入主要双边贷款人或发展融资机构打下基础，因为整体来看这些机构在发展融资体系中的作用已经大大加强。国际金融机构应与国际发展融资俱乐部和私人部门实体就正在推进的标准制定工作开展合作。① 在这方面,股东之间的合作至关重要。

需要特别考虑脆弱国家,因为标准方面需要根据这些国家的能力量身制定标准,并为标准的实施提供更多支持。②

如果政府能得到发展伙伴的协调与支持,国家发展合作平台往往更有效。协调员的选择应从该国优先发展领域的实际考虑出发。为了鼓励更广泛的主导权,协调员最好定期轮换。

同样重要的是,国家发展合作平台可确保区域开发银行从比较优势出发,特别是利用自身的区域知识和联系,继续发挥积极作用。

国家发展合作平台可促进协调和一致性,有助于大大提升私人部门投资。通过平台加强协调有助于增强政府在项目选择、准备和实施方面的能力,建立监管确定性,并实现合同文件标

---

① 发展融资俱乐部的成员是 23 家发展融资机构,资产为 3.5 万亿美元,每年发放超过 8 000 亿美元的贷款,它们正在着手开展一项协调各机构政策的进程。它们的资产已超过所有多边开发银行的总和。
② 考虑到脆弱国家的情况,多边开发银行可以优先开展有助于启动就业创造、增加基本医疗和教育机会(从而帮助各国政府获得持续改革支持)的业务,同时致力于逐步提高标准。参见伦敦政治经济学院和牛津大学国家脆弱性、增长与发展委员会 2018 年 4 月《摆脱脆弱性陷阱》的报告(特别是建议 7 的讨论)。

第二章 加大跨系统合作：实现更强有力的全球发展效应

准化，从而促进基础设施资产类别的形成。① 这些平台还将使国际金融机构自身整合其项目筹备设施。②

国家发展合作平台在发生危机时也是有效工具。在运转良好的情况下，国家发展合作平台将提供协调机制，以便在危机开始时就能将政府和相关国际金融机构、双边机构、联合国有关机构和其他非政府机构聚集在一起。此外，鉴于其促进实时协调与合作的操作原则，也可为人道主义和其他援助提供组织框架。

建议 3：落实区域发展合作平台，以促进重大跨境投资和互联互通。

区域性发展合作能使各国克服由地理因素造成的经济限制，例如无法接入港口，基础设施缺乏连通（特别是运输方面），以及能源和水资源供应不足等，从而有助于促进经济机会。

---

① 私人融资要求对基础项目说明、文件或模板，以及财务和非金融数据进行标准化，并以主要市场参与者（如 SOURCE 和 GEMs）已经认同的模板为基础。SOURCE 是多边开发银行和公私合作伙伴应 G20 要求而实施的一项全球联合倡议，旨在通过提供准备充分的项目来缩小基础设施差距。GEMs 是一个由欧洲投资银行维护的数据库，搜集 13 家发展融资机构的 B 类贷款违约历史和其他数据。

② 目前，国际金融机构的基础设施筹备设施包括：全球基础设施基金、阿拉伯基础设施融资基金、国际开发银行的基础设施基金、欧洲复兴开发银行的基础设施项目准备基金、亚洲开发银行的亚太项目准备基金、欧洲投资银行和欧盟雅斯贝尔斯东区和南区倡议、国际投资银行的项目筹备特别基金和非洲开发银行的非洲 50 基金。

区域性项目通常复杂、昂贵，需要多个国家和投资者参与，协调解决政策难题，解决复杂信托关系以及环境和社会问题。根据建立国际平台的原则建立区域平台，是加快区域项目实施的有效途径。

区域发展合作平台将促进区域内发展伙伴之间更好地合作和分工。[①] 如果一国规模过小难以建立国家平台，还可通过建立区域性平台同时推进具有多个效果的项目和计划。

建议4：建立系统性的降低和分散风险的发展融资框架，更多动员私人投资，包括基于投资组合的基础设施融资。

国际金融机构致力于帮助各国提升政府能力（建议1）以及通过运转良好的国家和区域发展合作平台在发展伙伴之间产生协同作用（建议2和建议3），这对改善投资环境和项目规划来说至关重要。然而，为了调动足够资源以应对未来的发展挑战，必须最大限度地发挥资本市场和机构投资者的潜力。在已达到债务可持续性限额的国家，必须在不显著增加主权债务的情况下，在基础设施方面获得更多的私人融资。

G20汉堡原则[②]表明，多边开发银行有必要通过增信和其他

---

① 这些区域平台的例子包括西巴尔干投资框架和非洲投资论坛。
② 汉堡原则关于动员私人部门金融的部分（《关于引入私人部门融资的汉堡原则》）于2017年4月发布，得到了G20的认可。它为多边开发银行提供了一个共同框架，以增加私人投资水平，从而支持发展目标。

第二章 加大跨系统合作：实现更强有力的全球发展效应

方式吸引私人投资者。目前，私人部门对发展中国家基础设施资产的投资微乎其微。投资者对发展中国家基础设施投资和预期回报的风险感知很高。因此，必须减少和管理风险，以使私人资本寻求的回报和定价降低到对发展中国家可行且可持续的水平。

在整个系统范围内，有很大空间降低、管理和分散风险，从而为私人投资打开大门，这必须包括以下三点。

◎ 重新定位多边开发银行的业务模式，重点关注风险缓释。
◎ 在全系统范围内使用政治风险保险和私人部门再保险市场。
◎ 构建大规模、多元化的新资产类别，使机构投资者能够投资于发展中国家的基础设施。

建议 4a：多边开发银行的基本运作模式由直接贷款转向提供以调动私人资本为目的的风险缓释工具。

传统上，多边开发银行将贷款作为主要业务，应转而利用其资产负债表来缓释风险。多边开发银行（以及双边开发伙伴）具有多边所有权，且有能力影响政府，在管理发展中国家风险方面具有独特能力。因此，其有条件提供增信（例如，在综合证券化结构中承担第一部分损失），从而吸引机构投资者入市，承担标准化的优先债务敞口，这些敞口的定价可以更低，反映更低的风险。

与直接贷款相比，多边开发银行提供增信可以更有效地利用其资本。此外，私人投资者并非增信服务的受益者，因为其降低了投资者的风险但也相应降低了投资回报。真正受益的是得到了较低融资成本的借款国。

建议4b：系统地开发政治风险保险工具，并加大利用私人再保险市场。

国际投资者在考虑是否以外商直接投资、债务或股权融资等方式进入很多发展中国家时，是否有政治风险保险至关重要。

多边开发银行作为一个体系，应利用多边投资担保机构[①]作为发展融资方面的全球风险承保人。过去5年中，多边投资担保机构大幅增加了向发展中国家私人投资者提供的政治风险保险。[②]通过利用私人再保险市场，其能力得到了提升。可以在多边投资担保机构现有的风险保险能力基础上，应对多边开发银行整体面临的风险，以实现规模效应，并从全球多元化投资组合中受益。多边开发银行和多边投资担保机构之间的合作可以采取多

---

① 多边投资担保机构是一个国际金融机构，是世界银行集团的一部分，其主要业务是提供政治风险保险和信用增级担保。
② 2012—2017年，多边投资担保机构的总风险敞口增长了73%（75亿美元）。

第二章　加大跨系统合作：实现更强有力的全球发展效应

种形式。例如，多边开发银行可将投资者与多边投资担保机构联系起来，或多边投资担保机构为多边开发银行的保险或担保产品提供再保险。更多地利用私人再保险市场，也有助于扩大政治风险保险的使用。

多边投资担保机构应建立联合咨询委员会，由参与的多边开发银行指导与其共同开展的业务，并监督标准和定价规范，从而支持合作。

多边投资担保机构和多边开发银行应通过以下方式显著扩大现有的风险保险业务。

◎ **合同和流程的标准化**。标准化合同将有助于扩大风险保险的供给规模，并有助于在投资组合的基础上（而不是逐个进行项目审查）建立程序化的保险或再保险承保流程和定价流程，**从而提高效率和市场投放速度，并降低成本**。[1]
◎ **扩大私人再保险的使用**。从长远来看，要在全系统范围内建立一个风险保险平台，需要大幅增加切割给私人再保险公司的风险，以便多边投资担保机构和多边开发银行能够循环利用其资本并支持更多的项目。可通过遴选建立再保险专家小组，并通过竞争择优的方式更新小组成员。再保险可以根据预先商定的标准在投资组合基础

---

[1] 特殊风险可通过标准化合同的附加险来解决。

上进行安排。

建议4c：开发一种发展中国家基础设施投资新资产类别，使其规模和多元化水平足以吸引机构投资者。

机构投资者[①]资金实力雄厚，但迄今很少投资发展中国家基础设施。除少数专业参与者外，机构投资者仅投资于规模大、较简单、多元化的发展中国家基础设施资产。截至目前，部分国家已采取措施构建可供私人投资者投资的基础设施资产类别，但仍不成体系。阿根廷在担任G20轮值主席国期间，已经要求基础设施工作组寻求机会，将基础设施这一资产类别主流化。

我们只能通过全系统的解决方法来实现规模效应：将整个多边开发银行系统的投资集中起来，将其标准化，包装成对投资者更加友好的证券化资产或基金。国际金融公司的"联合贷款组合管理计划"即为一例，其成功吸引了私人部门兴趣。这还只是一家机构的贷款组合，如果实现整个系统的标准化和投资集中，将产生更大、更多样化的贷款组合，从而大大提高机构投资者的参与度。同样重要的是，通过推动商业纪律，为私人和机构投资汇集多元化的多边开发银行贷款组合，可给项目周期的上游带来巨大利益。

多边开发银行系统中有大量与基础设施相关的贷款，可以汇

---

① 可能还包括保险基金、主权财富基金和公共养老基金。

第二章 加大跨系统合作：实现更强有力的全球发展效应

集起来供私人和机构投资。可以从 2 000 亿~3 000 亿美元的非主权贷款[①]开始，建立一个规模合理的资产类别。符合条件的贷款池可以进一步扩大至包含商业银行的基础设施贷款，其规模大概是每年发放 2 000 亿美元。绿色债券和绿色债券基金的增长也为多边开发银行和商业银行应机构投资者需求发放基础设施贷款提供了机遇。

新的主权贷款也可以集中起来用于投资，理想情况下，可待市场熟悉这一资产类别后再予以推进。可通过向私人和机构投资者对贷款组合进行"清洁销售"（clean sale）来实现，这一过程不涉及优先债权人身份的转移（详见附录2）。

建议5：在考虑既有经验的基础上，使多边开发银行和其他基础设施投资者的资本金要求更加合理。

要根据多边开发银行的特点和违约经验量身建立一套具有针对性的审慎标准并适用于所有多边开发银行。目前适用于多边开发银行的监管资本、流动性标准以及评级方法都是在借鉴商业银行标准的基础上制定的，没有充分反映多边开发银行独特的股权结构、优先债权人地位和违约经验。不同的评级机构也对多边开发银行采取不同的评级方法。因此，多边开发银行适用的标

[①] 已知数据显示，非洲开发银行、亚洲开发银行、欧洲复兴开发银行、欧洲投资银行、国际复兴开发银行、泛美开发银行和国际金融公司平均有25%的贷款流向非主权实体。但非主权敞口比例在多边开发银行之间可能存在很大差异。

准和规范各不相同，资本及流动性缓冲也不一致。缓冲越充足，多边开发银行财务能力受到的限制就越大。

同样，适用于银行和保险公司等机构投资者的在基础设施投资上的监管资本要求与适用于公司债的要求并无区别。这就抑制了投资者投资基础设施的热情。但数据显示，发展中国家长期基础设施投资违约率要比公司债低。因此，应重新考虑将基础设施投资列为一个独立的资产类别，设置不同的资本要求，供保险公司和其他机构投资者投资。

建议 5a：为多边开发银行量身设定资本和流动性框架。

考虑到多边开发银行独特的经营模式，其应集体请巴塞尔委员会就监管资本和流动性标准提供有针对性的指导。巴塞尔委员会可针对多边开发银行开展独立评审，并为其量身制定监管框架。这有利于在整个多边开发银行系统适用协调的资本和流动性安排，并为评级机构审议针对多边开发银行的评级方法提供基础。这样做的目的在于让多边开发银行和评级机构能够更为准确地测算多边开发银行承担的风险，进而制定合理的资本和流动性监管要求。如果能释放一部分资产负债表能力，则可用于风险承担。可解决的问题包括以下三点。

◎ 考虑多边开发银行运营模式区别于普通商业银行的关键因素，包括对优先债权人待遇的认定，待缴资本和风险

第二章　加大跨系统合作：实现更强有力的全球发展效应

集中度。①
◎ 多边开发银行整体的实际违约率。
◎ 与较为传统的信贷工具相比，对信用担保、增信和保险的监管应当以风险和证据为基础。

目前，在流动性极度紧张的情况下，多边开发银行也没有任何渠道获得资金便利，评级机构在评级时也考虑了这一点。因此，如果将多边开发银行视为一个整体，则其持有的流动性（过度的自保）或者付出的资金成本（评级机构认为多边开发银行是背后无任何流动性支持的金融机构）比所需要的要多。② 如多边开发银行与巴塞尔委员会就建立新的监管框架进行接洽，也应在流动性要求的合理性上寻求一些指导。

为了增强整个系统的抗风险能力，并更好地理解正常时期和危机时期的资源需求，应当时不时地对整个系统进行压力测试。

建议 5b：重新审议机构投资者基础设施投资的监管待遇。

来自发达国家和新兴市场③的机构投资者的基础设施投资都

---

① 迈向建设性参与重要的一步是在多边开发银行之间进行集中公开敞口和违约数据，让其对股东、投资界和评估机构来说是透明的。
② 据估计，对于世界银行，这样的便利将允许它至少扩大 10% 的信贷规模，而区域性多边开发银行可扩张的规模更大。
③ 例如，这些监管规定经常会在经合组织国家和非经合组织国家或者投资级和非投资级经济体之间进行简单区分。

在一定程度上受到了监管标准的限制。如果监管规定能够促进并认可本地机构投资者对基础设施建设带来的潜在价值，本地机构投资者就能够提供丰富的背景知识，且更加符合投资目标（如满足本币投资的要求）。可通过循证决策审查监管规定，寻求机遇激励长期投资。

仍有空间对基础设施债的监管措施进行循证审议，并将其视为具有独特风险特征、区别于公司债的资产类型。同样，仍有空间区别对待建设和运营阶段的不同风险，运营阶段风险较小。

建议6：提高联合应对全球公共领域所面临挑战的能力。

全球共同目标面临一系列挑战，包括气候变化带来的环境威胁、生态系统退化、生物多样性的丧失、水资源匮乏和对海洋的威胁、流行病暴发和抗生素耐药性（AMR）快速发展导致的健康威胁等。穷人往往受到更多影响并且总是更脆弱。此外，冲突导致的人类迁移、自然灾害和安全匮乏也是一项挑战。这是所有国家共同面临的挑战，但是国际社会可在支持发展中国家并促进其自身采取措施实现全球共同发展目标方面发挥重要作用。

未来15年，全球基础设施资本将翻一番。如何开展投资对全球共同目标有深远影响。急需国际金融机构在确保基础设施投资的质量和可持续性方面发挥关键作用。

上述挑战全部是跨越国界的，需要国际社会共同努力提供（跨国的和本地的）公共产品和相关的政策、投资，以便更及时、

第二章 加大跨系统合作：实现更强有力的全球发展效应

大规模、连贯和有效地应对各种威胁。应对不同挑战的合适对策在规模、范围、实施的复杂度和速度上也极其不同。[①]

全球共同目标之间的差异也对如何协调合作以及各机构的职责分工有很大影响。受系统影响，应对措施的协调要关注溢出效应的范围，以及应对措施所需公共物品、政策和投资的性质。

虽然上述因素给全球公共目标带来了切实的挑战，但科学技术也一直在快速发展。在一系列对生活质量和可持续发展至关重要的问题上，存在巨大的进步空间。环境因素的限制凸显了改变的迫切性，但同时也督促人们有创意地思考如何设计更宜居的城市，让公民生活得更健康，工作质量高、持续性强。国际金融机构尤其有义务推广创新。在可持续发展中，创新已创造了许多增长机遇。[②]

建议 6a：将支持全球公共领域服务纳入国际金融机构的核心业务，并融入国家发展合作平台内部（建议 2）的协调。

[①] 每种威胁可能都需要多种公共物品来应对。例如，与气候相关的环境威胁需要预防和缓解环境变化，这是纯粹的公共物品，并需要每个人的努力，但同时也需要提高对环境变化的适应力和增强韧性，这主要包括私人物品或者国家和区域性公共物品。与健康相关的威胁常需关注"最薄弱的环节"，如预防病毒传播。但有时重要的是其中一个主体的努力，如针对某种疾病发明一种疫苗或治疗方法。

[②] The Global Commission on the Economy and Climate, *Unlocking the Inclusive Growth Story of the 21st Century: Accelerating Climate Action in Urgent Times*, New Climate Economy, 2018, Washington, DC.

在国别项目背景下，国际金融机构在制定全球标准和推出市场化方法、推动私人部门参与行动实现全球共同目标方面可发挥重要作用。世界银行曾在与私人部门的联合行动（如碳定价领导联盟）中发挥领导作用；区域性开发银行也在一些特定领域推动了类似的倡议。[1] 国际金融机构应鼓励制定标准，披露与全球共同目标所面临挑战有关的风险。在政府的支持下（或者在政府的要求下），投资者和公司已经开始落实2017年由金融稳定理事会牵头的气候相关财务信息披露工作组（TCFD）提出的建议。[2]

国际金融机构也应当帮助各国将全球共同目标项目作为其增长战略和投资计划的一部分，并协助各国政府采取一致的方法。

建议6b：建立全球平台，由联合国的相关机构及世界银行在支持全球公共领域的各项工作中进行协调并发动关键参与方。

如想有效地应对全球共同目标带来的挑战和机遇，则需要各国内部及各国之间、联合国有关机构之间、国际金融机构和其他相关组织（如慈善机构）和私人部门采取强有力的行动。鉴于挑

---

[1] 例如，欧洲复兴开发银行在2015年启动的绿色经济转型方法，旨在其部门间和业务相关国间降低气候变化和环境恶化带来的影响和增加应对这些影响的韧性。
[2] 到2017年12月，总市值逾6.3万亿美元的237家公司致力于支持气候相关金融信息披露工作组。大型机构投资者也开始披露相关信息。

第二章 加大跨系统合作：实现更强有力的全球发展效应

战紧迫且规模大，目前上述活动的规模远远不够。为每个共同目标而指定的联合国相关机构和在多边开发银行中影响范围最广的世界银行应当负责识别全球应对策略的不足，如在适应气候变化、协调和动用核心成员等方面。至于具体的共同目标，区域性开发银行和其他实力强劲的股东将发挥核心作用。

目前，各方在应对全球共同目标所面临挑战方面存在严重的职责重叠，有些领域人满为患，有些领域则无人问津。因此，需明确划分职责以增强影响力。

虽然该系统应能分散化地应对风险，但各方也必须更加紧密地协调，以使国际金融机构、联合国机构和其他发展伙伴更好地发挥合力。联合国机构可在多数领域制定规范，例如确定目标、制定标准和提供政治合法性。多数情况下，联合国机构也是突发状况和危机的第一响应者。国际金融机构则根据其比较优势在政策建议和去风险、调动资金、增强抗风险能力和提高各国执行力等方面发挥着不同的关键作用。私人部门也发挥着至关重要的作用，且应当加强其与多边开发银行系统的合作。经常与私人部门和非政府组织合作的慈善机构也在创新、实验和创建影响测量系统方面发挥重要作用。

各机构应根据其在不同活动"价值链"各阶段的比较优势来分工应对，相关活动包括：对研发和创新的投资、资金调集、风险防范、加强韧性和危机应对。以下的例子表明，合作有潜力带来更强的影响。

第一，在研发和创新方面，国际金融机构与联合国专业机构应当共同搜集并分析数据，这是开发早期预警指标、制定风险防范与韧性增强计划的基础。慈善机构风险承受力更强，故在研发和创新投资方面发挥着重要的作用。

几年前，为应对西非埃博拉病毒疫情，惠康基金会在疫苗开发方面发挥了重要作用。这项活动风险太大，多边开发银行很难参与。

比尔及梅琳达·盖茨基金会（简称盖茨基金会）与非洲开发银行、亚洲开发银行一起提供资金支持，为城市贫民区提供金融及环境可持续的卫生服务。基金会还为创新技术研发提供援助资金，非洲开发银行和亚洲开发银行计划在有关技术可行性得以证实后加大对这些技术的运用。

多边开发银行可以为推动创新做出贡献。目前这些创新已度过了最初的高风险发展阶段。

第二，在资金调集方面，多边开发银行擅长促使私人资金参与全球公共目标。除了常规融资，多边开发银行应当开发一些临时的公共融资便利和全系统保险工具，这些对于快速拨付和发起支持行动十分关键。例如，在双边救助机构和世界卫生组织的支持下，世界银行建立了"流行病紧急融资便利"；非洲联盟、双边机构和世界银行共同建立了"非洲风险能力机构"，这是一个旨在确保食品安全的气象保险机制。进一步推进这类倡议仍有很大空间。

第三，在风险防范与韧性增强方面，国际金融机构在数据和知识共享领域有很大潜力仍待发掘。有关数据和知识可用于开发

第二章 加大跨系统合作：实现更强有力的全球发展效应

早期预警指标，并设计合理的风险预防与韧性增强机制。国际金融机构的特点使其能确保在项目和计划中嵌入合理的风险防范、快速反应和韧性增强机制，包括帮助最脆弱的国家适应气候变化，及早、有效地应对传染病或饥荒。泛美开发银行的新兴和可持续城市项目就是一个很好的例子，其旨在通过整合环境、城市和财政的可持续性和治理来增强韧性，尤其是与可持续基础设施相关的部分。

第四，在危机应对方面，有效的危机应对离不开国际金融机构、联合国机构和其他发展伙伴之间紧密、快速的协调。世界银行的全球危机应对平台就是这种联合机制的一个重要组成部分。一场由世界卫生组织领导、全球疫苗免疫联盟支持的联合行动有效地抗击了近年来在刚果（金）暴发的埃博拉疫情，展示了如何使用统筹方法有效遏制一场危险疫情的暴发。

为了全球人类健康而构建的抗击流行病和抗生素耐药性的架构正不断演化，世界卫生组织在其中起到了规范和协调的作用。该架构提供了一个很好的模型，示范了如何为每项共同目标搭建一个全球平台（见附录3）。

在新型国际合作秩序下，必须围绕某个特定的全球或区域公共目标来灵活动员国家和机构建立联盟。成立联合国 – 世界银行水资源高层小组即为一例。在此基础上，孟加拉国出台了德尔塔规划2100（Delta Plan 2100），展示了多边机构、双边合作伙伴和国家当局如何为了更强的长期效应共同努力，避免各自为战。①2018年10月成立的全球气候适应委员会也证明了各方可以在面对重要挑战时走到一起。②

建议7：信托基金活动融入多边开发银行的核心业务，避免其碎片化。

多边开发银行目前运营所需的很多资金不在其资产负债表内，主要以信托基金的形式存在。③这些基金背后的捐赠者或者捐赠联盟愿意为实现一些特定的发展目标而提供额外的资金支持。然而，大量的信托基金及其另类的治理结构正在使多边开发银行的活动碎片化，导致由信托提供资金的活动与多边开发银行战略目标不匹配，并导致了行政和运营方面的低效。此外，信托基金活动使各国政府的参与复杂化并降低了其参与度，因为信托基金一般专款专用且不可替代。

一些信托基金正在重要的高难度领域取得成果，特别是存在脆弱性的领域，例如以下四个基金所做的努力。

---

① 孟加拉国的德尔塔规划2100是一项长期的综合规划，它集合了水资源和食品安全、经济增长和环境可持续性等项目。世界银行与荷兰在吸取后者的经验上进行合作，并根据孟加拉的需求进行了调整。
② 该委员会获得了全球气候变化适应中心和世界资源机构的支持，它也在与其他伙伴密切合作。
③ 世界银行集团持有的信托资金至2017财年年底共有105亿美元：世界银行（国际复兴开发银行/国际开发协会）有544只标准化信托基金，国际金融公司有217只。参见2018年3月23日发布的《2017年信托基金年度报告：简述》。

第二章　加大跨系统合作：实现更强有力的全球发展效应

全球减灾与恢复基金——由400个合作伙伴组成的全球伙伴关系——为20个易受气候相关危害影响的国家提供了及时援助，并在2017财年助其将气候抗灾措施纳入本国发展战略和计划。

阿富汗重建信托基金——由34个捐助方组成的伙伴关系——为阿富汗的所有发展支出输送了50%的资金，并通过向全国数千个村庄提供教育和医疗机会，使930万人受益。

然而，多边开发银行必须与股东合作，以确保信托基金不会产生平行结构，这会显著降低国别项目和多边开发银行行动的效率和有效性。[①]

关于整合其他资源，供多边开发银行开展核心行动，下文提供了一些可供参考的做法。

全球优惠融资基金是全球危机应对平台的一部分，将捐助方赠款资源与世界银行的非优惠国际复兴开发银行资源相结合，为约旦和黎巴嫩的难民提供支持。

国际教育融资基金是一项新倡议，旨在为无法获得优惠贷款的中低收入国家提供资金，对多边开发银行提供的资金予以补充。

建议8：填补数据和研究缺口，有效支持科学和实践的政策

---

① 目前，世界银行正试图提升信托基金组合的效率和一致性，通过与捐助方合作将其分组为伞形安排，并在信托基金捐助方与世界银行的对话中采取更具战略性的方法。

制定，尤其是在发展中国家。

基本的社会、经济和环境数据存在重大缺陷，特别是在发展中国家。我们必须解决这些缺陷，以便为包容性增长和人力资本发展制定和实施有效的国别项目。

国际金融机构在数据（包括大数据）生成、分析和传播以及政策研究方面可在全球范围内发挥独特和重要的作用。这些是真正的公共物品，对于理解和应对全球挑战，推进合理、循证决策的经济发展，实现可持续发展目标至关重要。国际货币基金组织和世界银行是履行这些职责最理想的机构，可与联合国机构和在相关领域发挥类似作用的区域性开发银行密切合作。①

随着数据和研究结果不断涌现，相关主体有责任进行分享。国际金融机构往往在提高透明度方面发挥主导作用，但要更进一步，改善国际金融机构之间与政府的信息共享，并在适当情况下与全体公众共享信息。②

建议 9：系统性地利用企业联盟、非政府组织和慈善机构的观点和运营网络。

---

① 在 2018 年 5 月签订的联合国 – 世界银行集团战略合作伙伴框架中，联合国和世界银行集团承诺与政府、开发银行、市民社会和私人部门合作，加强国家统计体系，强化各国数字数据能力，关注数据搜集、分析和使用，以进行基于证据的决策。

② 20 世纪 90 年代，泛美开发银行和世界银行合作，改进了在拉丁美洲的家庭调查及其便利性，这在衡量贫穷、不平等及其决定因素上发挥了重要作用。

第二章　加大跨系统合作：实现更强有力的全球发展效应

利用商业联盟、非政府组织和慈善机构来增强发展效应的空间很大。这些机构提供新的理念、基层视角，并且可以调动专业知识和资源，作为国际金融机构可用资源的补充。其还能在国际金融机构难以参与的情形（例如脆弱和冲突情形）中提高执行能力。

上述机构创造价值的例子也有很多。自雇妇女协会（SEWA）是由贫困自主就业女工组成的基层组织。20多年来，其成员已从3万增加到190万。自雇妇女协会致力于为妇女赋权，为穷人提供有组织的医疗服务，积极提供小额信贷。自雇妇女协会已成为在基层释放技术潜力以激发创新、培育企业的典范。

孟加拉国农村发展委员会（BRAC）是一个旨在帮助穷人的非政府组织，起源于孟加拉国，但现在活动遍及全球。通过创新的、循证决策的发展方法，孟加拉国农村发展委员会影响了数百万人的生活，并改变了关于发展的思路和做法。

千禧年之际，名为"使贫穷成为历史"的民间社会联盟在重债穷国计划（HIPC）推进中发挥了重要的促进作用。这项由国际货币基金组织、世界银行和非洲开发基金共同发起的倡议为实现相关国家教育和医疗目标做出了重要贡献。

国际金融机构已开始与市民社会和慈善机构加强合作。国际金融机构可以更系统地利用市民社会和慈善机构的现有工作和能力，识别关键需求和缺口，将其与官方倡议联系起来，为这些参与者充分发挥作用提供空间和融资。国际金融机构在这方面的关键作用是发动更多力量实现好的理念。

第三章

强化增强全球金融韧性的改革：
确保日益关联的全球金融市场服务全球

第三章 强化增强全球金融韧性的改革：确保日益关联的全球金融市场服务全球

全球金融危机爆发十年后，要继续推行改革以减少阻碍增长的一系列不稳定因素，使各国不断走向开放，避免另一场重大危机。

第一，加强对各国的支持，为充分受益于跨境资本流动，应进一步深化国内金融市场，并制定和发展政策指导框架，确保以下两点。

◎ 各国能够利用国际资本流动，而不会因市场过度波动产生风险。
◎ 资本输出国实现国内目标，同时避免重大溢出效应。

第二，为复杂、相互关联的全球金融体系建立更强劲的综合风险监控体系，并系统性地考虑主流以外的不同观点。

第三，建立强大且可靠的全球金融安全网，将割裂的各层次金融安全网拼接起来。

一、世界受益于国际资本流动，但须避免过度市场波动引发的风险

国际货币和金融体系的一个关键目标应是促进投资，使各国能充分实现增长和发展潜力，同时满足全球储户的需求。

实现这一目标需要更强大、更有利的国内和国际环境。特别是，需要发展中国家进一步发展国内金融市场，通过长期投资等方式更为有效地动员更多国内储蓄并利用全球储蓄。同样，必须设法缓解过度金融波动，特别是短期资本流动相关的金融波动，以减少其对国内经济的影响。

关注如下两个重点将加强系统的抗风险能力，同时解决两个

紧迫的国际挑战。

◎ 帮助发展中国家打破以下不稳定因素的恶性循环：长期投资不足和对短期资金流的过度依赖使发展中国家易受到全球风险情绪和资本流动突然转变的冲击，而冲击带来的不稳定性进一步抑制了长期投资。国际货币与金融体系改革需要与改善各国投资环境同时推进，且必须**使发展中国家实现可持续的经常账户赤字，这是其充分发挥增长潜力的基础**。

◎ 为储户，特别是老龄化且预期寿命不断延长的群体提供分散风险并获得可靠长期回报的机会。①

第二次世界大战后工业化国家的经验表明，对外开放〔尤其是对贸易和外商直接投资（FDI）的开放〕已使全世界切实受益，有助于加强物质和人力资本，提高生活水平。在过去15年中，新兴和发展中国家的资本流动规模也显著增加（见图3.1），为能有效利用资本的国家带来了巨大潜力。特别是，在所有经济体中，外商直接投资都在知识和最佳做法的传播方面发挥了重要作用，是增长和发展的有效引擎。

---

① 金融市场改革也应确保风险分担机制的设计能使风险承受能力最强的主体承担更多风险。

第三章 强化增强全球金融韧性的改革：确保日益关联的全球金融市场服务全球

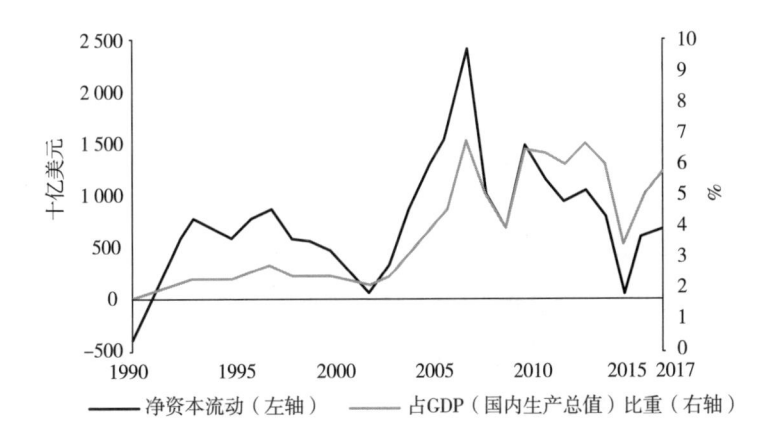

图3.1 非居民对新兴市场与发展中国家的净资本流动

注：这其中包括外商直接投资、证券投资、衍生品和其他资金流动，也包括跨境银行业资金流动。

资料来源：国际货币基金组织。

如果一国金融市场更有深度且实施可信的宏观经济战略，则能最大程度促进境内和境外融资并用于发展，同时在金融冲击下表现出更强的抗风险能力。

然而，受主要经济体政策溢出效应和全球风险偏好变化影响，跨境资本流动激增或骤停，部分国家汇率和国内资产市场也出现多轮大幅波动（详情见专栏3）。这些波动可能会干扰合理的政策制定，或导致不利于增长的干预措施。通常，资本流出或流入国制定了不合理的政策，或者当今全球市场的结构性或技术性因素是导致这种不稳定性的根源。

关于上述问题的政策思路往往跳不出流出国和流入国视角。

我们需要超越这一思路，建立以规则为基础的国际框架，全面考虑不断变化的证据并据此提供政策建议，使各国避免出台溢出效应严重的政策，提高市场的抗风险能力，在受益于资本流动的同时管理金融稳定风险。

国际货币金融体系必须确保各国能够从全球的相互依存中受益，持续开放并将此作为长期目标，同时管理金融稳定风险。国际货币与金融体系需要适应经济体（包括流出国和流入国）的不同发展阶段。特别是这一体系应该具备以下三点。

◎ 支持各国深化国内金融市场、在利用国际市场的同时管理波动。这将确保当前资本流动自由化的节奏和次序符合该国国情，经合组织最初为发达国家制定的《资本流动自由化准则》在此方面提出了愿景。
◎ 建立定期对话，从而围绕政策框架达成国际谅解，该框架旨在**实现国内目标**，同时避免大规模的负面国际溢出**效应**压缩他国的可用政策空间。
◎ 确保政策完善的国家可以获得临时流动性支持。

建议 10：各国际金融机构应强化并加速努力，帮助各国发展有深度、有韧性和有包容性的国内金融市场。

有深度、有韧性和包容性的国内金融市场对增长和发展至关重要，必须成为关键的优先事项，对新兴和发展中经济体尤其

第三章　强化增强全球金融韧性的改革：确保日益关联的全球金融市场服务全球

如此。有深度、有韧性和包容性的国内金融市场能够帮助各国更好地吸收资本流动，确保资金有效分配给实体部门。

专栏 3　新兴市场资本流动波动性

广义上讲，资本流动表现为少数几种主要形式：外商直接投资、证券投资和主要通过银行发生的其他流动。

◎ 外商直接投资是所有市场中传播知识、技术和最佳做法的主要动力，因此是增长的有效引擎。

◎ 证券投资和其他流动在为投资提供资金、加强金融市场流动性和确保风险得到对冲方面发挥重要作用。然而，除与流入国相关的因素外，证券投资和其他流动的波动性远强于外商直接投资*（见图3.2），且受到全球风险偏好转向的影响。

短期流动的激增和突然停止可能导致一系列剧烈波动，并可能大幅压缩政策制定的操作空间。

这对新兴市场尤为重要，因为其资本流动的波动性总体高于发达市场。市场微观结构和行为的变化，例如交易所交易基金（ETFs）的增长和算法交易的使用也凸显了这些波动性。此外，虽然近年新兴市场资本流动的波动性总量指标与21世纪第一个十年中期的平均值总体相当，但许多新兴市场国家的波动性增加，特别是在部分较大的新兴市场。

研究表明，"推动"因素（反映了流出国的发展和全球风险情绪的变化）在资本流动和资产价格波动中的作用越来越大。与此同时，"拉动"因素（如流入国自身的政策和情况）仍然解释了为什么全球波动事件对不同新兴市场国家的影响存在差异。

* 证券和其他投资的波动性分别比外商直接投资高 2 倍和 4 倍。见 Pagliari, M. and S. Ahmed Hannan, *The Volatility of Capital Flows in Emerging Markets: Measures and Determinants.* IMF Working Paper WP/17/41, Feb 2017.

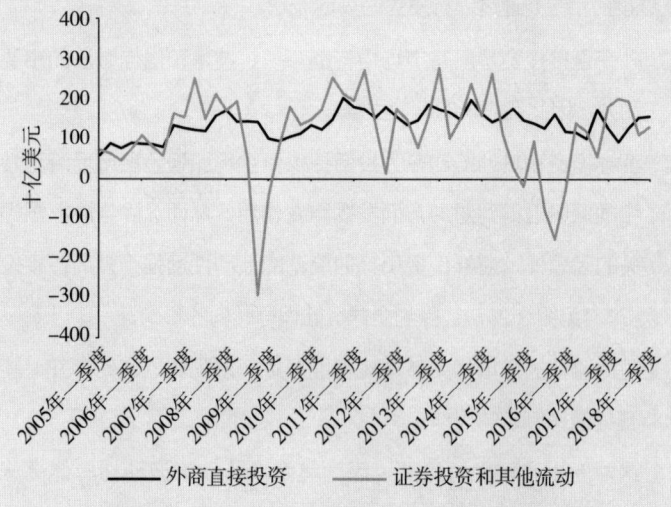

图 3.2 非居民向主要新兴市场的净资本流动

注：数据涵盖了非洲、中东、亚太、欧洲和拉丁美洲的 25 个最大的新兴市场经济体。

资料来源：国际金融协会。

为满足这一要求，国际货币基金组织、世界银行和区域性开发银行应与各国政府共同努力并加强协调。能力建设应强调以下政策和监管框架的制定。

第三章　强化增强全球金融韧性的改革：确保日益关联的全球金融市场服务全球

- ◎ 健全的银行和本币债券市场。这应包括实施国际标准制定机构建议的审慎监管，这也将降低资本流动波动性带来的风险。
- ◎ 强大的国内机构投资者基础。
- ◎ 借助技术应用、加快普惠金融发展的生态系统。

这方面的努力应与建议 11a 所描述框架的政策建议密切配合。

建议 11：国际货币基金组织的政策指导框架应帮助各国逐步迈向资本流动开放的长期目标，并更好地管理金融波动风险。

要建立更全面的政策指导框架，帮助各国维护宏观经济和金融稳定，确保不断推进开放。经验表明，要保持开放导向，各国必须能够管理资本流动和汇率的过度波动，并维持国内金融稳定。政策指导框架应帮助其预防正常时期的风险累积，并避免在紧张时期出现市场混乱和风险传染。[①]

建议 11a：制定基于实证的政策选项，使各国从资本流动中获益，同时维护金融稳定，并向市场保证所采取的措施是恰当的。

---

① 虽然建议提及的框架赞成各国根据国情渐进、适度地推进资本账户自由化（即开放道路因阶段而异），但其同样强调在面临金融稳定风险时须在每个阶段采取适当的措施（即基于状态的政策行动），目标是在压力消退后回到原来的开放道路上。

国际货币基金组织应将多次评估和政策建议的多项要素结合起来，促进机构观点的演变和扩展。

◎ 全面了解资本流动的驱动因素及其与货币、汇率和宏观审慎政策的相互作用。
◎ 可靠地评估流入国**存在风险的资本流动和宏观金融稳定性**。
◎ 评估来自流出国的"**推动因素**"，特别是周期性因素和潜在的资本流动逆转。
◎ 第四条款磋商应根据上述评估制定政策选项，指导各国在吸收资本流动的同时实现互利，应在充分考量各种工具，特别是宏观审慎政策有效性的基础上询证制定。这些选项应定期更新，确保一国在面临突发金融压力时能立即获得选项清单。

随着条件的成熟，可在全球范围内推动这一框架。该框架还应在各国采用符合框架的政策组合时向市场提供保证。

建议 11b：为使资本输出国既实现国内目标，又能避免大的负面国际溢出效应，要加强对政策选项的研究和宣传。

我们需要一个国际公认的政策框架，使流出国能实施自己的政策来实现国内目标（部分情况下由法定职能限定），同时避免

第三章　强化增强全球金融韧性的改革：确保日益关联的全球金融市场服务全球

大规模国际溢出效应压缩其他国家的政策空间。该框架应评估不同国内政策选项与资本流动、汇率和全球风险偏好转向的相互作用。这涉及不同政策组合（包括货币政策、财政政策和宏观审慎政策）如何对国际溢出效应造成不同影响。

这仍然是国际货币金融体系中一个棘手的问题。该框架虽然雄心勃勃，但为支持开放的国际体系，其重要性怎么强调也不过分。

应由国际货币基金组织制定该框架，各国政府和国际清算银行提供信息。这可以作为国际货币基金组织溢出效应有关工作的延伸，并纳入系统性国家的第四条款磋商。

政策框架应随着证据和经验的发展而演变。一个成功的例子是，在G20的支持和金融稳定理事会的推动下，审慎标准在全球范围内得以落实和发展。值得注意的是，巴塞尔委员会、国际保险监督官协会和国际证监会组织的框架虽然不具有强制性，但提供了一个基准来评估不同国家金融机构缓冲的充足性。若有国家偏离这一框架，同行和市场判断将对其构成约束。

我们必须在现有倡议的基础上，发展建议11描述的国际框架。国际货币基金组织的机构观点旨在解决资本流动波动性的问题，并考虑了各国经验。机构观点应该演变并扩展，并且包括如下要点。

◎ 该框架的目标是确保各国将资本账户可兑换作为**长期目标**，根据本国国情确定改革节奏和顺序，同时管理金融稳定风险。
- ◎ 制定更全面的资本流动评估框架，将**存在风险的资本流动、汇率政策和宏观金融稳定评估**纳入政策建议。该框架需要为各国提供最有效的政策以应对过度的短期波动及其影响，以帮助各国从持续推进开放中受益。[①]

在发展和扩展机构观点的同时，还应制定适当的政策框架，确保流出国实现其国内目标，同时避免重大的国际负面溢出效应。

完善全球金融架构还需要为实施稳健政策的国家提供临时流动性支持。随着金融关联性不断增强，更多经济体面临全球因素导致的流动性、资本流动和风险偏好的大幅波动，政策空间受到限制。有证据表明，灵活的汇率只能在一定程度上保护经济体不受这种波动的影响。因此，政策框架完善的新兴经济体决策者担忧，如果没有可靠的国际流动性支持来源，其需要积累更多储备或采取其他可能拖累增长的政策。

上述流动性便利的设计应该支持各国制定合理的政策，降低各国积累过多预防性储备的动机。此外，流动性便利仅供相关国家在全球或区域性流动性冲击中短期使用。

建议15阐述了该流动性便利的主要特征。

[①] 此外，还应建立一个评估以及建议的综合数据库，如建议11a和11b所述。

第三章　强化增强全球金融韧性的改革：确保日益关联的全球金融市场服务全球

国际货币基金组织的职责形成于资本流动规模较小的年代，仅包括经常账户。此外，经合组织虽然具有指导各国资本流动政策的职责，但其成员国覆盖面不够广泛。而成员国覆盖面广泛的机构均不具备指导各国资本流动政策的职责。在贸易和金融深度互联互通的当今世界，这是全球金融治理领域的一个空白。

长期来看，随着国际货币基金组织和国际社会就建议 11 所述的政策框架不断积累经验，一旦各国高度认可国际货币基金组织关于资本流动的政策建议，则应更新国际货币基金组织的职责，使其职责涵盖资本流动。

二、加强风险监督以避免下一次重大危机

我们不知道下一次危机将从哪里开始。但如果我们没有做好准备，危机将全面爆发，造成更广泛的全球性影响。因此，急需加强早期风险识别能力，并预测风险如何通过复杂且高度互联的全球金融体系传播，以便在风险加剧前予以控制。[①]

政府部门没有预见到本轮全球金融危机的来临。虽然此后国际货币基金组织、金融稳定理事会、国际清算银行的监督能力已显著扩张，但要避免下一次重大危机仍任重道远。考虑到当前债务水平和资产价格高企，且货币条件将收紧，应努力弥补监督能

---

① 名人小组的职能不包括评估审慎监管。然而，我们要解决的问题包括国际货币基金组织与金融稳定理事会及国际清算银行在避免未来危机的风险监督和应对措施方面的关系。

力方面存在的差距，将之作为重中之重。

此外，随着商业模式的变化，更广泛地区出现新型市场主体以及新技术的涌现，系统的复杂性和关联性也在不断增加。考虑到这种快速变化的格局，不论国际货币基金组织、金融稳定理事会还是国际清算银行，没有国际机构能以一己之力全面识别整个系统的风险。然而，现有的全球金融稳定职责仍然过于分散。上一次危机说明了职责分散的严重后果。[①]

建议12：整合国际货币基金组织、金融稳定理事会和国际清算银行的监督工作，构建具有一致性的全球风险地图，同时保持各机构观点的独立性。

有效的、经整合的全球监督和风险识别将降低未来爆发危机的可能性。我们必须对国际货币基金组织、金融稳定理事会和国际清算银行的特有视角进行整合，同时保留其相对优势。国际货币基金组织的优势在处理经济和宏观金融风险、溢出效应和主权债务脆弱性；金融稳定理事会的优势在处理金融体系脆弱性，包括修改监管规则的影响和由此产生的激励机制；国

---

① 例如，全球金融危机之前，随着监管边界扩大，利用跨境监管套利的风险未得到充分重视。因此，美国的冲击迅速传播到欧洲，尤其是以美元为中介的国家。随着全球范围内银行清算美元头寸，传染进一步蔓延，影响了新兴市场的美元流动性。国际清算银行相对较早地指出了这一问题，但金融稳定论坛（金融稳定理事会的前身）忽略了其根本原因，国际货币基金组织也很晚才开始认识到向全球各国的溢出渠道。

第三章　强化增强全球金融韧性的改革：确保日益关联的全球金融市场服务全球

际清算银行的优势在优化全球资金流动和市场基础设施。附录4对这三家机构的贡献进行了简要说明。①

三家机构应共同绘制全球风险地图并定期更新，涵盖以下各方的相互作用。

◎ 基本的宏观经济和金融条件以及政策溢出效应。
◎ 技术引发的金融稳定风险[2]，及其对不断演变的监管边界的影响。
◎ 银行和非银行金融中介机构商业模式的变化。[3]
◎ 资本市场结构的变化，这种变化可能加强顺周期性或降低市场预防大规模下跌的能力。[4]
◎ 上述情况对资本流动及其波动性的影响。
◎ 上述情况对市场基础设施（例如支付、结算系统和清算存管机构）的影响。

只有合作开展监督才能捕捉上述因素相互作用产生的风险。

---

① 附录4描述的作用反映了国际货币基金组织、金融稳定理事会和国际清算银行在风险识别各方面的相对优势。该描述完全是说明性而非限定性的。
② 例如，高频金融市场活动带来的潜在风险，人工智能的更多应用，加密资产和新的支付机制，以及网络入侵。
③ 这还包括研究各国落实改革的不同进度和方法是否/如何为金融机构创造套利机会（例如将某管辖区的交易记录在另一个管辖区）。
④ 例如，从主动向被动或趋势投资模型转变，主要股指的部门集中度增加，以及做市流动性减少。

全球风险地图将突出一系列风险，并指出可能诱发新危机的潜在脆弱性。

三家机构可成立联合小组，负责绘制全球风险地图并定期更新。该小组可系统性地从各种官方[①]和非官方渠道获取信息，但在分析中保持独立。至关重要的是，三家机构在此过程中必须保持自身评估和工作人员意见的独立性，并标明每项风险由哪家机构识别。必须避免为达成共识而放弃自身观点。[②]虽然经过统一的全球风险地图有助于整合三家机构识别的风险，但如果联合评估能够指出三家机构的分歧，也会很有裨益。

建议12a：系统性地纳入非官方部门和反对观点，提高风险监督的稳健性。

传统的官方智慧往往落后于现实，这在识别全球金融体系的重大扰动时尤为明显。上次危机就是个很好的例子，仅少数观点警告即将出现动荡。此外，考虑到当今全球金融体系的复杂性和去中心化特征，需要系统性地利用市场关于潜在扰动的观点和情报。[③]建议12中的监督框架应寻求这样的观点。

---

① 特别是来自金融稳定理事会全会和国际货币基金组织《世界经济展望》（WEO）和《全球金融稳定报告》（GFSR）的信息。还应寻求金融中心央行的信息。
② 关于机密性和披露的制度安排阻碍了当前的系统性风险监测。为克服这些障碍，须与信息来源当局和国际金融机构制定有力的知识和数据共享协议，以解决上述担忧。
③ 还可向区域性系统性风险委员会寻求信息，其在全球金融危机后不断发展。

第三章　强化增强全球金融韧性的改革：确保日益关联的全球金融市场服务全球

建议13：以国际货币基金组织和金融稳定理事会早期预警演练为基础，在政策上跟进处理全球风险地图识别的风险。[①]

以国际货币基金组织和金融稳定理事会早期预警演练为基础，由部长和央行行长就全球风险开展政策讨论。[②]

根据建议12描述的全球风险地图，各方可通过早期预警演练对风险驱动因素和结果展开讨论，以更好地认识全球体系中存在的主要同步风险和尾部风险。最重要的是，各方可就政策方向和具体行动开展讨论，以缓解主要风险和脆弱性。如可能，国际货币基金组织、金融稳定理事会和国际清算银行应进一步合作，区分仅需个别国家关注的风险和需国际协作应对的风险。

上述讨论应效仿早期预警演练，进行闭门讨论，以便参与方评估和讨论敏感问题，从而避免引发市场反应并使风险自我强化。尽管如此，为提高透明度并加强问责，最初阶段之后，各机构应对信息披露的政策选项开展评估，例如披露已识别的风险和相关政策建议。此处讨论是否披露的信息不包括为绘制全球风险地图

[①] 自2009年年会以来，国际货币基金组织和金融稳定理事会合作每年开展两次早期预警演练。早期预警演练主要评估全球经济和金融体系中概率低但影响大的风险，在提高尾部风险意识方面发挥了重要作用。根据识别风险的类型，政策建议有时会超出国际货币与金融委员会成员的政策范畴。此外，长期以来议题的连续性也比较有限。

[②] 当前，国际货币基金组织和金融稳定理事会的合作基于2008年11月国际货币基金组织总裁与金融稳定理事会主席的联合信函。

已经披露的信息。[①]

国际货币基金组织应继续与其他相关机构，特别是经合组织和反洗钱金融行动特别工作组（FATF）密切合作，以应对全球金融体系完整性面临的挑战。逃税、洗钱和恐怖融资的威胁始终存在。而且，这些威胁可能与网络安全风险以及新支付平台和加密资产等创新相互作用。上述创新本身可能没问题，但整体来看需要密切关注，且未来可能需要就此实施更严格的全球治理。

三、将割裂的全球金融安全网络拼接起来

保持开放和旨在促进全球增长的政策需要更加可预测的全球金融安全网，安全网中各个层级应紧密结合，并基于明确阐述的角色、责任及可行的保障措施运作。全球金融安全网应具备充足的资源，对不同的压力情况（包括全球系统性危机事件）做出响应。我们目前还未建成这样的安全网。

[①] 作为全球风险地图要素的潜在信息，国际货币基金组织目前公布其《全球金融稳定报告》，《世界经济展望》，《对外部门报告》（ESR），《财政监测报告》和第四条款磋商报告。国际清算银行的全球金融体系委员会（CGFS）发布关于全球金融市场潜在压力来源的多份报告，而国际清算银行本身也设有以币种细分的全球金融流动的公共数据平台。金融稳定理事会的脆弱性评估委员会（SCAV）定期发布关于金融体系风险和脆弱性的报告。

第三章　强化增强全球金融韧性的改革：确保日益关联的全球金融市场服务全球

在过去十年中，随着国家储备、双边互换协议（BSAs）和区域金融安排的发展，多层次的安全网不断演变（见图3.3）。然而，目前的去中心化结构有几个重大缺陷。

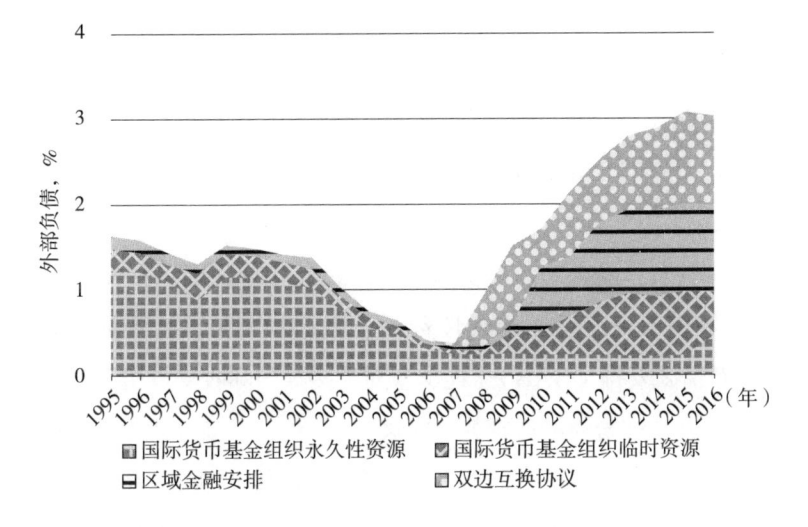

图3.3　全球金融安全网的发展

资料来源：国际货币基金组织，英格兰银行。

◎ 各地区安全网的规模和覆盖范围非常不均衡。全球大约70%的区域金融安排资源集中在欧元区，其具备政治基础和共同货币，确保了区域金融安排的快速和有效运作。其他区域金融安排缺乏类似的基础。还有大片地区无法获得区域金融安排，或者区域金融安排规模不足。

◎ 全球金融安全网的大部分增长由未经危机检验的双边互换协议和区域金融安排构成，并且受到提供国和地区普遍存在情况的限制。区域金融安排和双边互换协议也未覆盖几个系统重要性国家。[①]

◎ 整个系统缺乏必要的协调，难以有效利用其全部资金能力。

因此在下一次危机发生前，在全球金融安全网中建立一个强大、可靠的全球层级至关重要。

国际货币基金组织提供这一关键的全球层面的金融安全网。国际货币基金组织的永久性资源（即份额）和常备借款安排［即新借款安排（NAB）］能够应对大多数国际收支危机及危机蔓延，并能够扮演最后贷款人的角色。[②] 份额及新借款安排构成了国际货币基金组织[③]的第一道和第二道防线。国际货币基金组织还在全球金融危机发生后推出双边借款作为第三道防线。2008年全球金融危机之前，国际货币基金组织上述资源总和占全球金融安全网资源总和的90%，2016年这一比例降至1/3左右（见图

[①] 具有系统重要性的金融部门的国家和地区包括：澳大利亚、奥地利、比利时、巴西、加拿大、中国、丹麦、芬兰、法国、德国、中国香港特别行政区、印度、爱尔兰、意大利、日本、韩国、卢森堡、墨西哥、荷兰、挪威、波兰、俄罗斯、新加坡、西班牙、瑞典、瑞士、土耳其、英国和美国。
[②] 同时应尊重现行贷款政策，如超额贷款框架。
[③] 拟实施的流动性便利（建议15）也属于这一类。

第三章　强化增强全球金融韧性的改革：确保日益关联的全球金融市场服务全球

3.4）。① 当前的双边借款到期后，国际货币基金组织的资源将低于金融安全网全球层面的要求。

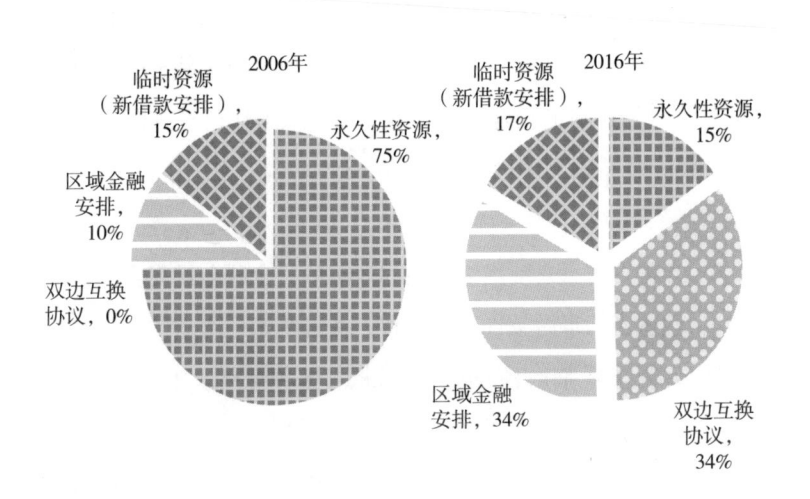

图 3.4　全球金融危机前后国际货币基金组织资源占比

资料来源：国际货币基金组织，英格兰银行。

建议14：将全球金融安全网的各个层面联结在一起，提高规模和可预见性。

在发生重大危机并需要资源之前，把安全网的各个层面连接起来至关重要。有效的治理框架应能促进稳健的国家政策，以

---

① 目前，国际货币基金组织资源中约 6 610 亿美元来自份额，约 2 530 亿美元来自新借款安排，另外，约有 4 500 亿美元双边贷款将于 2020 年到期。

及在特定情况下共享资金资源。一个设计合理且公平的体系可以避免道德风险，减缓危机蔓延[①]，并避免过度自我保护。

没有哪一种设计能够适合所有地区。然而，要使全球金融安全网有效，就需要明确国际货币基金组织和每个区域金融安排之间的责任划分并制定联合行动标准。[②] 这项工作已经开展，应尽快完成并应遵循以下关键原则。

◎ 当需要进行宏观经济调整和改革时，**全球金融安全网必须就适当的事后条件达成一致，并避免推迟调整。**
◎ 如果出现临时流动资金需求，应实行建议 15 中的规定且不附加任何条件。
◎ **国际货币基金组织是开展上述评估的最可靠的独立机构。**它的宏观金融监督分为全球和双边两个独立层面，还可通过借款活动提供所需的评估并发挥独特作用。

建议 15：国际货币基金组织建立常备流动性便利工具，在全球流动性冲击时为各国提供及时的临时性支持。

---

① 以 2011 年 G20 发布的关于国际货币基金组织与区域金融安排的合作原则为指导并汲取此前欧洲危机贷款项目的经验，国际货币基金组织与欧盟委员会以及欧洲稳定机制（ESM）在 2013 年国际货币基金组织对塞浦路斯的贷款项目中进行了合作，该合作被视为典范。合作各方在紧急危机救助知识、长期的结构性议程以及恰当的责任分担中相互补充，获益匪浅。
② 这项工作应以国际货币基金组织和区域金融安排之间的持续合作为基础，如就试运行、经验交流以及干预方式的一致性等开展定期对话。

第三章　强化增强全球金融韧性的改革：确保日益关联的全球金融市场服务全球

利用国际货币基金组织永久性资源建立一个常备的全球性流动性便利至关重要，各方应就此达成共识。如果没有可靠的流动性便利，各国将持有过多的储备，不利于全球增长。及时的流动性便利有助于提高各国抵御流动性冲击的能力，并避免更深层次的危机。

这一便利将遵循国际货币基金组织的正常额度政策，应为具备事前资格的国家提供可预见的支持。[①] 国际货币基金组织在设计这一循环便利时应确保以下两点：（1）贷款决策应根据单独的程序做出，而不是作为第四条款磋商的一部分，以此确保监督程序的完整性；（2）国际货币基金组织不应成为事实上的评级机构。[②]

这将使大多数政策稳健的国家无须与国际货币基金组织进行旷日持久的谈判即可及时获得临时流动性支持。这对于洗刷"国际货币基金组织污名"至关重要。

建议 15a：在启动区域金融安排支持时，以一国能够获得国际货币基金组织流动性便利工具为前提条件。

整合的全球金融安全网应通过区域金融安排提供临时流动性便利，这有助于：通过相互利用资源大幅提高服务各自成员的能力；在区域层面解决"国际货币基金组织污名"问题，从而鼓

[①] 每年将重新评估预先资格条件。
[②] 不同于评级机构，国际货币基金组织不会对国家进行单边评估，并且评估程序将保密，由此保护那些不具备资格或有兴趣加入的国家。

励成员国更迅速地获得支持；推广通用操作规程，提高危机应对速度。

建议16：允许国际货币基金组织在发生大规模及严重全球危机时迅速调动额外资源。

鉴于未来可能发生系统性和"尾部风险"性质的危机，急需弥补全球金融安全网的缺陷。这可能需要建立临时机制，并通过这些机制使国际社会可以迅速获得大量流动性，以确保或恢复金融稳定。

在上一轮全球金融危机期间，美联储通过与部分央行的流动性互换安排释放了约5 000亿美元流动性。虽然大多数新兴市场经济体并未直接从中受益，但是这些干预对于确保全球美元支付体系的完整性和稳定全球市场至关重要。重要的是，未来不一定会再出现这类操作。

此外，为了响应国际货币与金融委员会和G20的联合呼吁，危机期间，很多国家承诺向国际货币基金组织提供总计4 500亿美元的临时性资源，但并非所有成员国都提供了资金。为应对未来重大危机，必须能够快速动员该类双边借款。[①]

还应探索其他解决方案，以使国际货币基金组织能够在发

---

① 本轮临时融资于2012年4月启动。2012年6月，国际货币基金组织收到各国注资，同年10月，首批协议生效。2016年8月，双边借款期限延长至2019年末，并在到期后可再延期一年。

第三章　强化增强全球金融韧性的改革：确保日益关联的全球金融市场服务全球

生重大系统性危机时迅速调动足够规模的资源，维护全球稳定。备选方案见附录5。

然而，尽管从融资角度看这些方案是可行的，但却面临治理和政策方面的挑战，各界对此看法也不一。国际社会需要时间形成共识，从而克服这些困难。因此，名人小组不提供具体建议也不寻求快速通过建议方案。①

鉴于本章所提出的改革的重要性以及国际货币基金组织在实施改革方面的重要作用，国际货币与金融委员会应定期更新改革进展及面临的挑战。

---

① 同样，经评估，协调中央银行互换额度的方案在现阶段也不可行，目前也不予以考虑。

第四章

提升 G20 和国际金融机构的领导作用：维护系统整体有效运行

第四章 提升G20和国际金融机构的领导作用：维护系统整体有效运行

应重新设定G20在全球金融架构中的角色。它应当致力于在重大战略问题及危机应对方面达成政治共识。这就需要G20从现有的繁忙日程中解放出来，并把部分工作下放给国际金融机构。

我们需要一个能确保国际货币金融体系系统性运行的治理架构。

◎ 对发展融资进行系统性重新定位。以G20为首、涵盖主要非G20利益相关方的小组应当在未来三年促进这一转变，此后将协调职责移交给国际金融机构。这应包括在多个机构（多边、区域及双边机构）之间建立互补关系，并建立一个清晰的指标体系，用于跟踪资金使用效果及价值。

◎ **尽早解决发展面临的挑战。**在现有国际金融机构论坛的基础上，举办两年一次的战略对话，将国际金融机构与其他主要利益相关者聚集在一起，以便识别影响发展的风险，避免其造成持久损害，并对共同应对之策的充足性进行评估。

◎ 国际货币基金组织在与国际货币金融体系中其他不可或缺机构的互动中发挥关键作用，开展促进全球金融抗风险能力的治理改革，并定期向国际货币与金融委员会汇报最新情况。

国际金融机构开展自身治理改革，减少执行董事会和管理层在职责方面存在的大量重叠。应该促使执行董事会更多地关注战略优先事项，赋予管理层权力并对其进行问责。

国际金融机构体系的治理改革需要分两步走。第一步是确保在更加多样化和去中心化的世界中保持一致性和协同性。第二步是实现业务模式所需的根本转变，以拉动私人投资并产生更大的发展效应。

我们并非从原地出发。然而，尽管我们在促使各倡议和操作与新的优先事项保持一致方面取得了一些进展，但传统业务模式占比依然很大。我们在治理方面持续关注错误的领域，忽视了对战略问题的治理，导致职责重叠和决策效率低下。鉴于前几章涉及的需求规模大且具有紧迫性，需要在治理方面进行根本性转变，以推动全系统重新定位。

还需要重新定位G20在全球金融治理中的角色，以更高效地发挥其核心优势，避免重复工作，并最大限度地提高整个系统的有效性。

报告建议涉及以下三大变革。

◎ G20在前瞻性思维以及全球金融治理和危机应对方面的作用。
◎ 将国际金融机构作为一个整体来治理，使其总体贡献大于单个机构贡献的总和。
◎ 国际金融机构内部的治理，特别是简化执行董事会和管理层的职责，确保治理的有效性和建立以结果为导向的监督机制。

一、G20在全球金融治理中提供前瞻性战略指导

G20能够成为推动变革的强大动力，特别是在危机已经发生或迫在眉睫的情况下，它能够比单个机构更迅速地应对重大战

第四章 提升G20和国际金融机构的领导作用：维护系统整体有效运行

略挑战。各成员国在其共识框架内享有平等地位，这提高了G20在多极世界中的可信度。自全球金融危机以来，G20利用这一领导优势促进了多个重要领域的变革，例如，通过金融稳定理事会加强金融监管，通过经合组织实现税收透明化。

不过，G20与国际金融机构之间的治理关系对于实现有效的全球金融治理非常关键。G20并不包括所有国家，也不同于基于条约的组织，G20在履行决策方面缺少法律依据。它需要同国际金融机构及其他国际组织合作来实现目标。

就G20自身而言，人们感到随着时间的推移，其遗留议程及活动内容不断扩大，使其越来越难以专注于战略问题。

2018年，轮值主席国阿根廷采取了重要措施，征求了G20成员国对未来议程发展方向的意见。我们的建议就是本着这一理念提出的。

建议17：G20应重新聚焦长期战略性议程，工作流程应更加合理，把更多工作移交给国际金融机构。

随着时间的推移，G20会议数量和频率大幅增加（见表4.1）。[①] 日益增多的G20议程和活动与国际金融机构的治理存在重叠。各种倡议和活动的累积可能对需要G20战略指导的问

[①] 从2009年起，G20财长及央行行长会议平均每年举办4次，其他部长级会议也同样增加。2016年，G20各工作组共举行了50多次会议，而2009年G20仅召开了11次工作组会议。

题形成挤出——包括克服体系内的治理障碍问题，以及需要跨机构而不仅仅在个别机构内部实施才能产生决定性作用的情况。

G20需要重新关注全球战略目标，并更多地利用国际金融机构和其他国际组织。

从G20目标出发，G20内部的两级体系可以满足大多数目标，该体系包括侧重于战略挑战的部长级会议和为前者提供支持并确保贯彻落实的副手会。

◎ 部长会议应重新关注需要国际协调的重大战略问题及新出现的威胁。正常情况下，一年召开1~2次G20财长及央行行长会议就足够了，如果出现危机情况，则进一步提高会议频率。

◎ 随着工作任务转交给国际金融机构和其他主管机构，每年两次副手会应该成为常态。

G20工作组的大多数工作都可以且应该单独或合并下放给国际金融机构，下放依据是各机构的职责及比较优势，同时需要构建这些机构与G20之间的交流机制。

但是，为了推动重大的系统性举措，G20偶尔需要新成立工作组。此类工作组的存续时间应有限制。对此，G20应该有明确的目标，即在三年内开展初期工作，随后转交给现有机构。

根据名人小组的职责，我们的建议着眼于全球金融治理，但我们发现，这些建议可能与G20的其他工作都有关系。

第四章 提升G20和国际金融机构的领导作用：维护系统整体有效运行

表4.1 不同时期G20会议数量[1]

	1999年	2000年	2001年	2002年	2003年	2004年	2005年	2006年	2007年	2008年	2009年	2010年	2011年	2012年	2013年	2014年	2015年	2016年	2017年	2018年
峰会										1	2	2	1	1	1	1	1	1	1	1
协调人会议														5	6	4	4	5	5	4
财金渠道																				
财长及央行行长会议	1	1	1	1	2	1		1	1	2	4	4	4	3	4	5	2	4	3	5
财政和央行行副手会议				1	2	2	2	1			2	3	1	5	6	6	3	4	5	5
全球经济/架构															3	4	4	3	4	2
绿色/可持续金融											1						2	4	4	4
国际金融架构															4				5	3
基础设施																4	3	3		4
金融包容性																3	2	3	3	2
数据缺口																				4
非洲契约																			2	
协调人渠道												1	1	1						
劳动/就业部长会议																	1	1	1	1

[1] 对2008—2011年的会议数量估计基于现有数据。

097

未来全球金融治理

续表

	1999年	2000年	2001年	2002年	2003年	2004年	2005年	2006年	2007年	2008年	2009年	2010年	2011年	2012年	2013年	2014年	2015年	2016年	2017年	2018年
外交部部长会议													1	1	1		1		1	1
农业部部长会议													1	1			1	3	4	3
贸易部部长会议														1		1		1		1
能源部部长会议																		1	1	1
卫生部部长会议																			2	1
数字化部部长会议																			1	1
教育部部长会议																				1
发展											1		1		4	3	4	3	3	3
反腐败															3	3	3	3	3	3
就业															4	4	3	3	4	4
能源可持续性/转型															2	3	3	3	1	2
贸易及投资																		3	3	2
钢铁产能（M）																			4	3
数字经济																			4	2
可持续发展																			3	2
健康																			3	3
教育																				4

第四章　提升G20和国际金融机构的领导作用：维护系统整体有效运行

二、全系统改革治理

（一）实现更大的发展效应

将国际金融机构作为整体进行治理应当侧重于确保在更加多样化和去中心化的世界中保持一致性和协同性，共同拉动私人投资，从而产生更大的发展效应。

建议18：G20小组（包含来自非G20和国际金融机构的成员）在未来三年中指导发展融资重新定位，之后将该协调职能交给国际金融机构。应在各发展伙伴间建立互补性，构建一个清晰的指标体系，持续衡量发展效应和资金利用率。

需要一个有效的论坛来对发展融资系统进行重新定位。但是，目前还没有一个论坛拥有普遍成员资格，能够在发展中拥有系统性职权，并且可以引导重要转变，以确保国际金融机构之间以及与其他主要发展伙伴之间的一致性和互补性。由于主要国家在G20中拥有席位，因此G20具有系统性，但它的成员没有普遍性。而拥有普遍成员资格的发展委员会又只关注单个机构。

在国际金融机构现有举措的基础上，还需要三年时间来实现新的发展前景，并建立适当的体系和矩阵，确保在此之后继续深化改革。

由G20领导的、包含非G20成员国或国际金融机构的副手小组定期向部长汇报,这是在将协调职能移交给国际金融机构之前的三年里弥合上述缺口的最有效方式。由 G20 领导的小组最适合在多个机构(多边的、区域的及双边的)的利益相关方之间进行协调。此外,拟成立的小组应包括来自地区开发银行的代表及非 G20 成员的主要双边发展融资提供者。还应考虑包括国际开发金融俱乐部主席,该俱乐部由主要的开发性金融机构组成。

该小组的一项关键任务是提出系统性目标、时间表和相关进展的评估标准(见附录 6)。[1] 其应该关注以下三个方面。

◎ 关于**风险偏好**的战略指引,适合国际金融机构在实现发展效应方面的作用。[2]

◎ 加强**系统性协作**,包括利用所有发展伙伴优势的国家平台,并推动核心标准趋同。

◎ 转变多边开发银行**业务模式**和动员私人融资。

◎ 衡量**资金价值**,以确保多边开发银行单独和集体地为其

---

[1] 除了早期开发性金融机构私人部门项目混合优惠融资工作组外,2018 年 7 月多边开发银行联合工作组发布的关于额外性统一框架的报告是一次有用的尝试。需要进一步开展工作,制定共同指标,以便能够评价系统性进展和对国际金融机构进行比较。

[2] 需要特别注意的是国际金融机构在脆弱国家中的作用。在这种环境下,承担更高的风险启动投资和调动资源,可能会随着时间的推移产生更大的发展效应和潜在回报,例如国际开发协会私人部门窗口正在尝试参与的项目。

第四章 提升 G20 和国际金融机构的领导作用：维护系统整体有效运行

客户、股东和其他利益相关方实现最佳价值。[1]

建议 19：国际货币与金融委员会和发展委员会召开两年一度的战略论坛，识别潜在风险以及需要何种集体应对措施。

我们必须做得更好，在风险显现、风险跨国传播并造成持久损害之前预测风险。过去几十年，我们未能及时识别风险的例子不断重复。

财政部长也必须参与应对这些风险。国际货币与金融委员会和发展委员会（代表了 25 个选区）应每两年共同召集一次关于全球风险地图的对话，参会人员还包括国际金融机构、联合国发展系统、主要民间社会和慈善机构以及私人部门的代表。全球风险地图[2]应由世界银行、国际货币基金组织的联合秘书处与地区开发银行合作编制。它将着眼于新出现的趋势和挑战，还应包括关于制定全系统指标的见解。全球风险地图应使利益相关者能够评估应对措施的充分性和未来所需的集体努力。

---

[1] G20 国际金融架构小组（IFA）制定了一个衡量资金价值的框架。资金价值概念包括衡量多边开发银行实现其战略目标的效率，包括其在脆弱国家开展工作的情况。

[2] 广义上看，风险包括发展过程中面临的风险和错失机会后的风险。

（二）提高全球金融体系的抗风险能力

第三章在三个相互依存的领域提出了促进全球金融抗风险能力的改革建议，包括：（1）获得资本流动的收益，而不引发市场过度波动的风险；（2）加强对更复杂、互联互通的全球金融体系的风险监督；（3）建立强大可靠的全球金融安全网。为便于参考，现将第三章中阐述的治理要求总结如下。

关于资本流动。首先，国际货币基金组织、世界银行和地区开发银行应加快努力，帮助各国建立有深度、有韧性和具有包容性的国内金融市场。其次，国际货币基金组织的政策指导框架应使各国以迈向资本流动开放作为一个长期目标，开放的节奏和顺序应有利于维护金融稳定并管理好市场过度波动。这涉及：（1）发展和扩展国际货币基金组织的机构观点，以综合评估一国存在风险的资本流动和宏观金融稳定性、来自资本输出国"推动"因素的周期性背景及有关各种工具有效性的证据等，以此作为资本输入国制定政策选项的基础；（2）国际货币基金组织建立政策框架对此加以补充，使输出国能够采取政策，在实现其国内目标的同时避免产生巨大的负面溢出效应。为建立政策框架，国际货币基金组织应吸收各国和国际清算银行的信息。最后，我们必须在国际货币基金组织股东之间达成共识，建立国际货币基金组织常备流动性便利。

国际货币基金组织的正式职责确定时，资本流动较小，其职责只包括经常账户。随着时间的推移，国际货币基金组织和国际

第四章 提升 G20 和国际金融机构的领导作用：维护系统整体有效运行

社会就上述建议框架积累了经验。一旦有关资本流动的政策建议达成充分的国际共识，长期目标应该是更新国际货币基金组织正式职责，使其可以在资本流动方面发挥作用。

关于风险监督。国际货币基金组织、金融稳定理事会和国际清算银行应将其监督工作纳入全球风险地图，同时保持三个机构观点的完整性。这三家机构的联合小组应该从货币中心中央银行等各种官方和非官方渠道获取信息。国际货币基金组织－金融稳定理事会早期预警演练应为政策讨论和后续行动提供依据。

关于全球金融安全网。及时完成国际货币基金组织的份额检查对于确保金融安全网的全球层次拥有充足资源很有必要。[①] 此外，国际货币基金组织和区域金融安排应加强工作协调，明确责任分配并确立联合行动规范，以便建立更强大、更可靠的全球金融安全网。这包括在涉及宏观经济政策调整的案例中讨论事后条件的一致性、确定流动性需求以及国际货币基金组织流动性便利的信号作用。

此外，除了需要加强其永久性资源外，国际货币基金组织还应探索临时机制，以迅速调动资源，确保未来发生大规模系统性危机时获得足够规模的资源，维护全球稳定。

鉴于这三条改革措施的重要性以及国际货币基金组织在实施

---

① 国际货币与金融委员会曾呼吁国际货币基金组织执行董事会加快努力进度，争取在 2019 年春季会议之前、最晚于 2019 年年会之前完成第 15 次份额总检查。

这些改革方面的关键作用，国际货币与金融委员会应定期了解其执行情况和面临的挑战。

三、国际金融机构内部治理

国际金融机构本身的治理必须与时俱进。每家国际金融机构均应制定框架，简化执行董事会和管理层的作用，避免重叠，并确保每个部门有着明确的责任分工和问责制。

目前的治理安排是在传统银行业务时代制定的，因此需要转型。银行内部的公司治理有完善的监管标准，而当前国际金融机构治理结构和流程不符合这些既定标准，急需转型。[1]

治理改革的重点包括以下两个方面。

◎ 消除执行董事会（代表股东）与管理层之间职责的重叠，减少决策低效。[2]
◎ 将执行董事会的议程集中在战略问题和国家战略的治理上，而不是过多地把精力放在业务决策和交易职能上。

建议20：国际金融机构执行董事会应聚焦于本机构的战略优先事项，推进实现系统性目标。

---

[1] 过去对国际金融机构治理的研究也发现了这些差距。
[2] 《关于问责制框架的文件》中阐述的亚投行的新问责框架就是旨在提高决策效率和效果的一个案例。

第四章 提升 G20 和国际金融机构的领导作用：维护系统整体有效运行

执行董事会应重点阐明和实施系统范围内的政策和标准，并根据协商一致的目标为机构发展指引方向。多边开发银行执行董事会在重新定位责任时应考虑以下要素。

◎ 适合业务模式转变和实现发展效应的风险偏好。
◎ 资本充足率和流动性政策。
◎ 国家战略。
◎ 以风险为基础的适当框架，可将操作问题下放给管理层（建议 21），辅之以合规政策。

随着角色和责任进一步明确，股东还应根据有效性、成本结构和会议频率对国际金融机构执行董事会的不同模式进行评估（见表 4.2）。

表 4.2　国际金融机构执董预算情况

机构	执董数量	成员	预算（百万美元）	会议召开频率
国际复兴开发银行	25	189	88	一周 2 次
国际货币基金组织	24	189	70	一周若干次
欧洲复兴开发银行	23	69	20	一月 2~3 次
亚洲开发银行	12	67	34	一月若干次
泛美开发银行	14	48	23	一周 1 次
非洲开发银行	20	80	17.5	按需召开
欧洲投资银行	29+6	28	1.5	一年 10 次
国际农业发展基金	24	176	2.5	一年 3 次

续表

机构	执董数量	成员	预算（百万美元）	会议召开频率
亚洲基础设施投资银行	12	86	2.7	一年4次（外加4次虚拟会议）
伊斯兰开发银行	18	57	2.0	一年5次

注：欧洲投资银行除28名成员国和欧盟委员会（拥有投票权）外，其董事会还包括6名常任董事（无投票权）。

资料来源：Stilpon Nestor, 2018, *Board Effectiveness in International Financial Institutions*, AIIB Yearbook of International Law; and IFIs.

建议21：国际金融机构应采用切实可行、基于风险的方法，将更多责任下放管理层，并对管理层问责。

采用切实可行、基于风险的方法，国际金融机构董事会有较大空间进一步向管理层下放权力。作为综合评估的一部分，国际金融机构在必要时应考虑修改其章程，允许权力下放。①

明确具体角色和责任后，将使管理层获得授权并对相关工作负责，确保国际金融机构和整个系统的战略优先事项有效地转化为政策、操作和激励措施。如果没有组织文化的深刻变革，国际金融机构内部运营模式的主要战略转型将无法实现。政策、操作和激励措施等改革必须分两步走。

---

① 就多边开发银行而言，项目核准权的下放可根据项目规模以及项目的特性、是否需要开展更广泛讨论来确定。就国际货币基金组织而言，监督和贷款项目可能需要执行董事会进一步讨论。

第四章 提升G20和国际金融机构的领导作用：维护系统整体有效运行

◎ 通过共同参与国家平台的运作，发挥国际金融机构和其他发展伙伴之间的互补性和协同性。
◎ 推动多边开发银行业务模式的根本转变，重新关注各国的政策和机构能力以及风险缓释问题，促进私人投资。

每个机构的管理层必须指导这一转型过程。

建议22：各机构执行董事会和管理层应拥有多样化技能，更好地适应经营模式的转变和日益复杂的挑战。

执行董事会应采用现代化的公司治理做法，确保国际金融机构能够在更复杂的环境中有效运行。具体包括以下三个方面。

◎ 明确各选区选举执行董事、董事会遴选管理层应考虑的必备技能。
◎ 辅之以定期反馈和对执行董事会的有效性开展自我评估。
◎ 为专业化的执行董事会委员会寻求外部支持（例如审计和风险评估以及促进私人投资的战略），确保决策时将适当的因素考虑进来。

国际金融机构负责人的遴选程序应公开、透明和择优，这对国际金融机构的持续合法性和有效性至关重要。

附 录

附 录

附录1 现有平台安排分类

发展伙伴协作平台帮助政府制定全面的公共投资项目或计划，确定优先发展顺序，并基于各自的比较优势与发展伙伴的需求相匹配。成功的协作平台通常具有政府发挥较强的主人翁作用、透明度高以及与平台参与者协商等特点。（见专栏4关于卢旺达的例子）

> **专栏4：卢旺达——发展伙伴协作平台**
>
> 卢旺达政府已建立了一个成功的发展伙伴协作平台，该机制具有建议的国家发展合作平台的多个特点。卢旺达政府长期发展目标是通过实施一系列五年发展战略将卢旺达建设成为中等收入国家。该机制非常注重可持续性和包容性。发展伙伴通过一个体现若干良好治理原则的协调机制提供支持，具体包括：各国发挥较强的主人翁作用，由财政部长进行协调；使合作伙伴围绕发展战略保持协调一致；政府机构和发展伙伴间相互问责；透明度；政府内部（包括地方政府）建立发展成果的管理体系。这种协调机制还促进了发展伙伴之间协商分工，以降低交易成本并确保发挥比较优势。它使每个发展伙伴更加关注其发展项目的连续性和规模效率。迄今为止，协作平台主要涉及官方发展合作伙伴和非政府组织，但卢旺达政府正侧重于纳入开发性金

> 融机构和私人部门。这样做会扩大其影响范围。所有发展伙伴围绕核心标准进行融合，也将增强发展效应和可持续性。

重建发展合作平台着重解决具体的冲突后需求或脆弱性需求。近期发生的两个例子分别是：在冲突刚结束时，乌克兰重建活动由欧洲复兴开发银行和欧盟领导，欧洲投资银行和国际复兴开发银行/国际金融公司以及双边和慈善机构参与；叙利亚危机的约旦应对计划则汇集了主要多边开发银行、双边机构、联合国机构和非政府组织。

单一部门平台成功地将私人部门融资与官方融资相结合。哥伦比亚4G项目和开发性金融机构哥伦比亚国家开发银行合作就是一个成功的例子，该合作项目涉及一项投资计划，通过多达40个不同的公私合营项目（主要是在未经开发地区建设基础设施项目）创建了一个全国性收费公路网络。印度尼西亚国家贫民窟改造升级项目也具有指导意义（见专栏5）。由泛美开发银行、国际金融公司和巴西国家经济社会发展银行共同推出了巴西私人部门参与便利（Brazilian Private Sector Participation Facility），从技术和经济可行性研究到融资结束的全过程促进私人部门参与基础设施建设。欧洲复兴开发银行和国际金融公司刚刚启动了一个乌克兰港口计划或平台。

> **专栏5：印度尼西亚——国家贫民窟改造升级项目（NSUP）**
> 印度尼西亚政府采取设立发展合作平台的方式为其主要发展项

目进行融资，使政府能够将多边开发银行的资金以及政府的预算资金结合起来。国家贫民窟改造升级项目是一个典型的例子，这是一项全国性计划，旨在改善全国239个城市的2 900万印度尼西亚贫民窟居民的城市基础设施和服务。国家贫民窟改造升级项目融资来自四个多边开发银行（国际复兴开发银行、伊斯兰开发银行、亚洲基础设施投资银行和亚洲开发银行），以及社会和政府融资。世界银行在筹备项目和协调融资方面发挥了主导作用。项目实施由一个共同的项目管理单位监督，无论资金来自何方，该项目对所有投资适用相同的政策和保障措施。这是一个由国家驱动、大规模吸引资金、建设政府能力、使用共同标准并将所有层级政府结合在一起的例子。早期证据还表明，该计划在可持续和包容性增长的关键领域改善了政府预算支出的质量。虽然这种方法涉及政府和多边开发银行，但它确实说明通过设立平台的方法进行发展融资具有一些明显优势。

资料来源：世界银行工作人员和名人小组秘书处。

全球/区域基础设施合作平台是相对较新的举措，体现了全球基础设施融资平台方法的各个方面。

◎ 全球基础设施基金是指各国政府、多边开发银行、私人部门投资者和融资者之间建立的伙伴关系，旨在支持各国政府为市场提供精心准备和结构化的项目。它提供四项服务：基础设施项目优先排序、项目筹备、交易文档准备和融资收尾程序。

◎ 非洲开发银行正在创设非洲投资论坛——一个涉及多个利益相关方、多专业的区域平台。非洲投资论坛旨在筛选和加强项目，吸引共同投资者，降低中介成本，提高项目信息和文件质量，并促进非洲政府和私人部门之间达成积极和富有成效的合作。目的是在有利环境中提供可融资、低风险的项目。

◎ 西巴尔干投资框架是一个多利益相关方、政府主导的协作平台，参与方包括受益国政府、国际金融机构、20个双边资助机构和欧盟，共同支持西巴尔干地区经济社会发展。

附录 2　构建大型、多元化的发展中国家基础设施资产类别

从运作空间和实际需要看，可考虑将主要基础设施融资／投资主流化并纳入公认的资产类别，以促进机构投资者参与。通过开发简单易行和标准化的工具，允许投资者进行组合投资而不是参与单个贷款／实体。到目前为止，为缺乏必要规模的私人投资构建可投资产品已做出了一些令人鼓舞的努力，但仍是零敲碎打式的。未来发展空间可期。

为能够达到资产类别的规模并满足巨大的发展需求，必须将风险敞口标准化并从多边开发银行体系汇集起来，进行证券化

或基金化，以方便投资者投资。非主权贷款、与基础设施相关的贷款和其他贷款可作为一类较好的资产组合，先试先行。仅多边开发银行体系就有 2 000 亿~3 000 亿美元的此类贷款，可满足机构投资者对资产规模的要求。纳入商业银行贷款将极大地扩大资产类别。

单笔多边开发银行贷款和贷款组合可以通过"清洁销售"转移给私人投资者，换言之，将贷款敞口完全转移给私人投资者。多边开发银行最适合在基础设施项目的早期阶段管理国家和建设风险，因此应在此阶段"持有"贷款。这个早期阶段也正是多边开发银行增值最多的时期。建设项目完成后，投资风险大幅降低，多边开发银行可售出贷款，不保留投资权益。如果私人投资者要求的回报略高于多边开发银行对贷款的定价，则可以考虑提高定价，使贷款在建设阶段的定价较低，但随后在项目完成时提高到商业利率水平。

除了由多边开发银行和双边机构发起的贷款之外，贷款池还可以扩大至商业银行基础设施贷款或商业银行发行的债券。这样可以释放资产负债表空间或为商业银行提供资金以开展新的基础设施贷款。绿色债券和绿色债券基金的增长为多边开发银行和商业银行发起基础设施贷款提供了机会，可满足机构投资者的需求。

例如，国际金融公司-东方汇理资产管理公司成立了 20 亿美元的绿色基石债券基金，旨在为气候相关项目提供私人资金。该基金将投资于新兴市场金融机构发行的绿色债券，进而转贷给新兴市场气候相关项目。国际金融公司投资了总资金的 6.25%，以实现信用增级。

与商业定价的多边开发银行非主权贷款和商业银行贷款相比，多边开发银行主权贷款在汇集和再分配方面可能面临更多挑战。汇集主权贷款并将其再分配给私人投资者的一个挑战是多边开发银行贷款定价与商业贷款定价之间存在差异，并且多边开发银行具有优先债权人地位。虽然此类主权贷款向私人部门的销售不涉及优先债权人身份的转移，但可能必须以低于账面价值的方式进行。随着投资者对发展中国家风险认知逐渐改善以及名人小组的各项建议付诸实施，上述问题将逐渐消失。在后期阶段随着商业定价和多边开发银行定价缩小，可集合主权贷款并用于投资。

在名人小组讨论过程中，我们征集了大量关于利用私人资本市场和创建资产类别的反馈意见。关于如何成功创建资产类别，这些意见可概括为以下四个关键因素。[①]

◎ **明确承诺建立可靠的新资产类别。**投资者需要确定，多边开发银行将持续参与相关资产类别并支持其市场发展。

◎ **标准化贷款合同和标准。**标准化贷款文件和信息披露将使各多边开发银行的贷款更容易打包在一起，有助于吸引私人投资。多边开发银行还需要就可供私人机构投资

---

① G20基础设施工作组发布的资产类别报告指出，反馈证实了基础设施路线图中需要强调的许多要点。

者投资的统一的贷款承销框架达成一致，并且还要解决投资者对"可允许投资"和增信（例如担保、过度抵押和流动性便利）的预期。

◎ **建立关于贷款绩效的广义数据库。**为使发展中国家基础设施成为成熟的资产类别，相关资产的数据必须更容易获取，使投资者更加便利地获取相关信息。提高透明度[①]还将使多边开发银行与监管机构和信用评级机构加强协调，分析数据以识别阻碍投资的主要风险，并开发风险缓释产品以应对风险。

◎ **先小范围试点，再扩大规模。**首先，可指派2~3个多边开发银行（与私营金融机构合作）管理试点资金募集计划。与多边开发银行、投资界和信用评级机构合作，项目经理决定投资工具结构、资产募集标准和资本结构。从长远来看，应考虑在各机构之间募集资产以确保收益多样化。

附录3　为流行病和与抗生素耐药相关的突发公共卫生事件做准备

流行病和突发公共卫生事件是大概率、高风险事件，但预

[①] 多边开发银行可以匿名方式提供数据，保护借款人隐私。

防这些事件的资金严重不足。全球流行病年度成本估计为5 700亿美元，占全球GDP的0.7%。互通互联程度增强已加大了国家或区域事件迅速在全球蔓延的风险。

需要在全球、国家和当地层面积极应对上述威胁，确保在全球和各国国内尽早发现风险并采取足够的应对措施。这需要迅速地进行全球融资，以稳定的资金促进发展中经济体完善现有的公共卫生体系，特别是那些脆弱经济体。当然，采取何种应对措施取决于流行病疫情，但可能需要全球干预来研制疫苗和治疗方法，并主要通过国家卫生系统来实施。

当前的公共卫生突发事件应对架构在近期有所整合，但仍然不能完全实现预设目标。一系列流行病（如埃博拉病毒）和导致危险疫情的抗生素耐药性的幽灵促使公共卫生系统进行有效组织，建立切实可行的融资机制（有关参与方见图5.1）。

◎ 要建立抵御流行病和抗生素耐药性的堡垒，必须在国家主导的前提下发展国内医疗系统。国际社会，例如多边开发银行（尤其是世界银行）、双边机构、基金会和垂直基金需要提供资金和非资金支持。

◎ 世界卫生组织在控制流行病和抗生素耐药性方面发挥"守护人"的作用，识别全球卫生突发事件，组织其他联合国机构、垂直基金、官方机构和基金会做出迅速反应，提供药品、其他用品和服务。

附 录

图 5.1 全球公共卫生框架：结构和相关机构

◎ 世界银行牵头组织应急融资，具体方式包括由债券和衍生品融资的保险、现金窗口和捐资国关于未来提供额外保障的承诺。

将现有架构建成可持续、有效应对全球性卫生突发事件的应对机制需要各国采取强有力的行动，并要求各国、国际金融机构和联合国机构以世界卫生组织为中心开展合作。防范全球卫生突发事件的第一道防线是在多边开发银行国家方案的支持下建立国家卫生系统，并与资助者、基金会和垂直基金的资金相结合。为发挥世界卫生组织作为第一应对者的作用，国际金融机构还必须投资于数据、知识和分析，以便识别和降低风险，帮助各国提高抵御能力，提出改革方案。

近期为应对流行病而建立的新融资工具已经形成了一个可行的框架，但该框架仍然严重缺乏资金。因此，有必要注意以下两点。

◎ 扩大流行病应急基金规模，该基金已被证明性价比较高，但考虑到可能给全面紧急情况带来的损失，该基金的资源不足。
◎ 增强现有应急资源，以便能迅速拨付赠款资源应对危机，要么直接拨给受影响国家，要么拨给国际上最先采取应对措施的国家。

附录4　不同国际金融机构风险识别职能一览

以下反映了国际货币基金组织、金融稳定理事会和国际清算银行在风险识别不同方面的比较优势。职能分工纯粹是说明性质，并非限制性的（见表5.1）。

附 录

表5.1 不同国际金融机构风险识别职能一览

	信用风险	市场风险和流动性风险	国别风险（如新兴市场）	宏观经济风险
货币环境	[IMF/BIS] 放松或紧缩货币政策的影响	[IMF/BIS] 市场利率与利率平价之间的偏差	[IMF] 融资风险；资本流入 [BIS] 银行间（跨境）流动	[IMF] 宏观政策是否充分（例如过热）
监管条件和金融中介环境	[FSB] 信贷审慎标准的充足性（如：资本充足率） [BIS] 市场基础设施弹性 [FSB/BIS] 影子银行的范围及影响	[FSB] 资本充足率和流动性覆盖率 [BIS] 市场基础设施弹性 [FSB/BIS] 影子银行的范围及影响	[FSB] 资本缓冲的充足性 [BIS] 银行间（跨境）流动	[IMF/FSB] 整体金融稳定，如金融部门评估规划（FSAP）进程
金融环境	[IMF] 宏观金融状况：符合经济发展的信贷周期；杠杆率 [BIS] 银行间（跨境）信贷风险头寸	[IMF/BIS] 流动性过剩，银行放贷意愿和能力	[IMF] 融资风险；资本外流；债务可持续性 [BIS] 银行间（跨境）流动	[IMF/BIS] 整体金融稳定
风险偏好	[IMF/BIS] 资产价格运行趋势和投资者行为	[IMF] 金融中介调整投资组合的意愿	[IMF/FSB/BIS] 投资者行为评估（安全持有或谋求收益）	[IMF/FSB/BIS] 投资者行为评估（安全持有或谋求收益）

附录5　国际货币基金组织在大规模和严重的全球危机时提供资金的政策选项

附录5概述了国际货币基金组织可以通过什么样的临时机制迅速获得大量流动性,以确保在发生全球"尾部风险"事件时维护金融稳定。但是,为克服下述治理和政策挑战,还需要时间才能达成共识。因此,现阶段名人小组未提出解决方案并寻求各方支持。

方案1　从成员国储蓄中转借未使用的SDR(特别提款权)

国际货币基金组织成员国持有大量SDR(即余额为正),目前持有总额约为1 500亿~2 000亿美元。在危机期间,可启动SDR正余额用于国际货币基金组织贷款项目。SDR余额为正且有意向的国家可以暂时将SDR借给国际货币基金组织或由其管理的特殊目的工具,并收取适当的费用或其他激励手段。[①]这方面可额外动用的资金最多约2 000亿美元,可以支持中小国家的项目(或可获得区域金融安排强有力支持并与国际货币基金组织合作的项目)。该方案可在全面尾部风险情况下成为其他方案以外的另一道防线。

---

① 定价政策可以通过设计来确保:(1)SDR盈余国的利益;(2)国际货币基金组织融资可持续性(即低于贷款利率借款);(3)鼓励正常时期时恢复收支平衡。

方案 2　国际货币基金组织从市场融资

无论是否使用 SDR 分配额或现有 SDR 作为股本，国际货币基金组织都可以通过与成员之间的某种合作安排来进行市场融资，以利用成员国储备资产（或自己发行 SDR），构成一个特殊目的工具，然后在全球资本市场上发行高评级证券。[1]这与欧洲稳定机制利用欧元区国家缴存的资本通过市场发债的融资方式有一些相似之处。举例而言，如果国际货币基金组织采用 5 倍的杠杆率（较为保守，当前欧洲稳定机制[2]杠杆率为 6 倍），将从现有未使用的 SDR 余额中获得高达 1 万亿美元的额外资源。在此背景下，《国际货币基金组织协定》允许其在市场上融资。

国际货币基金组织市场融资面临着重要的治理挑战。首先，如果特殊目的工具使用 SDR 作为股本在市场上借款，则需要解决中央银行持有的 SDR 继续拥有储备资产地位的问题。此外，需要审查成员认缴资本的监管和财政处理情况，以确定 SDR 分配额可以使用。此外，还有一种方法允许国际货币基金组织利用其资产负债表直接进入市场融资，这也是《国际货币基金组织协定》[3]所允许的。

---

[1]　该机制基于国际货币基金组织员工立场报告 10/06 提出的建议并有所调整。
[2]　重要区别之一是欧洲稳定机制的股本由财政资源提供，国际货币基金组织的股本由央行储备（包括份额资源和 SDR 分配）提供。
[3]　《国际货币基金组织协定》第八条第 1 款允许国际货币基金组织从私人市场融资。与国际货币基金组织其他借款一样，国际货币基金组织执行董事会可做出决定，而不需要特别多数，但还需要借款涉及货币的发行国的同意。

> **方案 3　补充新借款安排，并在需要时扩大其规模**
>
> 过去曾动员有意愿的各方合作提供融资，虽然不能保证将来会再次出现这种情况，但经验表明，各国准备在必要时进行合作并提供更多的资源来克服全球挑战。没有逐步取消现有安排是有好处的，应考虑制定可快速扩张的应急计划，这方面应根据系统性危机的严重程度设置触发机制。

附录6　G20副手小组议程一览

G20领导的副手小组应认可多边开发银行作为一个系统的战略方向和优先事项。最初阶段，重点还在于跟踪建议的改革执行情况。主要优先事项包括：（1）对多边开发银行在实现促发展效应中应有的适当风险偏好进行战略指引；（2）确保加强全系统合作，包括建立利用所有发展伙伴优势的国家平台，以及促使核心标准趋同；（3）跟踪商业模式的转变，并通过全系统倡议动员私人融资。

通过在多边开发银行之间建立和完善共同指标体系来加强决策和问责制，项目的规划、监督和执行，稳健的风险管理。需要建立共同的原则和指标，以评估多边开发银行的效率和有效性，使其能够达到以下三个目标。

附　录

◎ 更好地衡量和跟踪关键结果，包括资金价值。
◎ 对多边开发银行进行比较，同时考虑到其在不同领域的作用，包括地理位置、知识创造以及项目和开发周期。
◎ 建立共同的统计基础。

副手小组应认可支撑国家平台的核心发展标准，并利用小组中的股东国身份促进多边开发银行和双边发展融资机构标准趋同。

对于多边开发银行来说，接受我们的建议有助于其完善风险管理实践。副手小组应建立一个框架供个别多边开发银行使用，以明确股东可接受的风险偏好和预期的发展效应，以及在两者之间进行权衡。实施这一共同风险管理框架将使多边开发银行能够实现以下三点。

◎ 在整体风险范围内做出决策，为更高的发展回报承担更高的风险。
◎ 实施包括保险业在内的全系统风险共担和多样化，旨在动员更高水平的私人资本。
◎ 考虑到多边开发银行的特点和专长，共同寻求巴塞尔委员会的指导，并让信用评级机构参与资本和流动性要求的评级。

缩略语

ADB	亚洲开发银行
ADF	非洲开发基金
AEs	发达经济体
AfDB	非洲开发银行
AIF	非洲投资论坛
AIIB	亚洲基础设施投资银行
AMR	抗生素耐药性
AU	非洲联盟
BIS	国际清算银行
BMGF	比尔及梅琳达·盖茨基金会
BNDES	巴西国家经济社会发展银行
BRAC	孟加拉国农村发展委员会
BRICS CRA	金砖国家应急储备安排
BSAs	双边互换协议
CDC	疾病预防控制中心
CEPI	流行病应对创新联盟
CGFS	全球金融体系委员会

DC	发展委员会
DFIs	开发性金融机构
EBRD	欧洲复兴开发银行
ECDC	欧洲疾病预防控制中心
EIB	欧洲投资银行
EMs	新兴市场
ESM	欧洲稳定机制
ESR	对外部门报告
ETFs	交易所交易基金
EU	欧盟
EWE	早期预警演练
FDI	外商直接投资
FDN	哥伦比亚国家开发银行
FSAP	金融部门评估规划
FSB	金融稳定理事会
G20	二十国集团
GEMs	全球新兴市场风险数据库
GFC	全球金融危机
GFSN	全球金融安全网
GFSR	《全球金融稳定报告》
GIF	全球基础设施基金
HIPC	重债穷国计划
IDB	泛美开发银行

IAIS	国际保险监督官协会
IBRD	国际复兴开发银行
IDA	国际开发协会
IDFC	国际开发金融俱乐部
IFAD	国际农业发展基金
IFC	国际金融公司
IFFEd	国际教育融资机构
IFIs	国际金融机构
IMF	国际货币基金组织
IMFC	国际货币与金融委员会
IMFS	国际货币金融体系
IOSCO	国际证监会组织
IsDB	伊斯兰开发银行
JASPERS	欧盟区域项目筹备联合资助计划
MDBs	多边开发银行
MIGA	多边投资担保机构
NAB	新借款安排
NDB	新开发银行
NGOs	非政府组织
NSUP	印度尼西亚国家贫民窟改造升级项目
OECD	经济合作与发展组织
PPPs	政府和社会资本合作
R&D	研究与开发

RDBs	地区开发银行
RFAs	区域金融安排
SCAV	脆弱性评估委员会
SDGs	可持续发展目标
SDR	特别提款权
SEWA	自雇妇女协会
TCFD	气候相关财务信息披露工作组
UN	联合国
UNICEF	联合国儿童基金会
WBG	世界银行集团
WEO	《世界经济展望》
WFP	世界粮食计划署
WHO	世界卫生组织

关于G20"全球金融治理名人小组"[①]

2017年4月，由G20财长和央行行长发起设立的"全球金融治理名人小组"正式成立，其职责是为改革国际金融架构和国际金融机构治理体系提供建议，以便在新时代背景下促进全球经济稳定和可持续增长，并讨论G20如何能够更好地为达到上述目标提供可持续的指导和支持。

成员

尚达曼（主席） 新加坡副总理、新加坡金融管理局主席、三十人小组主席、国际货币与金融委员会前主席、新加坡前财政部长

苏菲安·艾哈迈德 埃塞俄比亚总理顾问、埃塞俄比亚前财政与经济发展部部长、国际货币事务和发展二十四国政府间集团前副主席

阿里·巴巴詹 土耳其主管经济金融事务的前副总理、外交

[①] 以下所列名人小组成员的职务信息为本报告发布时（2018年）的情况。——编者注

部前部长和财政部前部长

马雷克·贝尔卡 波兰发展委员会前主席、波兰前总理、波兰国家银行前行长

雅各布·A.弗兰克 摩根大通国际董事长、三十人小组董事会主席、以色列央行前行长、泛美开发银行前主席、国际货币基金组织前首席经济学家和研究部主任

奥特玛·伊辛 歌德大学金融研究中心主任、欧洲央行执行委员会前成员兼首席经济学家

伊藤隆敏 哥伦比亚大学国际公共事务学院教授、日本财政部负责国际事务的副部长

诺拉·拉斯蒂格 美国杜兰大学拉丁美洲经济学塞缪尔·Z.斯通教授、公平承诺研究院主任、拉丁美洲和加勒比经济协会名誉主席、美洲开发银行贫困问题前高级顾问

恩戈齐·奥孔乔－伊韦拉 全球疫苗免疫联盟董事会主席、尼日利亚前财长兼经济统筹部长、世界银行前常务副行长

拉古兰·拉詹 芝加哥大学布斯商学院凯瑟琳·杜萨克·米勒金融学杰出贡献教授、印度储备银行前行长、国际货币基金组织前首席经济学家兼研究部主任

法布里齐奥·萨科曼尼 意大利联合信贷银行董事长、意大利经济与财政部前部长、意大利央行前司长

尼古拉斯·斯特恩 伦敦政治经济学院帕特尔经济学和政府学教授、世界银行前首席经济学家和高级副行长、欧洲复兴开发银行前首席经济学家

约翰·B. 泰勒 斯坦福大学玛丽和罗伯特·雷蒙经济学教授、斯坦福大学胡佛研究所乔治·舒尔茨高级经济学研究员、美国财政部前副部长

让-克劳德·特里谢 三边委员会欧元区集团主席、布鲁盖尔经济研究所董事会主席、欧洲央行前行长

安德烈斯·贝拉斯科 伦敦政治经济学院公共政策系主任、哈佛大学肯尼迪学院国际金融学教授、智利前财长

朱民 清华大学国家金融研究院院长、国际货币基金组织前副总裁

秘书处

悉达多·蒂瓦里（行政秘书） 李光耀公共政策学院杰出访问学者，国际货币基金组织战略、政策和审查部门主管

埃里克·伯格洛夫 伦敦政治经济学院全球事务研究所所长、欧洲复兴开发银行前首席经济学家

大卫·马斯顿 国际货币基金组织前首席风险官

R. 凯尔·彼得斯 世界银行运营部高级副行长

秘书处由克里斯蒂娜·科勒瑞斯积极协助，新加坡金融管理局和李光耀公共政策学院给予支持。

G20 全球金融治理名人小组职责

G20 全球金融治理名人小组由在全球金融框架和治理领域方面拥有丰富知识和经验的知名人士组成。

新加坡副总理尚达曼担任名人小组主席。名人小组所有成员均以个人身份开展工作。总体看，名人小组成员的职业经历体现出了地域和经济发展水平方面的多样性。

名人小组主要有以下三项工作任务。

◎ 审查当前和未来国际金融货币体系、全球金融框架和治理现状可能面临的挑战和机遇。

◎ 鉴于过去的审查情况，考虑国际货币基金组织、世界银行和其他多边开发银行组成的国际金融机构的最佳作用，包括这些国际金融机构与其他国际金融机构、G20 以及这些机构所属成员国如何相互作用和相互协调，促进私人资本流动，提高国内资源开发能力，优化机构治理和问责制结构，确保在应对确定性挑战方面更具效率、有效性和透明度。

◎ 建议通过实际改革改善全球金融框架和治理功能,从而促进经济稳定和可持续增长;讨论G20如何能够更好地为达到上述目标提供可持续的指导和支持。

名人小组工作不会与G20和国际金融机构开展的股权审议、国际货币基金组织份额总检查等工作相重叠。

名人小组将向G20财长和央行行长提供研究结果和建议供其讨论。涉及国际金融机构的任何建议方案则必须由各自机构做出决定。

名人小组在2017年国际货币基金组织与世界银行年会上向G20财长和央行行长提交了其工作大纲,并且在2018年国际货币基金组织与世界银行春季会议上提供进展报告。名人小组继续履行职责,并在2018年国际货币基金组织与世界银行年会之前提交了最终建议。

鸣　谢

名人小组感谢许多发展中国家和发达国家的政府部门给我们提供了宝贵的反馈意见，感谢国际金融机构与我们进行的广泛讨论。

我们也感谢许多在国别和国际政策制定方面有资深经验的人士、民间团体、学术界、智库和慈善机构的思想领袖、私人部门领袖以及基础设施投资、金融科技及其他领域的专家所做出的贡献以及提供的观点。名人小组感谢上述所有组织和个人以口头和书面形式表达了坦率和建设性的观点。我们在报告附件及网站（www.globalfinancialgovernance.org）列出了为本报告做出贡献的机构和人员名单。

此外，名人小组感谢英格兰银行、法兰西银行、德意志联邦银行、纽约联邦储备银行提供了慷慨支持，并感谢斯坦福大学胡佛研究所承办了数次会议。

发达国家和发展中国家都对名人小组的工作提供了宝贵意见。名人小组还在同以下机构的磋商中受益匪浅。

非洲开发银行

亚洲开发银行

亚洲基础设施投资银行

国际清算银行

欧洲复兴开发银行

欧洲投资银行

欧洲稳定机制

泛美开发银行

国际开发金融俱乐部

国际货币基金组织

伊斯兰开发银行

新开发银行

经济合作与发展组织

联合国发展系统

世界银行

感谢以下世界范围内政策制定者、思想领袖、私人部门和民间社会领导人士，他们凭借自身的丰富工作经历提出了意见和书面建议。

蒂莫西·安德慕（国际金融协会）

蒙特克·辛格·阿卢瓦利亚

马苏德·艾哈迈德（全球发展中心）

马克·安德森（美国风险投资公司 Andreessen Horowitz）

苏珊·阿西（瑞波币）

鸣　谢

阿比吉特·班纳吉（麻省理工学院）

蒂姆·贝斯利（伦敦政治经济学院）

阿马尔·巴塔查雅（布鲁金斯学会）

南希·博德塞奥（全球发展中心）

戈登·布朗（联合国全球教育特使）

夏朗·布劳（国际工会联盟）

麦克·卡拉汉（澳大利亚政府养老服务融资局）

尼基尔·达·维多利亚·洛博（瑞士再保险公司）

雅克·德·拉罗西埃

蒂埃里·德奥（麦格理基础设施投资公司）

拉斐尔·德尔·皮诺（法罗里奥集团）

曹文凯（美国国家医学院）

穆罕默德·埃里安（安联集团）

杰里米·法勒（惠康基金会）

丹尼尔·格罗斯（欧洲政策研究中心）

杰罗姆·海格里（瑞士再保险公司）

克里斯·希思科特（全球基础设施中心）

黄益平（北京大学）

比马尔·迦兰

哈罗德·詹姆斯（普林斯顿大学）

唐纳德·卡贝鲁卡（非盟可持续融资特使）

拉维·坎布尔（康奈尔大学）

德维什·卡普尔

加藤隆俊

河合正弘（东京大学）

维贾·科尔卡

霍米·卡拉思（布鲁金斯学会）

卡约·科赫－韦泽（欧洲气候基金会）

霍斯特·科勒

阿列克谢·库德林（圣彼得堡国立大学）

让-皮埃尔·兰多（巴黎政治大学）

南希·李（全球发展中心）

让·勒米埃尔（法国巴黎银行）

李飞飞（谷歌）

约翰·利普斯基（约翰·霍普金斯大学）

苏珊·兰德（麦肯锡全球研究院）

马克·梅钦（加拿大养老金投资协会）

理查德·曼宁（牛津大学）

普拉塔普·巴努·梅赫塔（印度阿育王大学）

拉客什·莫汉（耶鲁大学）

大卫·马尔福德（胡佛研究所）

泽维尔·穆斯卡（东方汇理资产管理公司）

阿德巴约·奥贡莱西（全球基础设施合伙公司）

吉列尔莫·奥尔蒂斯（巴西百达投资银行）

亨克·欧文克（荷兰王国国际水务局特使）

让·皮萨尼－费里（巴黎政治大学）

鸣 谢

马克·普朗特（全球发展中心）

娜丽莎·普里扎恩（英国海外发展研究所研究员）

埃莱娜·雷伊（伦敦商学院）

马克·苏兹曼（盖茨基金会）

亚当·波森（彼得森国际经济研究所）

鲍勃·普林斯（桥水公司）

亚历克斯·兰佩尔（霍洛维茨基金）

迈克尔·萨比亚（魁北克储蓄投资集团）

史蒂夫·施瓦茨曼（黑石集团）

阿尼什·沙阿（马恒达集团）

露西·夏皮罗（斯坦福大学医学院）

木下直之（东京大学）

乔治·舒尔茨（胡佛研究所）

阿文德·萨勃拉曼尼亚（哈佛大学）

杉崎重光（高盛日本）

达维德·塔利恩特（奥纬咨询）

阿尔温德·维尔马尼

戴维·韦纳（脸书）

马克·怀斯曼（贝莱德集团）

名人小组还在全球发展中心主办的圆桌会议上与以下其他民间社会代表进行了宝贵的交流。

相泽元子（人权与商业研究院）

南茜·亚历山大（伯尔基金会）

阿伦·贝特鲁（麦肯研究院）

林赛·科茨（国际行动志工协会）

莎拉·哈考特（公益组织ONE）

安德列斯·诺伯尔（C20国际金融框架）

保罗奥布莱恩（乐施会）

斯蒂芬妮·西格尔（战略与国际研究中心）

伊丽莎白·萨默斯（银行信息中心）

马克·乌赞（新布雷顿森林体系委员会）

路易斯·维埃拉（布雷顿森林项目）

MAKING THE GLOBAL FINANCIAL SYSTEM WORK FOR ALL

Report of the G20 Eminent Persons Group on Global Financial Governance

PREFACE

The challenges of global development and growth have never been more daunting, complex and urgent. It is no exaggeration to say that we face the risk of economic and social catastrophe in regions with large populations.

Since the G20 Eminent Persons Group presented its recommendations in October 2018, the COVID-19 pandemic has threatened to roll back the gains made by several developing countries in recent decades. It has also accentuated existing problems in development, and multiplied the challenges of achieving inclusive and sustainable growth in the coming decade.

We will need a much more forceful global effort to restart growth in the years to come. However, we also have to do so with fiscal resources that have been far more stretched as a result of COVID-19, and with much higher levels of indebtedness compared to a decade ago.

The EPG's recommendations are hence more relevant than ever. There has been some promising progress in implementing some of the recommendations. In particular, the G20 Finance Ministers and Central Bank Governors have endorsed a framework for country platforms that bring together all development partners and provide coherence in efforts to mobilise private investment. The Multilateral Investment Guarantee

Agency (MIGA) has also embarked on partnerships to offer political risk insurance and other products to multilateral development institutions beyond the World Bank Group, thereby enabling risk to be diversified and reduced. In response to the current pandemic, the International Monetary Fund has also introduced a short-term liquidity line to provide countries with a liquidity backstop during global shocks.

We must build on this momentum. We must use the urgency of today's crisis to solve not just the immediate threats we face, but the long-standing, legacy problems in international finance. We have put these issues off for too long, and the longer we postpone addressing them, the larger the challenge becomes, the higher the eventual costs, and the greater the risks of failure.

At the heart of the EPG's report was a call for a new cooperative international order. International governance and cooperation has however been weakened further in the face of COVID-19. We have witnessed more protectionist, 'my country first' measures, and escalating geopolitical tensions. Yet, it has never been more obvious that all nations have a mutual interest in international cooperation: to ensure a broad and equitable allocation of critical healthcare goods and services, to stimulate global growth, as well as to accelerate the implementation of sustainable practices.

COVID-19 will not be the last crisis the world will experience. We must strengthen the resilience of developing countries in response to crises. We can and must make improvements to the international financial architecture to deal with cross-border spillovers and volatility of capital flows. We must bolster the role of the IMF, stitch together the various

PREFACE

layers of the Global Financial Safety Net, and strengthen global financial surveillance for early identification of vulnerabilities.

I would like to thank Dr Zhu Min and colleagues from the People's Bank of China for this important initiative of translating the EPG report for the Chinese-speaking audience.

The EPG consulted widely, deliberated on the issues intensively, and made recommendations that we believed are practical and achievable within the next few years. It requires collective resolve among nations: built on the simple but powerful recognition that our interests in global growth, stability and the global commons are mutual, with benefits for all nations.

Tharman Shanmugaratnam

FOREWORD

WHY THE NEED FOR REFORM?

We were asked by the G20 Finance Ministers and Central Bank Governors in April 2017 to recommend reforms to the global financial architecture and governance of the system of International Financial Institutions (IFIs)[①], so as to promote economic stability and sustainable growth in a new global era; and to consider how the G20 could better provide continued leadership and support for these goals.[②]

At the heart of our review is the future of the open and competitive world order that has brought a large part of humanity out of poverty, raised living standards across nations, and provided the foundation for unprecedented global peace over the last 70 years. That open order remains critical to every nation's future. But the system of international governance and cooperation that underpins it is fraying. Left on its own, there is a real risk of drift into a fragmented world, with policies in different parts of the world working at odds with rather than

---

① The IFIs refer to the IMF and the Multilateral Development Banks, comprising AfDB, ADB, AIIB, EBRD, EIB, IDB, IsDB, NDB and the World Bank Group.
② Information about the G20 Eminent Persons Group on Global Financial Governance and its terms of reference can be found at the end of this report.

reinforcing each other, and with all nations ending up losing.

We cannot return to the past. Our central challenge is to create a cooperative international order for a world that has changed irreversibly: one that is more multipolar and decentralized in decisions, yet more interconnected, and with challenges ahead that are much larger and more pressing than we have seen in decades.

Getting national policies right is at the core of achieving inclusive societies and mutual prosperity. But international and national initiatives should reinforce each other in a way that creates a stronger future for all. An open, competitive and well-coordinated international order will enable win-win outcomes for nations. Its weakening will lead to lose-lose outcomes, as global growth and opportunities for new jobs are eroded over time, and as financial stability and the global commons become more fragile. Equally, cooperative internationalism will survive only if it helps the broad base of nations achieve inclusive growth.

The reforms that we propose in our report strengthen and add resilience to global financial governance for this new, cooperative international order. The present system lacks the coherence, joint capacity and effectiveness to support its most fundamental goals in global development and financial stability. It must be brought up to date with the realities of a new era.

We can achieve this by implementing decisive reforms to make the system work as a system. These reforms are within our reach.

They do not require new international bodies. They instead require that we take bold and defined steps to ensure that today's institutions–global, regional and bilateral–work together as a system. They require that we build trust and transparency among these different institutions, and leverage their combined strengths, so that the system as a whole delivers greater and more lasting development impact and reduces the frequency and damage of crises.

Our proposals build on various reforms that had been underway among the IFIs, and seek to take them further. But they also require a much greater sense of urgency and recognition among their shareholders of the need for consistency and joined-up efforts among the IFIs and all other stakeholders so we raise our whole game.

We need a step change in the pace and scale of reforms to enable the growth, job opportunities and sustainability that are critically needed in the next decade. The consequences of failure will not be simply economic. We also need further reforms to avert major, systemic crises; and to make it possible for developing countries to finance sustainable current account deficits, where they are fundamentally needed at their stage of development, without the recurring bouts of instability that set back growth.

As an Eminent Persons Group, our task was to provide an independent assessment of the changes needed. We focused especially on system-wide reforms, rather than those in individual institutions. Our mandate also excluded issues to do with the capital and shareholding structures of the IFIs, which we believe are of central importance but are covered by other ongoing reviews in the G20 and the IFIs.

Importantly, we were guided by the request that our proposals could be acted upon by the G20 and the IFIs in coordination with the other bodies integral to the international monetary and financial system. In this regard, besides drawing on our Group's collective experience in policy-making, our discussions benefited greatly from consultations with a broad range of national authorities, the IFIs, many other thought leaders from civil society, think tanks, academia and philanthropies, and private sector experts. These diverse interactions helped us arrive at proposals which we believe can be implemented within a reasonable time-frame, but which taken together should have a transformational impact.

The ambition is in the doing. Some of the reforms should be early wins in international coordination. Most are achievable within a few years, with focused effort. Some others go beyond current thinking. We urge that they be considered with an open mind, and developed further or adapted if necessary to enable their implementation.

We have deliberated intensively as a Group[1], supported by our very able Secretariat under the leadership of Siddharth Tiwari. We thank the G20 for the opportunity to review these important issues. We present our report with sober awareness of the challenges facing the international community, but also with hope for the collective resolve needed to take us into this new era of cooperative internationalism, with benefits for all.

---

[1] Over the last 15 months, the Group had eight plenaries and extensive interactions in between.

FOREWORD

Tharman Shanmugaratnam (Chair)

Jacob A. Frenkel

Ngozi Okonjo-Iweala

John B. Taylor

Sufian Ahmed

Otmar Issing

Raghuram Rajan

Jean-Claude Trichet

Ali Babacan

Takatoshi Ito

Fabrizio Saccomanni

Andrés Velasco

Marek Belka

Nora Lustig

Nicholas Stern

Zhu Min

ACKNOWLEDGEMENTS

The Eminent Persons Group received valuable feedback from national authorities from a broad range of developing and advanced countries, and benefited from extensive consultations with the international financial institutions (IFIs). We also benefited from the contributions and perspectives of individuals with deep experience in national and international policy-making; thought leaders from civil society, academia, think tanks and philanthropic organizations; and private sector leaders and experts in infrastructure investment, financial technology and other areas.

The Group would like to thank all these organizations and individuals for their candid and constructive views, in discussions and written submissions. A list of contributions is in the Annex and on the website: www.globalfinancialgovernance.org

The Group wishes to acknowledge the generous support from the Bank of England, Banque de France, Deutsche Bundesbank, the Federal Reserve Bank of New York, and the Hoover Institution, Stanford University for hosting some of its meetings.

KEY THRUSTS

I. Achieving Greater Development Impact: Collaborating Across the System

The next decade is critical.

We need substantially greater impact in helping countries achieve sustainable development and inclusive growth, and in managing the growing pressures in the global commons. The current pace of change will not get us there.

We need bolder reforms to harness complementarities and synergies in the development system:

- ◎ Refocus IFIs' efforts to help countries strengthen governance capacity and human capital, as the foundation for an attractive investment climate, job creation, and social stability.
- ◎ Exploit the largely untapped potential for collaboration among the IFIs as well as with other development partners to maximize their contributions as a group, including by convergence around core standards.
- ◎ Embark on system-wide insurance and diversification of risk, to create a large-scale asset class and mobilize significantly greater private sector participation.

◎ Strengthen joint capacity to tackle the challenges of the commons.

We must also leverage more actively on the work of the non-official sector, including NGOs and philanthropies.

II. Securing the Benefits of Interconnected Financial Markets: Reforms for Global Financial Resilience

A decade after the global financial crisis, further reforms are needed to reduce the bouts of instability that set back growth, to keep countries on the path toward openness and to avert another major crisis.

First, to get the full benefits of cross-border capital flows by strengthening support for countries in building deeper domestic financial markets; and developing and evolving a framework of policy guidance that:

◎ Enables countries to utilize international capital flows without risks arising from excessive market volatility.
◎ Enables domestic objectives to be achieved in sending countries while avoiding major spillovers.

Second, to create a more robust, integrated system of risk surveillance of a complex, interconnected global financial system, and systematically incorporate contrarian views.

Third, to create a strong and more reliable global financial safety net by stitching together its fragmented layers.

III. The G20 and the IFIs: Making the System Work as a System

The role of the G20 in the global financial architecture should be reset. It should focus on developing political consensus on key strategic issues and crisis response. This requires freeing up space from its current crowded agenda and devolving work to the IFIs.

We need governance to ensure that the system works as a system:

◎ Implementing the system-wide reorientation in development finance. A G20-led group, including key non-G20 stakeholders, should steer these shifts over the next three years, before handing the coordinating role to the IFI Heads. This should include achieving complementarity among multiple institutions (multilateral, regional and bilateral), and establishing a clear system of metrics to track impact and value for money.
◎ Addressing development challenges early. A biennial strategic dialogue, building on existing IFI fora, should bring together the IFIs and other key stakeholders to identify future development risks before they create lasting damage, and assess the adequacy of collective responses.
◎ The governance reforms to foster global financial resilience require the IMF to play a key role, in interactions with other institutions integral to the international monetary and financial system, and with regular

updates to the IMFC.

Governance reforms within the IFIs themselves should cut back on today's significant overlap between Board and Management responsibilities. They should enable Boards to focus more on strategic priorities, and empower and hold Management accountable for outcomes.

OVERVIEW[1]

A. Building a Cooperative International Order for a New Era

We are at a critical juncture. Our fundamental challenge is to build **a cooperative international order suited to the 21st century: one that delivers win-win outcomes for nations in a multipolar world.** It is within our reach to do so. We otherwise face the prospect of fragmentation, and the steady weakening of our capacity to respond to the much larger national and collective challenges of the future.

Our realities today are very different from those of a few decades ago, and vastly reordered compared to when the Bretton Woods institutions were formed.

◎ **Domestic economic, social and political divides have widened in most advanced nations, undermining longstanding social compacts.** There have always been winners and losers in technological progress and international trade. But slower growth has accentuated these divides, and they have been left unaddressed for too long in too many

---

[1] This Overview provides the larger context and reasoning behind the Proposals developed in the full Report. It also provides a summary of the Proposals.

countries. Trust in government and many other national institutions has declined. **These developments risk undermining support for international cooperation and an open world order.**

◎ A second, fundamental change has been the **steady and irreversible shift to a multipolar world**. This is the inevitable outcome of success through use of markets and greater openness, which both lifted global growth and led to convergence among nations in productivity and living standards–including a remarkable pace of catch-up among several emerging nations in the last three decades. We hence have new poles of global growth, more equal players and greater decentralization in international economic decision-making.

◎ Third, we however face a **challenge of unprecedented scale, urgency and complexity in the next decade**–especially in securing jobs and environmental and financial sustainability. The young populations that will enter the workforce–many in states with features of fragility–will be much larger than anything seen in past decades. So too the grave and multiple threats of environmental degradation, compounded by the growing risk of pandemics and other problems in the global commons.[1] Further, today more than ever before, we face a challenge of financial sustainability in a broad range of advanced and developing countries, due to the significant increases in public and private debts.

◎ Fourth, we live in a world much more **deeply connected by capital flows and ideas** today. Together with trade, they are powerful engines

---

[1] The Sustainable Development Goals (SDGs) and the 2030 Agenda that the global community has coalesced around aim to address these multiple challenges in growth and development.

of growth everywhere. But the complexity and interconnectivity of financial markets pose challenges to stability that cannot be tackled by nations on their own.

We need a credible and well-coordinated global financial architecture to meet the needs of a world that is **more decentralized in decisions, yet more interconnected, and more challenged in its future**.

There is no going back to the old multilateralism. There is no single conductor. There are already many more orchestras in play. The world needs a new harmony.

The new multilateralism must make this decentralized system more resilient and much stronger than the sum of its parts. We must leverage systematically on the strengths of the multilateral anchors, regional and bilateral institutions, and other key stakeholders that make up the system, and build trust and transparency amongst these different players. This new, cooperative international order must also help nations achieve more inclusive and sustainable growth, while enabling us to tackle collective challenges effectively.

Getting national policies right is at the heart of achieving inclusive societies and mutual prosperity. Most fundamentally, as the digital economy widens and advances in machine learning and big data gather pace, governments must help citizens equip themselves for the jobs of the future through both education and life-long learning. We must invest most urgently in skilling the large, youthful populations in developing nations, to avoid the prospect of new technologies derailing job creation and growth.

However, the interplay of international and national initiatives is essential to a stronger future for all. There are several core roles for cooperation in the international monetary and financial system (IMFS), and for the international financial institutions (IFIs)[①]:

◎ To **promote mutually reinforcing policies between countries and minimize negative spillovers**. Policies aimed at growth and financial stability are most effective nationally when they are undertaken widely or coordinated internationally.[②] However, it is also in the nature of today's highly interconnected markets that policies in some economies may have negative spillovers on others or reduce their policy space. A framework is needed to mitigate such spillovers and their effects as much as possible. There is also a role for international commitments to avoid 'beggar-thy-neighbor' policies, which benefit one country at the expense of another.

◎ To **take full advantage of the unique roles of the IFIs as multipliers of development**–especially by institution-building and spreading policy knowhow, by helping governments improve the investment environment,

---

[①] The IFIs refer to the IMF and the Multilateral Development Banks, comprising the African Development Bank (AfDB), Asian Development Bank (ADB), Asian Infrastructure Investment Bank (AIIB), European Bank for Reconstruction and Development (EBRD), European Investment Bank (EIB), Inter-American Development Bank (IDB), Islamic Development Bank (IsDB), New Development Bank (NDB) and the World Bank Group.

[②] For example, closer international cooperation on macro-economic policies during the Global Financial Crisis in 2008 was mutually reinforcing. Historically too, innovations and advances in productivity within nations have tended to feed into each other, and been a positive rather than zero-sum game.

and by mitigating risks to unlock private investment.

◎ To build joint capacity and coordinate actions to **avoid systemic financial crises, and tackle the growing challenges of the global commons**.

There is hence no either-or choice between cooperative internationalism and national strategies to secure growth and financial stability. An open, competitive and well-coordinated international order will enable win-win outcomes for nations. Its weakening will lead to lose-lose outcomes, as global growth and opportunities for new jobs are eroded over time, and as financial stability and the global commons become more fragile. Equally, cooperative internationalism will survive only if it helps the broad base of nations achieve inclusive growth.

The reforms that we propose in our report strengthen and add resilience to **global financial governance** for the cooperative international order that we believe is needed for a more decentralized and more challenged world. The reforms seek to **achieve significantly higher impact for sustainable and inclusive development**; to enable countries to preserve financial stability and **secure the benefits of interconnected financial markets**; and to focus governance on **making the system work as a system** rather than a set of individual agencies. We also propose **resetting the role of the G20 in the IMFS**, to free up space on its agenda for Ministers to focus on developing political consensus around the key strategic issues of the times and crisis responses.

B. Achieving Greater Development Impact: Collaborating Across the System

Bold and urgent reforms in development policies and financing are required to achieve the major step-up in growth, job opportunities and sustainability that the world needs in the next decade. **The current pace of reforms will not get us there.**

The challenges are complex, because they are interlocking. Conflict and insecurity, weak investment in human capital and infrastructure, and limited growth of jobs and incomes feed into each other. Environmental vulnerabilities and infectious disease threats, if not addressed, will also push large numbers into extreme poverty and forced migration. The required doubling of the world's infrastructure in the next 15 years to achieve the needed growth and jobs, highlights the risk of locking in unsustainable infrastructure for the much longer term. The interconnectedness of the system also means that success or failure in achieving sustainability in one part of the world will have profound effects on development prospects elsewhere.

There are at the same time major positives on the horizon. **A wave of entrepreneurship and innovation is sweeping across the developing world**, spreading into low-income countries too. Mobile technologies, cloud computing and e-commerce are opening up markets for small producers everywhere, improving productivity, and making finance more inclusive. Global health R&D, if sustained, also has the potential to deal with malaria and other major diseases, with important economic and social dividends. Technologies for urban management are enabling transport, utilities and other services to be provided in a more citizen-centered way.

Reforms to tackle these challenges and maximize the potential of technologies and markets are needed in every continent. But to bend the arc of history, we must succeed in Africa, where the poverty, demographic and environmental challenges are the largest–and so too the opportunities to contribute to world growth and the global commons. **The consequences of failure will not be simply economic.**

The magnitude of the development challenge will require **greater resources than before, from every source**–domestic savings and public revenues, and external financing from private, official and philanthropic sources. Even by conservative projections, the gap in infrastructure financing alone is well over US$1 trillion annually. **This gap in financing must be closed**, to ensure the quality and scale of investments in economic and social infrastructure that will be critical in the next decade.

However, strategies to scale up development finance must also reckon with the **reality that public sector debts (including contingent liabilities) are reaching unsustainable levels in several developing countries**. The aspirations of the 2030 Development Agenda can be achieved only if financial stability is sustained. Primary reliance cannot be placed on sovereign loans to achieve development goals.

Two key strategies therefore need much greater priority. First, to strengthen public finances and domestic resource mobilization. There is significant potential to strengthen tax collection and reduce leakages through corruption and waste, at the levels of both central and local governments. These public resources underpin efforts to develop human capital and strengthen the investment climate. Together with efforts to build up local currency markets and stimulate domestic savings, they also provide the domestic financial resilience on which long-term investment depends. The international community must also support these national efforts by **closing opportunities for tax evasion and money laundering**.

Second, it is equally clear that we must stimulate a much larger scale of private investment than has been achieved historically. Given the significant increase in debt ratios in many countries, **much greater emphasis will have to be given to equity financing**. However, private investment in developing country infrastructure has so far been only a small fraction of its potential. On current initiatives, private funding is unlikely to scale up significantly, despite ample supply globally. **Investment risks, actual and perceived, remain too high** for all but the most specialized players, and the required returns are hence also too high for countries to bear. The market for infrastructure investments is too fragmented, and the tools to diversify project and country risks are limited.

We must therefore organize the world's multilateral development capabilities and resources in a new way to tackle these challenges and achieve greater and more lasting development impact. There is much potential to be unlocked by governing the system as a system rather than as individual institutions.

We have to **put risk at the center** of strategies to boost development finance, given the need for much larger volumes of private investment, and in particular equity financing. We must **maximize the IFIs' unique ability to help reduce and manage risk:**

OVERVIEW

- By helping countries to **de-risk their whole investment environment** (besides de-risking projects). The IFIs must collaborate to help countries take advantage of best practices in governance and regulation, and persist in reforms.
- By **pioneering investments in low-income countries and states with features of fragility**, in critical areas such as energy infrastructure, to reduce perceived risks and pave the way for private investments.
- By **mitigating risk** through instruments such as first-loss guarantees, and co-investments to catalyze private investment. Importantly, they must use their risk-mitigation tools to harness the **full potential of private investment in low-income countries**–not just in the middle-income countries where blended finance has so far been heavily concentrated.
- By **leveraging on the largely untapped potential to pool and diversify risks across the development finance system**, so as to create new asset classes for private investors.

The scale and urgency of needs require decisive, **system-wide shifts**. We believe significantly greater development impact can be achieved by:

Proposal 1: *Re-focus on governance capacity and human capital, as foundations for a stronger investment climate.*

- **Refocusing on governance capacity and human capital.** Supporting countries' efforts in these areas will provide the critical foundations for an attractive investment climate, job creation and economic dynamism, and social stability, as decades of experience show.

- Governance reform lasts only when it comes from within. But the IFIs, as trusted partners in the adoption of best practices and institutional innovations, have to work more closely together, and with countries' other development partners, to support enduring reforms.
- The IFIs must also support governments in ensuring the broadest base in human capital development: providing equality of opportunity for all, regardless of gender, ethnicity and social backgrounds.

Proposal 2: *Build effective country platforms to mobilize all development partners to unlock investments, and maximize their contributions as a group, including by convergence around core standards.*

◎ **Joining up IFIs' operations**, as well as with those of other development partners, to enhance development impact:

- Country platforms can be transformational in their impact. **Effective country platforms will maximize the contributions of development partners as a group and scale up private investments, including by convergence around core standards.**[1]

---

[1] This would be a set of five/six core development standards with appropriate sequencing for states with features of fragility. They could include debt sustainability, ESG standards, coherent pricing policies, local capacity building, procurement, and transparency and anti-corruption. As a pragmatic first step, the IFIs should agree to use each other's standards within a platform, which would enable early implementation and help provide a path towards consensus. Convergence towards core standards must be done in close collaboration with shareholders.

OVERVIEW

» A country platform must be owned by its government, encourage competition, and retain the government's flexibility to engage with the most suitable partners. However, transparency within the platform is essential to avoid zero-sum competition, such as through subsidies or lower standards.
» Coherent and complementary operations between development partners will help scale up private sector investment. The adoption of core standards can also lower the private sector's costs in working with a range of partners.
» Priority has to be given to linking up security, humanitarian and development efforts in states with features of fragility, working with UN agencies and other partners.
» Cooperation within the country platforms would enable rapid response in times of crisis.
» Cooperation at the country level should be supported by global platforms for IFIs to cooperate on key thematic issues such as sustainable infrastructure.

Proposal 3: *Implement regional platforms to facilitate transformational cross-border investments and connectivity.*

◆ **Implement regional platforms to facilitate transformative cross-border infrastructure projects** that enable regional connectivity and open up new supply chains and markets.

Proposal 4: *Reduce and diversify risk on a system-wide basis* to mobilize significantly greater private investment, including portfolio-based infrastructure financing.

Proposal 4a: Shift the basic business model of the MDBs from direct lending towards risk mitigation aimed at mobilizing private capital.

Proposal 4b: Develop system-wide political risk insurance and expand use of private reinsurance markets.

Proposal 4c: Build a developing country infrastructure asset class with the scale and diversification needed to draw in institutional investors.

◎ **Multiplying private capital** by adopting **system-wide** approaches to risk insurance and securitization. Institutional investor participation in developing country infrastructure has so far been miniscule. The development of a standardized, large-scale asset class, that diversifies risk across the development finance system, will help mobilize this huge untapped pool of investments.

Proposal 5: 'Right-size' capital requirements for MDBs and other investors in infrastructure, given their default experience.

Proposal 5a: Establish tailor-made capital and liquidity frameworks for the MDBs.

Proposal 5b: Review the regulatory treatment of infrastructure investment by institutional investors.

◎ **Reassessing regulatory capital and other prudential norms for the Multilateral Development Banks (MDBs),** as well as institutional investors in infrastructure[1], based on the evidence of their default experience.

Proposal 6: *Strengthen joint capacity to tackle the challenges of the global commons.*

Proposal 6a: *Integrate activities in support of the global commons into the IFIs' core programs, and coordinate them within country platforms.*

Proposal 6b: *Create global platforms with the UN guardian agency and the World Bank coordinating and leveraging on the key players in each of the commons.*

◎ **Strengthening joint capacity to tackle challenges of the global commons, through global platforms that bring together the players in each field–** coordinated by the designated UN guardian agency and the World Bank, which has the broadest reach amongst the MDBs. For specific commons, there will be Regional Development Banks (RDBs) and other stakeholders with significant capabilities that should play key roles.

Proposal 7: *Integrate trust fund activities into MDBs' core operations to avoid fragmentation.*

◎ **Mainstreaming activities in support of the global commons into IFIs'**

---

[1] Institutional investors currently face some regulatory disincentives in investing in infrastructure.

core country-based operations. We must likewise **integrate trust fund activities with the MDBs' strategies and operations**, to avoid parallel structures that pose significant costs to efficiency and impact.

Proposal 8: *Plug shortfalls in data and research that hamper effective policymaking, especially in developing countries.*

◎ **Investing in data and research** to support sound, evidence-based policies. Basic data still falls short in many developing countries. These are public goods in their own right. The International Monetary Fund (IMF) and World Bank should work with UN agencies and RDBs to strengthen efforts in these areas.

Proposal 9: *Leverage more systematically on the ideas and operating networks of business alliances, NGOs and philan-thropies.*

◎ **Achieving stronger synergies with business alliances, NGOs and philanthropies** so as to benefit from their on-the-ground perspectives, innovations and delivery capacity. The IFIs must work with governments to collaborate with and leverage on these actors more systematically, identifying key needs and providing space and co-funding where required so they can play their full roles.

These system-wide shifts will enable the international community to meet the vastly larger development needs of the future. **They will help mobilize private capital, which is a potential game-changer in development**

finance. However, private capital is unlikely to engage on the scale required without the involvement of the IFIs–in project origination, risk participation, and staying engaged with governments on reforms.

While the G20 Eminent Persons Group's (EPG) mandate does not include making specific proposals to enhance the IFIs' capital bases, we underline the need for their official shareholders to review periodically the need for capital replenishments to ensure that they achieve their full potential in a world of growing challenges in development, growth and stability. The capital reviews must be supported by the reforms to the IFIs to ensure they can most effectively perform their roles as catalysts for private investment and multipliers of development. It is equally necessary for the effectiveness of the IFIs that their shareholding structures are updated regularly to reflect an evolving world economy.

C. Securing the Benefits of Interconnected Financial Markets: Reforms for Global Financial Resilience

Governance of the IMFS should be focused on its most fundamental goals: **enabling countries to reach their full growth and development potential; and averting the damage caused by financial crises.**

The IMFS has been strengthened in important respects since the crisis, especially through more robust prudential regulations and standards. But the system still has features that lead to crises occurring too often–in individual countries or in groups of similar countries through contagion, or globally. Reforms are needed to **make it possible for developing**

countries to finance sustainable current account deficits, where they are fundamentally needed at their stage of development, without the recurring bouts of instability that set back growth. Such reforms should support countries' own efforts to strengthen the environment for long-term, reliable flows of capital.

To achieve the fundamental goals of the IMFS, we must repair and strengthen three interdependent pillars of the system.

1. Getting the Benefits of International Capital Flows Without Risks Arising from Excessive Market Volatility

Both domestic financial markets and cross-border investments have brought major benefits globally. There is considerable potential yet for the developing world to utilize them to finance investments and growth.

Countries with sound macroeconomic policies, reliable rule of law and deep domestic financial markets have been best able to benefit from openness to international capital. However, **even well-run economies are exposed to spillovers from policies in advanced countries and shifts in global risk sentiment in today's highly interconnected global financial markets**. Excessive volatility reduces the room for maneuver in policy-making, and can lead to responses that hurt growth, both nationally and regionally. Experience has also shown that countries will only remain on a path towards openness if they can manage episodes of excessive volatility in capital flows and exchange rates, and protect domestic financial stability.

This remains a vexing issue in the IMFS. However, **policy thinking on the issue has often been shaped by whether one sits in sending or receiving**

OVERVIEW

countries. We have to move beyond this. A rules-based international framework, drawing on a comprehensive and evolving evidence base, is needed to provide policy advice through which countries seek to avoid policies with large spillovers, develop resilient markets, and benefit from capital flows while managing risks to financial stability.

Our proposals aim at **enabling countries to move towards openness as a long-term goal**, at a pace and sequence that enables them to preserve financial stability:

Proposal 10: *The IFI community should strengthen and accelerate efforts to help countries develop deep, resilient and inclusive domestic financial markets.*

◎ The IMF, World Bank and RDBs should strengthen and coordinate their technical assistance and partnership with the national authorities to **deepen domestic financial markets**. Efforts should focus on policy frameworks, including the legal and regulatory infrastructure, for development of sound banking, capital markets and the domestic institutional investor base, macro-financial stability, and financial inclusivity.

Proposal 11: *The IMF's framework of policy guidance should enable countries to move toward the long-run goal of openness to capital flows and to better manage the risks to financial stability.*

Proposal 11a: *Develop evidence-based policy options to enable countries to benefit from capital flows while maintaining financial stability, and to provide assurance to the markets that measures taken are appropriate.*

Proposal 11b: *Develop an understanding of policy options that enable sending countries to meet domestic objectives while avoiding large adverse international spillovers.*

◎ **The IMF should evolve and extend its Institutional View to enable countries to benefit from capital flows while managing risks to financial stability.** It should involve a reliable assessment of a receiving country's capital flows at risk and macro-financial stability, and of 'push factors' and possible reversal of flows from sending countries. It should build on experience on the effectiveness of various instruments, including macro-prudential policies in particular. It should also aim at providing assurance to the markets when countries are pursuing a policy mix consistent with the framework.

◎ **The IMF should also develop a policy framework for sending countries** that enables them to meet their domestic objectives while avoiding large international spillovers. While ambitious, the importance of such a framework for sustaining support for an open international system, and for receiving countries to continue to liberalize, cannot be overemphasized.[1] The development of this framework–with inputs from national authorities and the Bank for International Settlements (BIS)–should be built upon an

---

[1] The global adoption and evolution of prudential standards is a successful example of an internationally accepted policy framework agreed under the umbrella of the FSB, where the Basel, IAIS and the IOSCO standards–while not mandatory–provide a benchmark to assess the adequacy of financial institutions' buffers in different countries.

extension of IMF's spillover work and integrated into the Article IV consultations of key systemic countries.

◎ The global financial architecture also needs **a standing IMF facility for temporary liquidity support**, as part of the package that enables countries to benefit from openness to capital flows. The facility should support good policy-making, and be accessed only in the event of global liquidity shocks or those arising from contagion.[1]

2. Strengthening Risk Surveillance to Avoid the Next Major Crisis

Every financial crisis has lasting costs. They disrupt investments in the future, tend to hurt poorer citizens most, and have consequences that can last a generation or longer.

We will not know where the next crisis will start. But **it will become a full-blown crisis, with broader global consequences, when we are not prepared for it**. It is therefore critical that we strengthen our ability to detect risks early, and anticipate how they can be transmitted through a complex and highly interconnected global financial system, so that we can contain them before they escalate.

Proposal 12: *Integrate the surveillance efforts of the IMF, FSB and BIS in a coherent global risk map, while preserving the independence of each of the three institutions' perspectives.*

---

[1] See Proposal 15.

Proposal 12a: *Incorporate non-official and contrarian views systematically for more robust risk surveillance.*

The official community did not see the Global Financial Crisis coming. **Ten years on, risk surveillance has advanced, but is still too diffused. Much remains to be done to avert the next crisis.** We need a more integrated system of risk surveillance. It should bring the distinct surveillance lenses of the IMF, Financial Stability Board (FSB) and BIS together, to construct and continually update a global risk map of financial linkages and vulnerabilities.[1] **An integrated risk assessment must nevertheless preserve the independence of perspective of each of the three institutions**, and **avoid converging on a diluted consensus**. It must also solicit regular inputs from central banks and regulators, and **look out for contrarian views**, including those from the non-official sector.

Proposal 13: *Build on the IMF-FSB Early Warning Exercise (EWE) to ensure policy follow-up from the global risk map.*

This global risk map should also be used to facilitate regular discussion of **policy actions to pre-empt crises**. The IMF-FSB Early Warning Exercise (EWE) should be extended to enable this follow-through.

---

[1] An integrated system of surveillance should retain the comparative advantages of the three institutions–the IMF focused especially on economic and macro-financial risks and sovereign vulnerabilities, FSB on financial system vulnerabilities, and BIS on global flows and market infrastructure risks.

3. Stitching Together the Fragmented Global Financial Safety Net

Proposal 14: *Stitch together the various layers of the GFSN to achieve scale and predictability.*

We also need an effective global financial safety net (GFSN), to sustain open markets and support global growth. A decentralized, multi-layered structure of global, regional and bilateral arrangements has evolved over the last decade. But it is highly uneven in scale and coverage across regions, has major components that are untested in crisis, and lacks coordination. As a result, it lacks the predictability essential to an effective financial safety net. **The incentive hence remains for countries to 'self-insure' by accumulating more reserves, or for developing countries in particular to avoid or reduce current account deficits even where they are fundamentally needed to achieve their full growth potential.**

It is critical to put in place a reliable GFSN before the next crisis. First, we must ensure an adequately-resourced global layer in the IMF through timely conclusion of quota reviews.[1] Second, the IMF must work with Regional Financial Arrangements (RFAs) to enable consistent actions during a crisis so as to achieve the necessary scale and global impact. A

---

[1] The International Monetary and Financial Committee (IMFC) has called on the IMF Executive Board to work expeditiously towards the completion of the 15th General Review of Quotas by the Spring Meetings of 2019 and no later than the Annual Meetings of 2019.

properly designed and predictable GFSN can avoid moral hazard, minimize contagion between countries, and promote openness and growth.

Proposal 15: Establish a standing IMF liquidity facility to give countries timely access to temporary support during global liquidity shocks.

Proposal 15a: Use a country's qualification for the IMF's liquidity facility in considering the activation of RFA support.

Third, it is important to **put in place a standing global liquidity facility**[①], drawing on IMF permanent resources, to strengthen countries' ability to withstand global liquidity shocks and avoid deeper crises. A reliable liquidity facility will also help them avoid building up excessive reserves as the price for being open to capital flows, and hence avoid hampering growth. The facility should be designed for countries with sound policies, and to minimize 'IMF stigma' when they draw on it.

Proposal 16: Enable the IMF to rapidly mobilize additional resources in large and severe global crises.

We must also address the global safety net requirements in the event of a large and severe future crisis. Such needs are not catered for in the permanent resources of the IMF. There is no assurance that the solutions effected in the

---

① The support provided should be in line with the IMF's normal access policies, and for short durations.

midst of the last crisis, especially the large liquidity swaps between selected central banks, will be available in future.[1] We have to explore temporary mechanisms to mobilize resources on the scale required to ensure global stability in such systemic 'tail risk' events. However, the available solutions face governance and policy challenges, on which there are differing views. These must first be resolved through a process of consensus building. The EPG is hence not proposing a solution for endorsement at this stage.

D. The G20 and the IFIs: Making the System Work as a System

The G20 has been a powerful impetus for change. Its members have equal standing within its consensus-based setting, which gives the G20 added credibility in a multipolar world. The G20 has used these advantages to promote several initiatives following the global crisis, for example in strengthening financial regulation through the work of the FSB and achieving tax transparency via the OECD.

However, the G20 does not have universal membership and unlike

---

[1] During the last global financial crisis, around US$500 billion were deployed through the US Federal Reserve's liquidity swaps with selected central banks. These interventions were critical in ensuring the integrity of the global US$ payment system and in calming global markets–although the majority of emerging market economies did not directly benefit from them. Importantly, such actions cannot be taken as assured in the future. Furthermore, in response to a joint call by the IMFC and G20, a significant group of countries pledged US$450 billion to temporarily augment IMF resources during the crisis. Participation was not universal. This option of bilateral borrowings for future major crises will require swift mobilization.

the treaty-based organizations, is not legally constituted to deliver on decisions. It has to work in coordination with the IFIs and other international organizations to advance many of its aims. The governance relationship between the G20 and the IFIs is hence key to effective global financial governance.

It is widely felt that the accumulation of initiatives and multiplicity of meetings within the G20 risks crowding out issues that require its strategic guidance and political consensus-building. The growth of the G20 agenda and activities has also meant an overlap with the governance and roles of the IFIs and other international organizations.

Our proposals fall in three areas and benefited from discussions with a range of stakeholders. First, for effectiveness in **the G20's role** in developing forward-looking thinking on global financial governance and crisis responses. Second, on the **governance of the IFIs as a system**, so that they collectively deliver much more than the sum of their individual contributions. Finally, to streamline the roles of **Executive Boards and Management within IFIs** to ensure greater effectiveness and outcome-driven oversight.

Proposal 17: The G20 should refocus on a multi-year, strategic agenda, rationalize workstreams, and devolve more work to the IFIs.

The G20 should refocus on building consensus on strategic global goals, prune its agenda significantly, and leverage more on the IFIs and other international organizations. G20 Ministerial meetings on the finance track should be convened once or twice a year in normal times, and focus on strategic issues and emerging threats that require international coordination, or on overcoming governance hurdles within the system. In a similar vein, two Deputies meetings a year as a norm would be adequate to support and ensure follow through of the Ministerial agenda. This two-tier system within the G20 should be sufficient for most purposes, and enable much of the work currently done in working groups to be devolved to the IFIs and other competent bodies. If the G20 needs to constitute a working group to drive major new system-wide initiatives, the group should ideally operate for a period of no more than three years.

Governance of the system of IFIs itself requires **two significant step-changes** to deliver a much greater scale of development impact: to ensure synergy and complementarity in a more diverse, decentralized world; and to achieve an important shift in business models within the system as a whole so as to effectively catalyze private investments.

Proposal 18: *A G20-led group, with representation from key non-G20 constituencies and the IFIs, should steer the reorientation of development finance over the next three years before handing the coordinating role to the IFI Heads. This should include building complementarity among all development partners, and a clear system of metrics to track impact and value for money.*

An effective forum is required to ensure this major reorientation of the system of development finance. However, there is currently no effective forum with universal membership that has the necessary system-wide remit–to steer the shifts required to ensure coherence and complementarity among the IFIs as well as with other major development partners. **It will require dedicated steering over three years to move to this new landscape, building on current initiatives in the IFIs. A clear system of metrics to track impact and value for money should be established, which will also ensure continuity of the reforms beyond that period.** A G20-led Group of Deputies, with representation from key non-G20 constituencies and the IFIs[1], reporting periodically to Ministers, will be the most effective way to fill this gap over the next three years before handing the coordinating role to the heads of the IFIs.[2]

We must also strengthen system-wide collaboration to respond to major challenges and anticipate risks in development before they create lasting damage or spiral across countries. There are repeated instances where we have failed to do so in the recent decades.

Proposal 19: *A biennial strategic forum convened by the IMFC and DC should identify development risks before they manifest,*

---

[1] Apart from the IMF and the World Bank, this should include representation from the RDBs. Consideration should also be given to include the Chair of the International Development Finance Club, which comprises the major DFIs.

[2] The principal focus of the G20-led Group would be to endorse objectives, milestones and associated system-wide metrics to evaluate progress made on achieving coherence and complementarity among the IFIs and with other development partners, and the crowding in of the private sector. The Group should also aid in removing the governance hurdles that impede progress, while operating in a manner that does not undermine the governance structure of individual institutions.

OVERVIEW

and the required collective responses.

It is critical that Finance Ministers be engaged in addressing these risks. A biennial dialogue on a **Global Development Risk Map** should be convened, comprising members of IMFC and Development Committee[①] (who together represent 25 constituencies), as well as representatives from IFIs, the UN Development System, key civil society and philanthropic players, and the private sector. The risk map should enable stakeholders to assess the adequacy of responses and the future collective effort required.[②]

Reforms are also needed to the governance of the IMFS to foster **global financial resilience**. Responsibility for pursuing these reforms in three interdependent areas identified in Section C above, and discussed more fully in the Main Report, are summarized below for ease of reference:

◎ **On capital flows.** First, **the IMF, World Bank and RDBs** should accelerate efforts to help countries develop **deep, resilient and inclusive domestic financial markets**. Second, the IMF's framework of policy guidance should enable countries to move toward openness as a long-term goal, at a pace and sequence that

---

[①] The IMFC is the key ministerial forum for providing strategic direction to the work and policies of the IMF. The Development Committee (DC) is a ministerial forum of the World Bank Group and the IMF for intergovernmental consensus-building on development issues.

[②] The World Bank and IMF could provide the secretariat for the development of the Global Development Risk Map.

enables them to preserve financial stability, and to manage episodes of excessive volatility. This involves (i) **evolving and extending the IMF's Institutional View** as a basis for developing policy options for receiving countries; and (ii) the IMF complementing this by developing a policy framework that **enables sending countries to meet their domestic objectives while avoiding large adverse spillovers**. This is best undertaken with inputs from national authorities and the BIS. Third, we must achieve consensus to put in place a standing IMF liquidity facility.

◎ **On risk surveillance.** The **IMF, FSB and BIS** should integrate their surveillance efforts in a coherent global risk map, while preserving the integrity of the three institutions' perspectives. A joint team from the three institutions should take inputs from various official sources including the money-center central banks, as well as from non-official sources. The **IMF-FSB Early Warning Exercise should provide the home for policy discussions and resulting follow-up**.

◎ **On the global financial safety net.** Timely conclusion of IMF quota reviews is necessary to ensure an adequately-resourced global layer of the GFSN. Further, **the IMF and the RFAs** should intensify their work to establish a **clear assignment of responsibilities and protocols for joint actions**, so as to create a stronger and more reliable GFSN. This includes discussions on coherence of ex-post conditionality in adjustment cases, the determination of liquidity needs, and the possible signaling role of an IMF liquidity facility. Further, the IMF should also explore **temporary mechanisms** to

OVERVIEW

swiftly mobilize resources on the scale required to ensure global stability **in future crises of a large, systemic nature**.

Given the significance of these three sets of reforms and the key roles of the IMF in effecting them, the **IMFC should be regularly updated** on the status of their implementation and challenges faced.

Proposal 20: *The Executive Board of each IFI should focus on strategic priorities for the institution and advancing system-wide goals.*

Proposal 21: *Adopt a practical, risk-based approach to delegate greater responsibility to IFI Management, and hold them accountable for outcomes.*

The governance of IFIs themselves has to be brought up to date, reflecting the complexity of the strategic challenges and the needed shifts in MDBs' business models for a new era. Individually, the IFIs should develop a framework to **streamline the roles of the Executive Board and Management** to avoid overlaps and ensure clarity of responsibilities and accountability. Boards should focus on strategic issues and directions and move away from a disproportionate tilt towards operational decision making and transactional functions. **Management should be empowered and held accountable** for ensuring that the strategic priorities of the IFI and the system as a whole are effectively translated into policies, operations and incentives.

In keeping with this objective, consideration should be given to IMF, World Bank and other MDBs amending their Articles of Agreement where necessary, to allow for delegation of appropriate decision-making responsibilities to the Managements of the respective institutions. A practical and risk-based approach should form the basis for such delegation of responsibilities.

Proposal 22: *Ensure diversity and better match the skills available to IFI Boards and Management to the shift in the business models and increased complexity of challenges.*

For Boards to optimally perform their roles, they need access to the **right skills, diversity and expertise**. The Boards should define skills sets relevant for constituencies' own selection of Executive Directors; as well as to guide processes for selection of Management. The Boards should also invite external experts to contribute in Board committees requiring specialized knowledge (for example, in audit and risk assessments and strategies to catalyze private investment).

With a new clarity of roles and responsibilities, shareholders should also consider the different models of Executive Boards across IFIs, with a view to evaluating their effectiveness, cost structure and frequency of meetings.

An open, transparent and merit-based process for the selection of IFI Heads is also essential to the sustained legitimacy and effectiveness of the IFIs.

E. Conclusion

Taken as a whole, the reforms serve a common agenda: to enable nations to create the jobs of the future and achieve more sustainable and inclusive growth, to eliminate extreme poverty and enable youthful populations to achieve their aspirations, to avert financial crises and the lasting damage they inflict on societies, and to tackle the pressing challenges in the global commons that affect us all.

The present international monetary and financial system lacks the coherence, joint capacity and effectiveness to support these goals. It must be brought up to date with the realities of a new era. We can achieve this by implementing decisive reforms to **make the system work as a system.** These reforms are within our reach.

They do not require new international bodies. They require that we take bold and defined steps to ensure that today's institutions–global, regional and bilateral–work together as a system. They require that we build trust and transparency among these different institutions and leverage on their combined strengths. These changes will be critical to meeting the development challenges of the decade ahead, and helping countries experience fewer crises that set back reforms and growth.

The proposals in this report build on reforms that had been underway among the IFIs, and take them further. But they also **call for a much greater sense of urgency and recognition among their shareholders of the need for consistency and joined-up efforts among the IFIs and all other stakeholders, so that we raise our whole game.**

The ambition is in the doing. Some of the reforms are low-hanging fruit. Most are achievable within a few years, with focused effort. Some others go beyond current thinking. We urge that they be considered with an open mind, and developed further or adapted if necessary to enable their implementation.

Achieving these reforms will also contribute to **a larger goal that every nation has a vested interest in.** They enable us to build **a cooperative international order for a new**, **multipolar era**–one that enables nations everywhere to fulfil the aspirations of their citizens, and serves the global good.

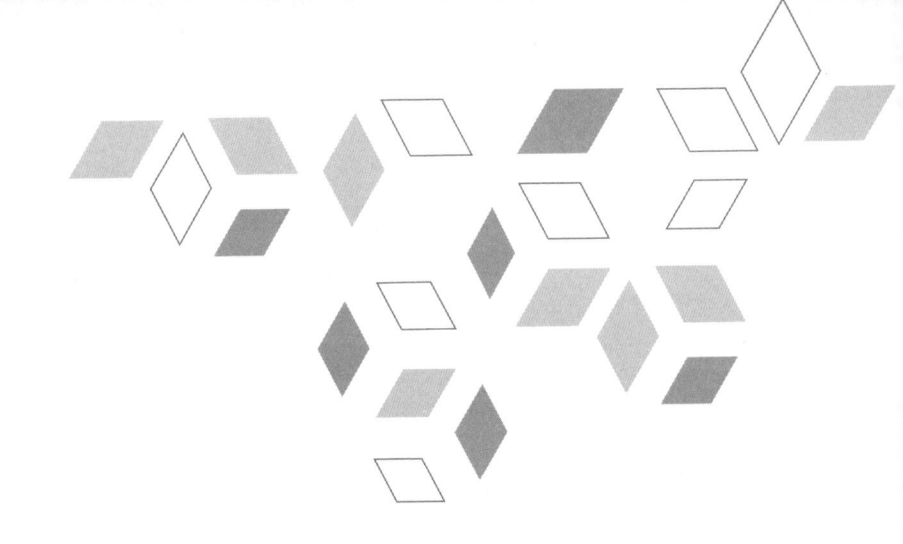

01
ACHIEVING GREATER DEVELOPMENT IMPACT: COLLABORATING ACROSS THE SYSTEM

01 ACHIEVING GREATER DEVELOPMENT IMPACT: COLLABORATING ACROSS THE SYSTEM

The next decade is critical.

We need substantially greater impact in helping countries achieve sustainable development and inclusive growth, and in managing the growing pressures in the global commons. The current pace of change will not get us there.

We need **bolder reforms to harness complementarities and synergies** in the development system:

- Refocus IFIs' efforts to help countries strengthen **governance capacity and human capital**, as the foundation for an attractive investment climate, job creation, and social stability.
- Exploit the largely **untapped potential for collaboration** among the IFIs as well as with development partners to maximize their contributions as a group, including by convergence around core standards.
- Embark on **system-wide insurance and diversification of risk**, to create a large-scale asset class and mobilize significantly greater private sector participation.
- Strengthen **joint capacity** to tackle the **challenges of the commons**.

We must also leverage more actively on the work of the non-official sector, including NGOs and philanthropies.

Bold and urgent reforms in development policies and financing are required to achieve the major step-up in growth, job opportunities and sustainability that the world needs in the next decade.

We must achieve significantly greater development impact in every continent. The road to achieving the Sustainable Development Goals (SDGs) must pass through Africa, in particular. It has great potential to contribute to global growth in the coming decades. But Africa also faces unprecedented poverty, demographic, jobs and environmental challenges (see Box 1). **The consequences of failure will not be simply economic.**

We must **organize the world's multilateral development capabilities and resources in a new way to address these challenges and achieve greater and more lasting development impact**. The IFIs are uniquely positioned as multipliers of development–by supporting good policies, strengthening institutions, promoting innovation, taking programs to scale and mobilizing private sector investment. **There is much further potential to be unlocked by governing the system as a system rather than as individual institutions.**

Given the critical need to attract much larger volumes of private risk capital, and in particular equity financing, we must **maximize the IFIs' unique ability to help reduce risk in order to draw in private investment by**:

◎ Helping countries to **de-risk their whole investment environment** (besides de-risking projects). The IFIs must collaborate to help countries take advantage of current best practices in governance and regulation.

01 ACHIEVING GREATER DEVELOPMENT IMPACT: COLLABORATING ACROSS THE SYSTEM

◎ **Pioneering investments in lower income countries and states with features of fragility**, in critical areas such as energy infrastructure, to reduce perceived risks and pave the way for private investments.

◎ **Mitigating risk** through instruments such as first-loss guarantees, and co-investments to catalyze private investment.

◎ **Leveraging on the largely untapped potential to pool and diversify risks across the development finance system**, so as to create new asset classes for private investors.

To achieve these objectives, IFI governance must place **rigorous emphasis on additionality**–ensuring that guarantees and concessional resources are deployed where they have the greatest catalytic role in attracting private capital and addressing market failures. Importantly, they must use their risk-mitigation tools to **attract private investment to the least developed countries**, in addition to the middle-income countries in which blended finance has been heavily concentrated so far.

Box 1: Africa's Opportunities and Challenges

Africa has grown well over the past decade, expanding at over 4 percent on average. But there are major challenges ahead, and setbacks in some parts of the continent that need to be overcome.

The coming decades offer great opportunity. With strong reforms in governance, human capital, and the investment climate, an environment can be created that brings greater job opportunities for Africa's burgeoning youth population and spurs sustainable and inclusive growth.

However, poverty and environmental challenges remain severe and could worsen without continuous reforms and investments to create jobs, and to pre-empt the implications of climate change for food security and the spread of diseases.

The pace of growth in the young, working age population in Africa will be unprecedented in global history. It offers the possibility of a significant market for global goods and services, with Africa's middle class expected to grow by 100 million.

However, at the current pace of economic growth, job creation will still be short of needs, which in turn implies a persistent difficulty in reducing extreme poverty. By 2030, nine in ten of the world's poor are expected to be in Africa. A young population that is not gainfully employed could also become a source of instability.

Growth in agriculture has tremendous potential, given Africa's vast tracts of arable land. Its realization will depend on the adoption of improved techniques, commercialization, and better utilized water resources. There are also huge opportunities for digitalization of Africa's economies and developing resource-based manufacturing to increase domestic value-added.

Mobilizing the private sector to support these goals will be critical. Thriving African economies, connected to global markets, can become a new engine of growth and will contribute to tackling the challenges of the global commons.

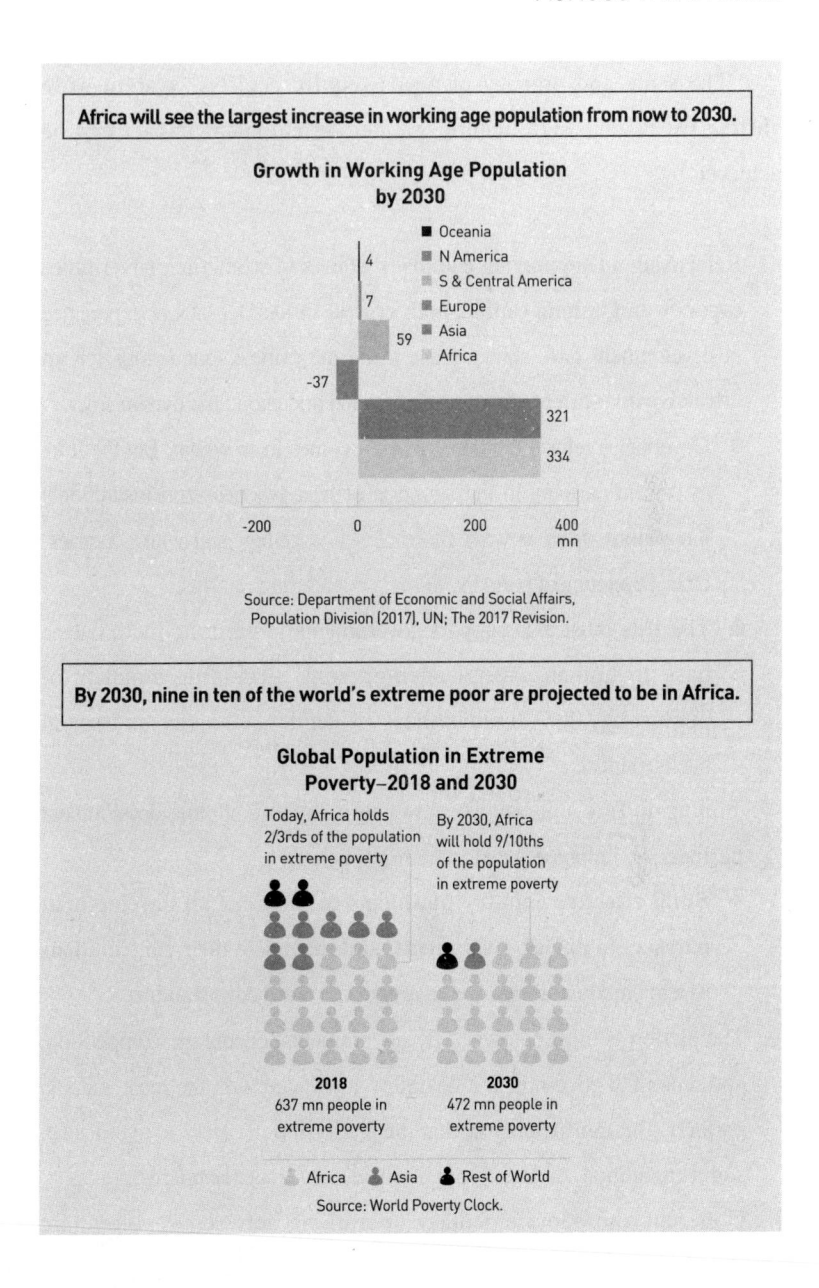

01 ACHIEVING GREATER DEVELOPMENT IMPACT: COLLABORATING ACROSS THE SYSTEM

Africa will see the largest increase in working age population from now to 2030.

Growth in Working Age Population by 2030

- Oceania: 4
- N America: 7
- S & Central America: 59
- Europe: -37
- Asia: 321
- Africa: 334

(mn)

Source: Department of Economic and Social Affairs, Population Division (2017), UN; The 2017 Revision.

By 2030, nine in ten of the world's extreme poor are projected to be in Africa.

Global Population in Extreme Poverty—2018 and 2030

Today, Africa holds 2/3rds of the population in extreme poverty

By 2030, Africa will hold 9/10ths of the population in extreme poverty

2018
637 mn people in extreme poverty

2030
472 mn people in extreme poverty

Africa Asia Rest of World

Source: World Poverty Clock.

The scale and urgency of needs require decisive, **system-wide shifts**. We believe significantly greater development impact can be achieved by:

◎ **Refocusing on supporting countries' efforts to strengthen governance capacity and human capital, both critical tasks.** Decades of experience in development have shown these to be the critical foundations for **an attractive investment climate**, job creation and economic dynamism.
   ◆ Governance reform lasts only when it comes from within. But the IFIs, as trusted partners in the adoption of best practices and institutional innovations, have to work more closely together, and with countries' other development partners, to support enduring reforms.
   ◆ The IFIs must also support governments in ensuring the broadest base in human capital development: providing equality of opportunity for all, regardless of gender, ethnicity and social backgrounds.
◎ **Joining up IFIs' operations**, as well as with those of other development partners, to enhance development impact:
   ◆ **Build effective country platforms to mobilize all development partners to unlock investments, and maximize their contributions as a group, including by convergence around core standards.**
» The platforms must be owned by governments, encourage competition, and retain the government's flexibility to engage with the most suitable partners. But transparency within the platform must serve to avoid zero-sum competition, such as through subsidies or lower standards.
» Coherent and complementary operations between development

partners will help scale up private sector investment. The adoption of core standards can lower the private sector's cost in working with a range of development partners.

» Priority has to be given to linking up security, humanitarian and development efforts in states with features of fragility, working with UN agencies and other partners.

» Cooperation within the country platforms would enable a rapid response in times of crisis.

» Cooperation at the country level should also be supported by global platforms for the IFIs to collaborate on key thematic issues such as sustainable infrastructure.

- ◆ **Implement regional platforms to facilitate transformative cross-border infrastructure projects, that enable regional connectivity and open up new supply chains and markets.**
- ◎ **Multiplying private capital** by adopting **system-wide** approaches to risk insurance and securitization. Institutional investor participation in developing country infrastructure has so far been miniscule. The development of a standardized, large-scale asset class, that diversifies risk across the development finance system, will help mobilize this huge untapped pool of investments.
- ◎ **Reassessing regulatory capital and other prudential norms for the MDBs, as well as institutional investors in infrastructure**[1], based on the evidence of their default experience.

---

[1] Institutional investors currently face some regulatory disincentives in investing in infrastructure.

- **Strengthening joint capacity to tackle the challenges of the global commons through tighter and more effective coordination mechanisms** among the diverse organizations in each field, to enhance response capacity and to ensure adequate financing.
- The IFIs must also **mainstream activities in support of the global commons into their core country-based operations**. We must likewise **integrate trust fund activities** with the MDBs' strategies and operations, to avoid parallel structures that pose significant costs to efficiency and impact.
- **Investing in data and research** to support sound, evidence-based policies. Basic data still falls short in many developing countries. These are public goods in their own right. The IMF and World Bank should work with UN agencies and RDBs to strengthen efforts in these areas.
- **Achieving stronger synergies with business alliances, NGOs and philanthropies** so as to benefit from their on-the-ground perspectives, innovations and delivery capacity. The IFIs must work with governments to collaborate with and leverage on these actors more systematically, identifying key needs and providing space and co-funding where required so they can play their full roles.

Proposal 1: Re-focus on governance capacity and human capital, as foundations for a stronger investment climate.

Governance and human capital development have been at the core of the successful development stories of the last half century.

01 ACHIEVING GREATER DEVELOPMENT IMPACT: COLLABORATING ACROSS THE SYSTEM

This agenda succeeds only when it is owned by countries themselves. However, the IFIs should refocus their efforts, individually and collectively, on assisting countries in strengthening governance capacity, spreading best practices more quickly, and spurring the adoption of new technologies that improve productivity and enable more inclusive access to education and healthcare.

Strengthened governance capacity is essential to mobilizing domestic financial resources and creating an attractive investment climate, both at the national and local levels, by:

◎ **Improving domestic tax administration** and reducing leakages.
◎ **Reducing corruption** which is a major constraint on economic development.
◎ Developing the domestic financial system, particularly by **deepening local currency capital markets.**
◎ **Strengthening the rule of law and increasing regulatory certainty** to provide confidence for long-term investors.

The IFIs can also be effective in sensitizing governments to a **critical unfinished task in human capital development**: the need for equality of opportunity for all, regardless of gender, ethnicity and social backgrounds.[1] They should also encourage governments to **leverage on the initiatives of the non-official sector,** including NGOs

---

[1] The recent compilation of a comprehensive Human Capital Index by the World Bank will help countries benchmark their policies and measure progress.

and philanthropies, and the private sector, to spread opportunities widely.

However, building governance capacity and developing human capital take time. Special attention must be paid to countries with significant elements of fragility, to help reformist governments to achieve progress in creating jobs and widening access to services, and thereby build public support for continuing reforms. There is otherwise a real risk of governance reforms being undermined by a lack of demonstrated success in improving welfare.

Proposal 2: Build effective country platforms to mobilize all development partners to unlock investments, and maximize their contributions as a group, including by convergence around core standards.

Country platforms, owned by governments, will enhance contributions from all development partners including the private sector. They can be transformational in their development impact:

- **Exploiting the complementarity among a country's development partners**–the IFIs, UN agencies, bilateral official agencies, and in some cases philanthropies and NGOs–hence taking advantage of their combined strength and knowledge.
- **Enabling development partners to provide more consistent and better coordinated support for policy and institutional reforms.**
- **Scaling up private sector investment** through coherent and

01 ACHIEVING GREATER DEVELOPMENT IMPACT: COLLABORATING ACROSS THE SYSTEM

complementary operations between development partners.

◎ **Facilitating adoption of common core standards** to ensure sustained development impact and lower the cost of working with the range of partners.

◎ **Strengthening crisis response capacity** as they provide a coordinating mechanism that can be utilized for immediate response.

Importantly, the platforms **must not be a straitjacket on either the government or development partners**:

◎ To be effective, they must have strong **government ownership**, preserving the government's flexibility to engage with partners with appropriate strength. The platforms should also be able to evolve differently across countries, depending in part on governments' planning capacities.

◎ However, country platforms also have the potential to help governments in **planning through the life cycle of public assets, and to enhance coordination across agencies within government** with Ministries of Finance usually playing a coordinating role.

◎ For development partners, transparency within the platform and convergence on core standards will encourage **healthy competition around innovation, efficiency and speed to market and improve the investment climate**.

The use of country platforms has so far been fragmented and

selective.[1] They have been mainly used in post-conflict reconstruction or at a sectoral level (see Annex 1 for an overview of existing forms). None yet combine the transparency, convergence around common development standards, and the standardized approaches needed to achieve a major step-up in private sector investment. Developing such country platforms will hence **require a significant shift in the way the development community operates.**

Effective country platforms require **a high level of transparency**, to ensure that all partners have access to and share relevant information. They will involve **the partners adopting a set of agreed core standards** to ensure sustainability, and to **avoid competition of a zero-sum nature** such as in subsidies.[2] The adoption of common core standards will improve the **ease with which the private sector can collaborate with different development partners** (see Box 2).

> **Box 2: Core Standards**
> Core standards should aim at achieving coherence amongst the multiplicity of today's actors in development finance, and

---

[1] Rwanda, for example, has developed a well-functioning donor coordination mechanism encompassing many of the key attributes of an effective country platform. Other examples exist of mechanisms that capture different key elements of the EPG's proposal, such as sectoral platforms in Brazil for private sector participation, the 4G in Colombia, and the National Slums Upgrading Program in Indonesia (see Annex 1 for further illustration).

[2] As a pragmatic first step, the IFIs should agree to use each other's standards within a platform, which would enable early implementation and help provide a path towards consensus.

enable them to focus on unlocking synergies in the system. It would also enable both governments and the private sector to work more effectively with different development partners and at lower cost.

This would involve the system agreeing to a set of five/six core development standards with appropriate sequencing for states with features of fragility. They could include:

1. Debt sustainability.
2. Environmental, social and governance standards.
3. Coherent pricing policies.
4. Local capacity building.
5. Procurement.
6. Transparency and anti-corruption.

Currently the IFIs broadly adhere on the principal components of the core standards. The development of and **convergence towards core standards must be done in close collaboration with shareholders. With regard to certain standards (e.g. transparency and anti-corruption, debt sustainability and pricing policies)–convergence needs to be accelerated. In other areas, convergence should start with a broad equivalence approach, with agreement on principles and outcomes**. This would allow for different approaches aimed at the same objective of protecting citizens today and in the future, and enable convergence over time.

Importantly, this effort to converge on a set of core standards should **form the basis for bringing on board major bilateral lenders/ development finance institutions (DFIs)**, as they have collectively become much larger players in development finance. The IFIs should collaborate with the International Development Finance Club (IDFC) and private sector entities in their ongoing work on standards.[1] Cooperation among shareholders is critical in this regard.

Special consideration will need to be given to **states with features of fragility**, as they will require a more customized approach to standards, tailored to their capacity, and with greater support for implementation.[2]

Country platforms are often more effective when governments have the support of coordinating development partners. Selection of such coordinators should be based on practical considerations regarding the country's development priority areas. To encourage wider ownership, the coordinator role should ideally be rotated on a regular basis.

Importantly too, the country platforms will **ensure that the RDBs continue to play active roles based on their comparative strengths–**

---

[1] Members of the IDFC–23 DFIs with assets of US$3.5 trillion and loans of over US$0.8 trillion annually–have recently embarked on a process to align policies across their institutions. Their assets are larger than all the MDBs together.

[2] Acknowledging the circumstances of states with fragility, MDBs could prioritize operations that help kick-start job creation and enhance access to basic healthcare and education–and hence help governments win support for continuing reforms– while working on raising standards over time. See also Report of the Commission on State Fragility, Growth and Development, *Escaping the Fragility Trap*, April 2018 (in particular the discussion at Recommendation 7).

01 ACHIEVING GREATER DEVELOPMENT IMPACT: COLLABORATING ACROSS THE SYSTEM

especially their regional knowledge and relationships.

The coordination and coherence achieved on such platforms will help significantly scale up private sector investments. This would follow from coordination to strengthen government capacity in project selection, preparation and implementation; to build regulatory certainty; and to **standardize contract documentation** to enable the development of an infrastructure asset class.[1] The platforms will also enable the IFIs themselves to integrate their project preparation facilities.[2]

Country platforms will also be effective instruments in the case of crises. When they are functioning well, they will provide a coordinating mechanism to bring together the government and relevant IFIs, bilateral agencies, relevant UN agencies and other non-governmental actors at the onset of a crisis. They can provide organizing frameworks for humanitarian and other assistance as their operating principles will

---

[1] Private financing requires the standardization of the underlying project descriptions, documentation/templates, and financial and non-financial data and build upon templates already agreed by major market participants, such as SOURCE and GEMs. SOURCE is a joint global initiative of the MDBs and private-public partners, in response to the G20, to close the infrastructure gap by delivering well-prepared projects. GEMs is a database which collects default histories and other data on B-loans from 13 development finance institutions and is maintained by the European Investment Bank.

[2] Currently, the IFIs' infrastructure preparation funds include: the Global Infrastructure Facility; the Arab Financing Facility for Infrastructure; IDB's InfraFund; EBRD's Infrastructure Project Preparation Facility; ADB's Asia-Pacific Project Preparation Facility; EIB and EU JASPERS initiative for the Eastern and Southern neighborhood; AIIB's Project Preparation Special Fund; and AfDB's Africa 50.

facilitate coordination and collaboration in real time.

Proposal 3: Implement regional platforms to facilitate transformational cross-border investments and connectivity.

Regional approaches help promote economic opportunity by allowing countries to overcome economic constraints resulting from geography such as lack of access to ports, lack of infrastructure connectivity especially in transport, and poor energy and water availability.

Regional projects are usually complex and expensive. They require the involvement of multiple countries and investors, coordination of difficult policy issues, and the resolution of complicated fiduciary, environmental and social arrangements. **Establishing regional platforms, based on the same principles as country platforms, offers a good approach to accelerating the implementation of regional projects.**

The regional platforms will allow for better collaboration and division of labor among the development partners operating in a region.[1] They can also be used to accommodate small countries' projects and programs, where individual country platforms may not be as viable.

Proposal 4: Reduce and diversify risk on a system-wide basis to mobilize significantly greater private investment, including portfolio-

---

[1] Examples of such regional platforms include the Western Balkans Investment Framework and the Africa Investment Forum.

01 ACHIEVING GREATER DEVELOPMENT IMPACT: COLLABORATING ACROSS THE SYSTEM

based infrastructure financing.

The IFIs' efforts to help countries to strengthen government capacity (Proposal 1) and to derive synergies among development partners from well-functioning country and regional platforms (Proposals 2 and 3) are critical to strengthening the investment environment and project pipelines. However, **to mobilize the vastly greater resources required to meet the coming development challenges, we must maximize the potential of capital markets and institutional investors**. Greater private financing in infrastructure must also be achieved without adding significantly to sovereign liabilities in countries where debt sustainability limits have been reached.

The G20 Hamburg Principles[1] affirm the need for MDBs to crowd in private investors through credit enhancement and other means. Private investments in developing country infrastructure assets are today minimal. Investors' risk perceptions of developing country infrastructure investment and expected returns are high. **Risk must be reduced and managed so that returns and pricing sought by private capital can be brought down** to a level that is viable and sustainable to developing countries.

There is **significant scope for system-wide approaches to reduce, manage and diversify risk, to open the gates to private investment**. These must involve:

---

[1] The *Hamburg Principles on Crowding-in Private Sector Finance* were issued in April 2017 and endorsed by the G20. They provide a common framework for MDBs to increase private investment levels to support development objectives.

- Re-orienting MDBs' business models to focus on risk mitigation.
- Using system-wide political risk insurance and private reinsu-rance markets.
- Developing a large and diversified asset class that enables institutional investors to deploy funds in developing country infrastructure.

Proposal 4a: Shift the basic business model of the MDBs from direct lending towards risk mitigation aimed at mobilizing private capital.

The MDBs, which have traditionally focused on lending, should shift to using their balance sheets to mitigate risk. MDBs (and bilateral development partners) have a **unique ability to manage risks** in developing countries through their multilateral ownership and ability to influence governments. They are hence well placed to provide credit enhancement (e.g. taking the first loss piece in a synthetic securitization structure) with institutional investors coming in to take a standardized senior debt exposure which can be priced lower to reflect the lower risk.

MDB credit enhancement can be a more efficient use of their capital than direct lending. Further, **the benefit goes not to private investors–who receive a lower return commensurate with the lower risk they bear– but to the borrowing country through a lower financing cost.**

Proposal 4b: Develop system-wide political risk insurance and expand use of private reinsurance markets.

01 ACHIEVING GREATER DEVELOPMENT IMPACT: COLLABORATING ACROSS THE SYSTEM

Political risk insurance coverage is critical to draw international investors into many developing countries–through FDI and both debt and equity financing.

The MDBs should, as a system, leverage on MIGA[1] as a global risk insurer in development finance. MIGA has significantly expanded its political risk insurance coverage provided to private investors in developing countries over the last five years.[2] Its capacity has been boosted by utilizing the private reinsurance market. We can build on MIGA's existing risk insurance capabilities to take on risk from the MDB system as a whole, and achieve the benefits of scale and a globally diversified portfolio. Collaboration among the MDBs and MIGA can take different forms, e.g. the MDBs connecting investors to MIGA; or MIGA reinsuring MDBs' insurance/guarantee products. Greater use of private reinsurance markets will also allow the scaled-up use of political risk insurance.

MIGA should establish a joint advisory board involving participating MDBs to guide joint activities and oversee standards and pricing norms to support collaboration.

MIGA and the MDBs should significantly scale up current risk insurance operations by:

◎ **Standardizing contracts and processes.** Standardized contracts will

---

[1] Multilateral Investment Guarantee Agency (MIGA) is an IFI that is a part of the World Bank Group whose primary operational business is to provide political risk insurance and credit enhancement guarantees.

[2] MIGA's outstanding gross exposure grew by 73% (US$7.5 billion) between 2012 and 2017.

help facilitate scaling up the provision of risk insurance. They can aid in the creation of programmatic underwriting and pricing processes for insurance/reinsurance on a portfolio basis (instead of project-by-project review), **thereby improving efficiency and speed to market and lowering costs.**[1]

◎ **Expanding the use of private re-insurance.** A system-wide risk insurance platform would in the long term require a significant increase in the amount of risk ceded to private sector reinsurers so that MIGA and the MDBs can recycle their capital for more projects. A reinsurance panel could be selected and renewed through a competitive process. Reinsurance can be arranged on a portfolio basis using pre-agreed criteria.

Proposal 4c: Build a developing country infrastructure asset class with the scale and diversification needed to draw in institutional investors.

Institutional investors[2] represent an **enormous pool of potential investment that has so far evaded developing country infrastructure**. With the exception of a few specialized players, they can only be drawn into developing country infrastructure if markets provide a large, simple and diversified asset for them to invest in. Thus far there have been promising but piecemeal efforts to structure investible products for private investment. The Argentine G20 Presidency has asked the Infrastructure

---

[1] Idiosyncratic risks can be addressed through add-on cover to standardized contracts.
[2] These could include insurance funds, sovereign wealth funds and public pension funds.

01 ACHIEVING GREATER DEVELOPMENT IMPACT: COLLABORATING ACROSS THE SYSTEM

Working Group to look at opportunities for mainstreaming this asset class.

We can only achieve scale by taking a system-wide approach: by pooling and standardizing investment from across the MDB system into securitized assets or fund structures that enable easier investor access. The IFC's Managed Co-Lending Portfolio Program (MCPP) is an example of a loan portfolio from a single MDB that has successfully garnered private sector interest. Standardizing and pooling across the system will generate larger, more diversified loan portfolios that will significantly scale up institutional investor participation. Equally important, the pooling of diversified portfolios of MDB loans for private and institutional investment **confers significant benefits upstream in the project cycle, by driving commercial discipline**.

There is a significant amount of loans in the MDB system, infrastructure-related and others, that could be pooled for private and institutional investment. This could start with **the US$200-300 billion of non-sovereign loans**,[1] sufficient for an asset class of reasonable scale. The eligible loan pool can be further widened to include **commercial banks' infrastructure loans, of which there are about US$200 billion issued annually**. The growth of **green bonds and green bond funds** is another opportunity for MDBs and commercial banks to originate infrastructure loans that respond to the needs of institutional investors.

New sovereign loans can also be pooled for investment, which

---

[1] Based on reported data, AfDB, ADB, EBRD, EIB, IBRD, IDB and IFC have an average of 25% of their loans going to non-sovereign entities, although the proportion of non-sovereign exposures can vary significantly between MDBs.

should ideally be done once the market is familiar with the asset class. This can be done by clean sales of loan portfolios to private and institutional investors which would not involve a transfer of preferred creditor status (see Annex 2 for more details).

Proposal 5: 'Right-size' capital requirements for MDBs and other infrastructure investors, given their default experi-ence.

A set of prudential norms specific to and applied across all MDBs need to be established, based on their unique characteristics and default experience. Currently, the regulatory capital and liquidity standards and rating methodologies applied to MDBs are adapted from those developed for commercial banks and do not sufficiently reflect their distinctive shareholding structures, preferred creditor status and default experience. The different rating agencies also adopt varying methodologies for the MDBs. As a consequence, the MDBs each have different adaptations and capital and liquidity buffers. The larger the buffers, the more constrained the MDBs will be in their financial capacity.

In a similar way, the regulatory capital treatment for infrastructure investment applied to banks and institutional investors such as insurers do not differentiate such investments from generic corporate debt. This has acted as a disincentive to investors to take on infrastructure investments. Evidence however shows that long-term investments in developing country infrastructure have a better default experience than corporate debt. The case for carving infrastructure investment out as a separate asset class distinct from corporate debt in the capital treatment for insurers and certain other institutional investors should be revisited based on the evidence.

Proposal 5a: Establish tailor-made capital and liquidity frameworks for the MDBs.

MDBs should collectively **approach the Basel Committee to seek guidance on the regulatory capital and liquidity standards for MDBs, considering their unique operating models**. An independent review by the Basel Committee and the development of a tailor-made regulatory framework would promote the adoption of harmonized capital and liquidity approaches across the system, and provide a basis for rating agencies to also review their rating methodologies for MDBs. The aim is for MDBs and rating agencies to more accurately quantify the risk taken on by the MDBs and so determine the appropriate capital and liquidity requirements. Should some balance sheet capacity be freed up, this can be deployed to take on risk. The issues that could be addressed include:

◎ Taking into account the key elements that differentiate MDB operating models from commercial banks, including the recognition of preferred creditor treatment, callable capital and concentration risk.[1]
◎ Actual default experience across the MDBs.
◎ The treatment of credit guarantees/enhancement and insurance as

---

[1] An important step towards productive engagement is to pool exposure and default data across MDBs and to make these transparent to shareholders, the investment community and rating agencies.

compared to more traditional loan instruments should be risk and evidence-based.

The MDBs also currently do not have access to any support facility in case of extreme liquidity stress and are treated by the rating agencies as such. As a result, they are holding more liquidity (excessive self-insurance) and/or pay a higher cost of capital (the rating agencies treat the MDBs as financial institutions without access to liquidity backstops) than needed if the MDBs were viewed as a system.[1] As part of their approach to the Basel Committee on the establishment of a regulatory framework for the MDBs, **they should also seek guidance on the appropriateness of a liquidity back-stop**.

From time to time, the system as a whole should be stress-tested with a view to strengthening its overall resilience, and better understanding resource needs both in normal times and in crisis.

Proposal 5b: Review the regulatory treatment of infrastructure investment by institutional investors.

Institutional investors from both developed and emerging markets[2] are constrained by regulatory standards from investing in infrastructure.

---

[1] Estimates suggest that for the World Bank such a facility would allow it to expand lending by at least 10 percent and the regional MDBs by significantly more.

[2] These regulations often make, for example, simple distinctions between OECD and non-OECD countries or between investment-grade and noninvestment-grade economies.

01 ACHIEVING GREATER DEVELOPMENT IMPACT: COLLABORATING ACROSS THE SYSTEM

Home country institutional investors can bring to bear superior contextual knowledge and a strong alignment in investment objectives (e.g. in a requirement for local currency investment), if regulation also facilitates and recognizes their potential value-add to the infrastructure development ecosystem. Using an evidence-based approach to review regulations may identify opportunities for incentivizing long-term investment.

There is scope to review the regulatory treatment of infrastructure debt based on the evidence, and to consider it as a distinct asset class from corporate debt with its own differentiated risk profile. There is also scope for risks to be differentiated between the construction and operation phases, with the latter posing a lower level of risk.

Proposal 6: Strengthen joint capacity to tackle the challenges of the global commons.

The global commons face a wide range of challenges, including environmental threats related to climate change, degradation of ecosystems, loss of biodiversity, water scarcity and threats to oceans and specific health-related threats from pandemics and the rapid spread of antimicrobial resistance. The poor are often more exposed and invariably more vulnerable. Another related challenge involves forced displacement of people because of conflict, natural disasters and lack of security. These are challenges for all countries, but the international community has **a critical role to play both in supporting developing countries in protecting the global commons and through their own national actions**.

Total infrastructure capital round the world will double in the next 15 years. How that investment takes place will have a profound influence on the global commons. The IFIs have an essential and urgent role to play in ensuring the quality and sustainability of that investment.

These challenges all span national borders and **require international action to provide the public goods (transnational and local) and relevant policies and investments to respond to these threats with greater urgency, scale, coherence and impact**. The appropriate responses for the different challenges differ greatly in scale and scope as well as in the complexity and speed of delivery.[①]

The differences across the global commons also have **important implications for how efforts should be coordinated, and for the allocation of responsibilities across institutions**. As the system shapes the response, coordination must look at the scope of the spillovers and the nature of public goods, policies and investments needed to respond.

While these challenges to the global commons are very real, technology has also been advancing at a rapid rate. There are **huge opportunities to make progress on a broad range of issues critical to quality of life and sustainable growth**. Environmental limits create

---

[①] Each threat may require the production of several public goods. For example, climate-related environmental threats must be met by climate change prevention and mitigation, which are pure global public goods where everyone's contribution matters, but also by adaptation and enhanced resilience to the changing climate, which involves mostly private goods or national and regional public goods. Health-related threats often require attention to the "weakest link", e.g., preventing the spread of viruses, but sometimes what matters is really the effort of one actor, e.g., to invent a vaccine or a cure for a specific disease.

01 ACHIEVING GREATER DEVELOPMENT IMPACT: COLLABORATING ACROSS THE SYSTEM

imperatives for change, but they also spur creative thinking on how to design livable cities with citizens living healthier lives and working in high-quality sustainable jobs. IFIs have a particular responsibility in spreading innovation. Innovation in sustainable development is already generating growth opportunities.[1]

Proposal 6a: Integrate activities in support of the global commons into the IFIs' core programs, and coordinate them within country platforms (Proposal 2).

IFIs have a critical role to play, in the context of country-based programs, in setting global standards and developing market-based approaches that would crowd in the private sector into action on the global commons. The World Bank has exercised leadership working in partnership with the private sector through, for example, the Carbon Price Leadership Coalition; and the RDBs have taken similar initiative in specific areas.[2] The IFIs should encourage the adoption of standards regarding the disclosure of risks associated with the challenges to the global commons. The 2017 recommendations of the FSB-initiated Task Force on Climate-related Financial Disclosures (TCFD) have begun to be implemented by

---

[1] The Global Commission on the Economy and Climate, *Unlocking the Inclusive Growth Story of the 21st Century: Accelerating Climate Action in Urgent Times*, New Climate Economy, 2018, Washington DC.

[2] For example, the EBRD's Green Economy Transition (GET) approach which was launched in 2015, aimed at mitigating and building resilience to the effects of climate change and environmental degradation across its sectors and countries of operations.

investors and companies, supported–and in some cases required–by their governments.[1]

IFIs should also help countries incorporate their programs for the global commons into their growth strategies and investment plans and assist them in adopting a consistent approach across the government.

Proposal 6b: Create global platforms with the UN guardian agency and the World Bank coordinating and leveraging on the key players in each of the commons.

An effective international response to the challenges and opportunities of the global commons requires strong action within and across countries, and across the UN agencies, IFIs and other relevant bodies including philanthropies and the private sector. The current scale of activities falls far short of what is needed given the urgency and magnitude of the challenges. The **designated UN guardian institution for each of the commons and the World Bank**, which has the broadest reach among the MDBs, should be responsible for identifying gaps in the global response, such as climate change adaptation, and coordinating and leveraging on the key players. For specific commons there will be **RDBs and other stakeholders with significant capabilities that should play key roles**.

The current global efforts to tackle the challenges of the global

---

[1] By December 2017, 237 companies, with a total market capitalization of over US$6.3 trillion, committed to support the TCFD. Large institutional investors are also starting to disclose.

01 ACHIEVING GREATER DEVELOPMENT IMPACT: COLLABORATING ACROSS THE SYSTEM

commons have significant degrees of duplication between agencies, overcrowding in certain fields and gaps in others. We need clearly delineated roles to strengthen impact.

While the system must be capable of responding in a decentralized fashion, it must be more tightly coordinated to leverage the joint capacity of the IFIs, UN agencies and other development partners. The **UN agencies** have a normative function in most areas, defining goals, setting standards and providing political legitimacy. They are also in many instances first responders in emergencies and crises. The **IFIs** play different key roles, based on their comparative advantage in policy advice and de-risking, mobilizing finance, building resilience and strengthening countries' implementation capacity. The **private sector** has a crucial role to play and its collaboration with the MDB system should be strengthened. The **philanthropies**, often working with the private sector and **NGOs**, are also a source of important innovation, experimentation and establishing systems for measuring impact.

The alignment of responsibilities of each institution should be based on its comparative advantage in each stage of the 'value-chain' of activities: investments in R&D and innovation, mobilization of finance, prevention, resilience and crisis response. The illustrations below indicate the potential of collaboration leading to greater impact.

a. R&D and innovation: The IFIs together with the specialized UN agencies, should collaborate to collect data and undertake the analytical work necessary to develop early warning indicators, and prevention and resilience plans. The philanthropies with more risk absorption capacity play an important role in funding R&D and innovation.

- In response to the West African Ebola virus epidemic (2013-2016), Wellcome Trust played an important role in the development of vaccines–a risky activity which is difficult for MDBs to engage in.
- The Bill and Melinda Gates Foundation (BMGF), in partnership with the AfDB and ADB, is funding efforts to scale up financially and environmentally sustainable sanitation services for urban poor communities. The BMGF is providing grant funding to support R&D in innovative technologies, and AfDB and ADB plan to scale up deployment of those technologies that prove viable.

MDBs can contribute to scaling up innovations which have passed the initial high-risk development stage.

b. Mobilizing finance: The MDBs are best positioned to crowd in private resources into the global commons. In addition to their regular financing, MDBs should develop contingent public finance facilities and system-wide insurance instruments which are key to fast disbursement and launching support operations. Important examples are the World Bank Pandemic Emergency Financing Facility, supported by bilateral aid agencies and the WHO; and the Africa Risk Capacity, a weather-based insurance mechanism to enable food security and involving partnership between the African Union (AU), bilaterals and the World Bank. There is substantial scope to scale up such initiatives.

c. **Prevention and resilience**: There is significant untapped potential in the combined data and knowledge of the IFIs that can be used to develop early warning indicators and design appropriate prevention and resilience programs. IFIs are also uniquely positioned to ensure that their programs and projects embed appropriate prevention, preparedness, and resilience mechanisms, including helping the most vulnerable adapt to climate change, and early and effective response to pandemics or famine. A good example is the IDB's Emerging and Sustainable Cities Program which aims at strengthening resilience by combining environmental, urban and fiscal sustainability and governance, particularly in relation to sustainable infrastructure.

d. **Crisis response**: Intrinsic to effective crisis response is tight and speedy coordination between the IFIs, UN agencies and other development partners. The World Bank's Global Crisis Response Platform is an important element of such an integrated approach. The WHO-led, Gavi-supported, effort to combat the recent outbreak of Ebola in the Democratic Republic of the Congo is an example of how an integrated approach can effectively staunch a dangerous pandemic outbreak.

The evolving architecture for global health to combat pandemics, and anti-microbial resistance (AMR), with the WHO playing a normative role and performing a coordinating function, provides a good model for how a global platform could be structured for each of the commons (see Annex 3).

A new cooperative international order must also enable mobilization of flexible coalitions of countries and institutions around specific global or regional commons. One such initiative is the UN-World Bank High Level Panel on Water. The Bangladesh Delta Plan 2100 was launched on this common undertaking and is an example of how multilateral organizations, bilateral partners and national authorities can join forces and avoid fragmented efforts for greater long term impact.[1] The Global Commission on Adaptation, soon to be established, is another example of how a coalition of partners can come together on a critical challenge.[2]

Proposal 7: Integrate trust fund activities into MDBs' core operations to avoid fragmentation.

MDBs currently operate with considerable resources outside of their balance sheets, mostly in the form of trust funds.[3] These funds represent donors or coalitions of donors that are willing to provide additional financial support to achieve specific development objectives. However, **the large number of trust funds and their alternative governance structures are fragmenting MDB activities**, driving a misalignment between trust-

---

[1] The Bangladesh Delta Plan is a long-term integrated plan that brings together programs for water and food security, economic growth and environmental sustainability. The World Bank and the Netherlands have worked together to draw on the experience of the latter and adapted to Bangladesh's need.

[2] The Commission is being supported by the Global Center on Adaptation and the World Resources Institute in close collaboration with other partners.

[3] The funds held in trust for the World Bank Group totaled US$10.5 billion at end-FY17: there were 544 standard trust funds in the World Bank (IBRD/IDA) and 217 at the IFC. See *2017 Trust Funds Annual Report A Brief Overview*, March 23, 2018.

01 ACHIEVING GREATER DEVELOPMENT IMPACT: COLLABORATING ACROSS THE SYSTEM

funded activities and the MDBs' strategic objectives, and engendering administrative and operational inefficiencies. Moreover, trust fund activities can complicate and reduce country-ownership as they are generally earmarked for specific purposes and are non-fungible.

Some trust funds are achieving results in important and difficult areas, especially in situations of fragility. For example:

◎ The *Global Facility for Disaster Reduction and Recovery*–a global partnership of 400 partners–has provided just-in-time assistance to 20 countries vulnerable to climate-related hazards and helped them integrate climate resilience measures in their development strategies and programs during FY17.
◎ The *Afghanistan Reconstruction Trust Fund*–a partnership of 34 donors–channels 50 percent of all development expenditures in Afghanistan and has benefited 9.3 million people by providing access to schools and health clinics in thousands of villages across the country.

However, the MDBs must work with shareholders to ensure that trust funds do not create parallel structures, at significant cost to the efficiency and effectiveness of countries' programs and MDBs' operations.[1]

---

[1] Currently, the World Bank is attempting to improve the efficiency and alignment of its trust fund portfolio by working with the donors to group them into umbrella-type arrangements and to take a more strategic approach in the dialogue between trust fund donors and the World Bank.

There are some examples of approaches that integrate additional resources with MDBs' core operations:

- The ***Global Concessional Financing Facility***, which is part of the Global Crisis Response Platform, blends donor grant resources with World Bank non-concessional IBRD resources to provide support to refugee populations in Jordan and Lebanon.
- The ***International Finance Facility for Education (IFFEd)*** is a new initiative targeted at supplementing MDB financing for lower-middle income countries as they lose access to concessional financing.

Proposal 8: Plug shortfalls in data and research that hamper effective policymaking, especially in developing countries.

There are major deficiencies in basic social, economic and environmental data, especially in developing countries. We must address these deficiencies in order to design and implement effective national programs for inclusive growth and human capital development.

The IFIs have a unique and globally important role to play in the generation, analysis and dissemination of data (including big data) and policy-relevant research. These are true public goods that are critical to understanding and tackling global challenges, fostering sound, evidence-based approaches to economic development and meeting the SDGs. The IMF and the World Bank are ideally placed to undertake these roles, and to work closely with the UN agencies and the RDBs

01 ACHIEVING GREATER DEVELOPMENT IMPACT: COLLABORATING ACROSS THE SYSTEM

that play similar roles in areas related to their specific mandates.[1]

With the production of data and research come a responsibility to share. The IFIs have often played a leading role in promoting transparency, but they must go further, particularly in sharing information with each other, with governments, and, wherever appropriate the public at large.[2]

Proposal 9: Leverage more systematically on the ideas and operating networks of business alliances, NGOs and philanthropies.

There is significant scope to leverage on business alliances, NGOs and philanthropies to improve development impact. They contribute new ideas, grassroots perspectives, and can mobilize expertise and resources that complement those available to the IFIs. They can also enhance delivery capacity in situations where the IFIs have difficulty engaging, such as in situations of fragility and conflict.

There are numerous examples of the value created by such actors. For example:

---

[1] The UN-WBG Strategic Partnership Framework signed in May 2018 includes a commitment by the UN and WBG to work with governments, development banks, civil society and the private sector to strengthen national statistical systems and enhance countries' digital data capacity, focussed on collection, analysis and use of data for evidence-based decision making.

[2] The IDB and World Bank's joint work in the 1990s to improve household surveys and their accessibility in Latin America has been instrumental in the measurement of poverty, inequality, and their determinants.

- Self Employed Women's Association (SEWA) is a grassroots organization and movement of poor, self-employed women workers. It has grown from 30,000 to 1.9 million women as members in two decades. SEWA has worked to empower women, organized health services for the poor and been active in micro-finance. It has served as a model for unleashing technology to spark innovation and enterprise at the grassroots level.
- BRAC is a non-governmental organization to help the poor originally in Bangladesh but now with activities around the world. Through innovative, evidence-based approaches to development it has affected the lives of millions and changed both thinking and practice around development.
- The campaign for debt relief for heavily indebted developing countries around the turn of the millennium provides a powerful example of how a civil society coalition, Make Poverty History, built momentum for the IMF, World Bank and ADF's HIPC initiative that made important contributions to achieving education and health objectives.

The IFIs have begun working more with civil society and philanthropic actors. The IFIs can **leverage more systematically on their efforts and capabilities**, identify key needs and gaps, connect them with official initiatives, and provide space and co-funding for these actors to play their full roles. A key role of the IFIs in this context is to take good ideas to scale.

02

SECURING THE BENEFITS OF INTERCONNECTED FINANCIAL MARKETS: REFORMS FOR GLOBAL FINANCIAL RESILIENCE

02 SECURING THE BENEFITS OF INTERCONNECTED FINANCIAL MARKETS: REFORMS FOR GLOBAL FINANCIAL RESILIENCE

A decade after the global financial crisis, further reforms are needed to reduce the bouts of instability that set back growth, to keep countries on the path toward openness and to avert another major crisis.

First, to get the full benefits of cross-border capital flows by strengthening support for countries in **building deeper domestic financial markets**; and developing and evolving a **framework of policy guidance** that:

◎ Enables countries to utilize **international capital flows without risks arising from excessive market volatility**.
◎ Enables domestic objectives to be achieved in sending countries while **avoiding major spillovers**.

Second, to create a **more robust, integrated system of risk surveillance** of a complex, interconnected global financial system, and systematically incorporate contrarian views.

Third, to create a **strong and reliable global financial safety net** by stitching together its fragmented layers.

A. GETTING THE BENEFITS OF INTERNATIONAL CAPITAL FLOWS WITHOUT RISKS ARISING FROM EXCESSIVE MARKET VOLATILITY

A key goal of the international monetary and financial system (IMFS) must be to facilitate investments that allow countries to achieve their full growth and development potential, while meeting the needs of savers worldwide.

Achieving this **requires a stronger enabling environment, both domestic and international**. In particular, it requires stronger domestic financial markets in developing countries, so as to mobilize greater domestic savings as well as utilize global savings in the most productive ways, especially in long-term investments. Equally, we must find ways to mitigate excessive financial volatility, especially that associated with short-term capital flows, and reduce its effects on domestic economies.

Focusing on these two priorities will strengthen the resilience of the system, and address two pressing international challenges:

◎ Helping developing countries to break out of recurring cycles of instability that hamper growth: inadequate long-term investments and overdependence on short-term flows; vulnerability to sudden shifts in global risk sentiment and capital flows; and consequent instability that deter long-term investment. Reforms to the IMFS, together with efforts to strengthen countries' investment environment, must **enable developing countries to run sustainable current account deficits where they are fundamentally needed to achieve their full growth potential.**

◎ Enabling savers, especially in populations that are ageing and seeing

02 SECURING THE BENEFITS OF INTERCONNECTED FINANCIAL MARKETS: REFORMS FOR GLOBAL FINANCIAL RESILIENCE

extended longevity, with opportunities to diversify risks and earn reliable long-term returns.①

The post-World War II experience of industrialized countries demonstrates that **openness, particularly to trade and foreign direct investment (FDI), has brought substantial benefits worldwide, contributing to enhanced physical and human capital and the rise in living standards**. Capital flows have also grown significantly for emerging and developing countries over the last 15 years (Chart 1) and **offer considerable potential to countries that can utilize** them effectively. In particular, FDI has been a major force in the spread of knowledge and best practices in all economies, and an effective engine for growth and development.

Chart 1: Non-resident Net Capital Flows to EMDCs*

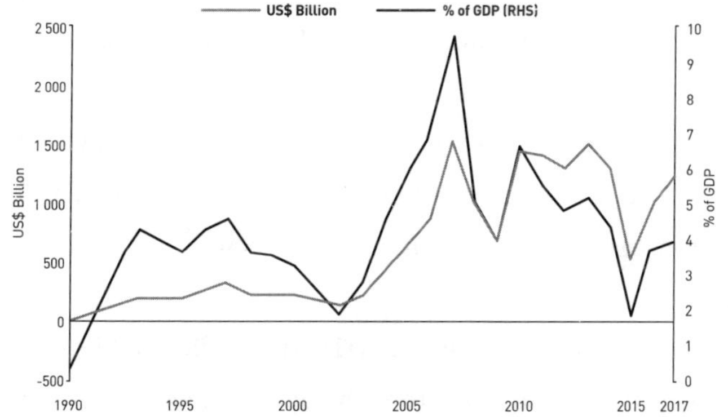

Source: IMF

* This comprises FDI, portfolio investment, derivatives, and other flows, including cross-border banking flows.

---

① Financial market reforms should also enable risk to be shared in such a way that those best able to bear the risk take on more of it.

Countries with deeper domestic financial markets and credible macroeconomic strategies have been best able to catalyze local and foreign financing for development, while demonstrating greater resilience to financial shocks when they occur.

However, spillovers from policies in major economies and shifts in global risk appetite have led to surges or sudden stops in capital flows, and bouts of excessive volatility in exchange rates and domestic asset markets (see Box 3). **These fluctuations can interfere with sound policy-making or lead to interventions that hurt growth.** The sources of such instability include deviations from sound policies in either sending or receiving countries for capital flows, as well as the structure and technologies of today's global markets.

Policy thinking on the issue has often been shaped by whether one sits in sending or receiving countries. We need to move beyond this. A rules-based international framework, drawing on a comprehensive and evolving evidence base, is needed to provide policy advice through which countries seek to avoid policies with large spillovers, develop resilient markets, and benefit from capital flows while managing risks to financial stability.

The IMFS must **enable countries to benefit from international interdependence and move towards openness as a long-term goal, while managing risks to financial stability**. It needs to accommodate economies at each stage of development, and include both sending and receiving countries. In particular, it should:

◎ Support countries' efforts to deepen domestic financial markets, and to

02 SECURING THE BENEFITS OF INTERCONNECTED FINANCIAL MARKETS: REFORMS FOR GLOBAL FINANCIAL RESILIENCE

tap international markets while managing volatility. This would enable an ongoing liberalization of capital flows at a pace and sequence in line with a country's circumstances; the OECD's Code of Liberalization of Capital Movements, originally developed for advanced countries, offers an aspiration in this regard.

◎ Develop a regular dialogue aimed at building international understanding around a policy framework for **achieving domestic objectives while avoiding large adverse international spillovers** that reduce the policy space available to other countries.

◎ Ensure the availability of temporary liquidity support for countries with sound policies.

Proposal 10: The IFI community should strengthen and accelerate efforts to help countries develop deep, resilient and inclusive domestic financial markets.

Deep, resilient and inclusive domestic markets are critical to growth and development and must be a key priority, especially for emerging and developing economies. They help countries to better absorb capital flows and enable an efficient allocation of funds to productive uses in the real sector.

> **Box 3: Capital Flow Volatility in Emerging Markets**
> Broadly speaking, capital flows take a few predominant forms: foreign direct investment (FDI), portfolio investments and other flows which take place mainly through banks.

- FDI has been a major force in the spread of knowledge, techniques and best practices in all markets, and hence an effective engine for growth.
- Portfolio and other flows play an important role in financing investments, enhancing liquidity in financial markets and enabling risk to be hedged. However, they are significantly more volatile than FDI* (see chart) and subject to swings in global risk appetite, besides factors associated with the receiving country.

Surges and sudden stops of short-term flows can lead to sharp bouts of volatility, and may significantly reduce the room for maneuver in policy-making. This is particularly pertinent for emerging markets (EMs), where capital flow volatility has generally been higher than in advanced markets. Those bouts of volatility have also been accentuated by changes in market microstructures and behavior, such as the growth of exchange-traded funds (ETFs) and use of algorithmic trading. Further, while aggregate measures of EM capital flow volatility have in recent years been broadly comparable to their mid-2000s average, volatility has increased for many individual EMs, especially among some of the larger EMs.

Studies show that 'push' factors (reflecting developments in sending countries and shifts in global risk sentiment) have been playing an increasingly active role in volatility of capital flows and asset prices. At the same time, 'pull' factors (e.g. a receiving country's own policies and circumstances) still explain a significant part of why the impact of a global volatility event varies across EMs.

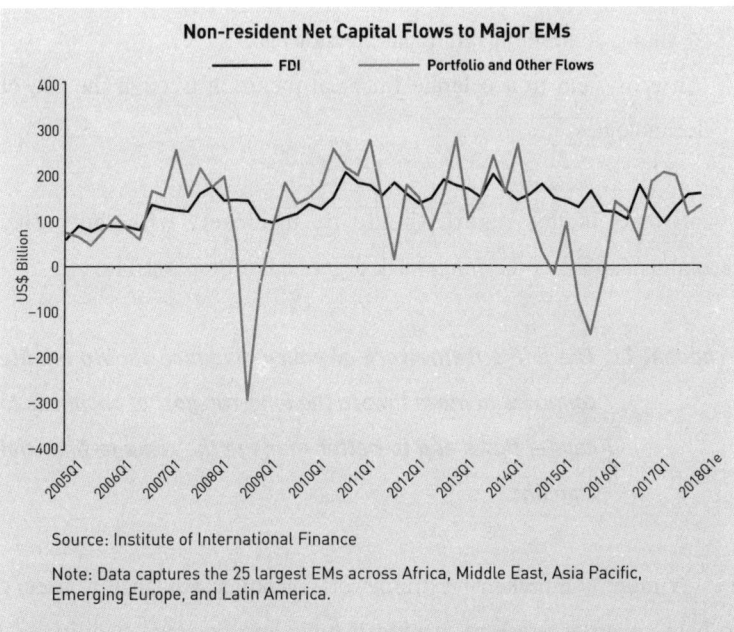

02 SECURING THE BENEFITS OF INTERCONNECTED FINANCIAL MARKETS: REFORMS FOR GLOBAL FINANCIAL RESILIENCE

Non-resident Net Capital Flows to Major EMs

Source: Institute of International Finance

Note: Data captures the 25 largest EMs across Africa, Middle East, Asia Pacific, Emerging Europe, and Latin America.

* Portfolio and other investments are respectively two and four times more volatile than FDI. See Pagliari, M. and S. Ahmed Hannan, *The Volatility of Capital Flows in Emerging Markets: Measures and Determinants*. IMF Working Paper WP/17/41, Feb 2017.

The IMF, World Bank and RDBs should strengthen and coordinate their efforts in partnership with national authorities to meet this need. Capacity building should give emphasis to developing policy and regulatory frameworks for:

◎ Sound banking, and local currency debt markets. This should include implementation of prudential regulations as recommended by international standard-setters, which will also reduce risks stemming from capital flow volatility.

◎ A strong domestic institutional investor base.
◎ An ecosystem to accelerate financial inclusion through the use of technologies.

Efforts in this regard should tie in closely with the policy recommendations of the framework described in Proposal 11a.

Proposal 11: The IMF's framework of policy guidance should enable countries to move toward the long-run goal of openness to capital flows and to better manage the risks to financial stability.

A more comprehensive framework of policy guidance is needed to help countries preserve macroeconomic and financial stability, and thereby enable them to make consistent progress towards openness. Experience has shown that countries will only remain on such a path if they can manage episodes of excessive volatility in capital flows and exchange rates and protect domestic financial stability. A framework of policy guidance should help them prevent the build-up of risks in normal times, and to avoid market disruptions and contagion during times of stress.[1]

---

[1] While the proposed framework subscribes to a gradual and appropriate liberalization of the capital account in line with country circumstances (i.e. a time-dependent path towards openness), it equally emphasizes the need for appropriate measures at each stage if financial stability is at risk (i.e. state-dependent policy actions), with the objective of returning to the original path of openness after pressures have receded.

02 SECURING THE BENEFITS OF INTERCONNECTED FINANCIAL MARKETS: REFORMS FOR GLOBAL FINANCIAL RESILIENCE

Proposal 11a: Develop evidence-based policy options to enable countries to benefit from capital flows while maintaining financial stability, and to provide assurance to the markets that measures taken are appropriate.

The IMF's Institutional View should evolve and be extended by bringing several assessments and elements of policy advice together:

◎ A comprehensive understanding of the drivers of capital flows and their interaction with monetary, exchange rate and macro-prudential policies.
◎ A reliable assessment of the receiving country's **capital flows at risk and macro-financial stability**.
◎ An **assessment of 'push factors' from sending countries**, especially with regard to the cyclical context and possible reversals.
◎ The Article IV process should develop policy options from the above assessments on how countries can absorb capital flows to mutual advantage, building on evidence on the effectiveness of various tools and instruments, including in particular macro-prudential policies. These options should be updated regularly so that a country has a readily available menu of options in the event of sudden financial pressures.

Over time, adopting such a framework would aim to achieve broad international acceptance. It should also aim at providing assurance to the markets when countries are pursuing a policy mix consistent with the framework.

Proposal 11b: Develop an understanding of policy options that enable sending countries to meet domestic objectives while avoiding large adverse international spillovers.

We need an internationally-accepted policy framework that enables sending countries to **adopt their own policies to meet domestic objectives (in some cases set by legislative mandates), while avoiding large international spillovers that reduce the policy space available to others**. The framework should evaluate the different domestic policy options with regard to their interactions with capital flows, exchange rates and shifts in global risk appetite. **This includes how different policy mixes–including monetary, fiscal and macro-prudential policies–have different implications for international spillovers.**

This remains a vexing issue in the IMFS. **While ambitious, the importance of such a framework for sustaining support for an open international system cannot be overemphasized.**

The IMF should develop this framework, with inputs from national authorities and the BIS. This can be an extension of the IMF's work on spillovers, and integrated into Article IV consultations for systemic countries.

The policy framework should evolve with evidence and experience. The global adoption and evolution of prudential standards, supported by the G20 and driven by the FSB, is a successful example. Notably, the Basel, IAIS and the IOSCO frameworks–while not mandatory–provide

02 SECURING THE BENEFITS OF INTERCONNECTED FINANCIAL MARKETS: REFORMS FOR GLOBAL FINANCIAL RESILIENCE

a benchmark to assess the adequacy of financial institutions' buffers in different countries. Peer and market judgments act as a disciplining device when countries depart from such a framework.

We must build on existing initiatives to develop the needed international framework as described in Proposal 11. The IMF's Institutional View has been developed to address issues of capital flow volatility and has taken into account countries' experiences. The Institutional View should evolve and be extended to include:

◎ The objective of enabling countries to move toward the **long-run goal** of openness to capital flows at a pace and sequence in line with country circumstances, while managing risks to financial stability.
◎ A more comprehensive framework for evaluating capital flows, including the incorporation of **assessments of capital flows at risk, exchange rate policy, and macro-financial stability** into policy recommendations. It needs to support countries' efforts to derive the benefits of maintaining consistent progress on a path to openness, by advising them on the most effective options for managing excessive short-term volatility and its consequences.[1]

The evolved and extended Institutional View should also be

---

[1] As well as an integrated repository for the assessments and advice as set out in Proposals 11a and 11b.

complemented by the development of a policy framework that enables **sending countries** to meet their domestic objectives while avoiding significant adverse international spillovers.

A further need in the global financial architecture is temporary liquidity support for countries with sound policies. Increasing financial interconnectedness has also exposed more economies to significant fluctuations in liquidity, capital flows and risk appetite influenced by global factors, which could reduce their policy space. Evidence shows that flexible exchange rates provide only partial insulation from such fluctuations. **Policy makers from emerging economies with sound policy frameworks have hence had concerns that in the absence of predictable sources of international liquidity support, they need to build up further reserves or adopt other policies that will hurt growth.**

The liquidity facility should be designed to support good policy-making in countries, and help to reduce incentives to accumulate excessive precautionary reserves. It should also be accessed only in the event of liquidity shocks of a global or regional nature and for a short duration.

The key features of the liquidity facility are set out in Proposal 15.

The IMF's formal mandate, established in an era when capital flows were small, includes only the current account. On the other hand, the OECD, which has a formal mandate to guide country policies on capital flows, does not have universal membership. There is hence no institution with universal membership that has a formal responsibility to guide countries' policies on capital flows. This is a lacuna in global financial governance, in a world deeply interconnected by finance, not just trade.

Over the long term, as the IMF and international community build up experience with the proposed framework (Proposal 11), and **once there is strong international acceptance developed around its policy advice on capital flows, the goal should be to bring the IMF's formal mandate up to date** to include its role with regard to capital flows.

B. Strengthening Risk Surveillance to Avoid the Next Major Crisis

We will not know where the next crisis will start from. But it will become a full-blown crisis, with broader global consequences, when we are not prepared for it. It is therefore critical that we strengthen our ability to detect risks early, and anticipate how they can be transmitted through a complex and highly interconnected global financial system, so that we can contain them before they escalate.[1]

The official community did not see the Global Financial Crisis (GFC) coming. While the IMF, FSB, BIS and major central banks and regulators have significantly expanded their surveillance capacities, much remains to be done to avert the next major crisis. We should seek to fill the remaining gaps as a key priority, especially in view of

---

[1] The mandate of the EPG excluded review of prudential regulation. However, the issues we address include the IMF's relationship with the FSB and the BIS in the surveillance of risks and in responses aimed at averting future crises.

current elevated debt levels as well as asset prices, and the prospective tightening of monetary conditions.

Further, the complexity and interconnectivity of the system are continually evolving–with changing business models, new players spread out more widely geographically, and new technologies. Given this rapidly changing landscape, **no one international body–the IMF, FSB or the BIS alone–can have a comprehensive grip on the risks in this system. However, existing responsibilities for global financial stability are still too diffused.** The last crisis illustrated the consequences.[1]

Proposal 12: Integrate the surveillance efforts of the IMF, FSB and BIS in a coherent global risk map, while preserving the independence of each of the three institutions' perspectives.

Effective and integrated global surveillance and risk identification will reduce the likelihood of future crises. We must **bring the distinct lenses of the IMF, FSB and BIS together, while retaining their comparative advantages–the IMF on economic and macro-financial risks, spillovers and sovereign vulnerabilities; the FSB on financial**

---

[1] For example, in the run up to the GFC, the risks associated with a widened regulatory perimeter exploiting cross border regulatory arbitrage were under-appreciated. As a consequence, shocks in the US transmitted rapidly to Europe especially to countries intermediating in US$. Contagion spread further as banks liquidated US$ positions globally affecting US$ liquidity in emerging markets. The BIS had pointed out the cascade relatively early, but the root causes were missed by the Financial Stability Forum (the predecessor to FSB), and the IMF was late in recognizing the spillover channels to countries globally.

02 SECURING THE BENEFITS OF INTERCONNECTED FINANCIAL MARKETS: REFORMS FOR GLOBAL FINANCIAL RESILIENCE

system vulnerabilities, including the effects of regulatory adaptations and resulting incentives; and the BIS on global flows and market infrastructure. Illustrative contributions by the three institutions are sketched in Annex 4.[1]

The three institutions should develop jointly a global risk map that is continually updated and incorporates the interactions between:

◎ Underlying macroeconomic and financial conditions, and policy spillovers.
◎ The emergence of technology-enabled risks to financial stability[2], and their implications for an evolving regulatory perimeter.
◎ Changes in business models of bank and non-bank financial intermediaries[3].
◎ Shifts in the structure of capital markets that may lead to greater pro-cyclicality or reduced ability of markets to prevent large

---

[1] The roles described in Annex 4 reflect the comparative advantages of the IMF, FSB and BIS in the various dimensions of risk identification. They are purely illustrative and not intended to be confining.

[2] Examples include potential risks arising from high-frequency financial market activity; the growing use of artificial intelligence; crypto assets and new payment mechanisms; and cyber intrusions.

[3] This also includes studying if/how the differential speed and approaches to meeting the reforms in countries create opportunities for arbitrage by financial institutions (e.g. booking transactions from one jurisdiction to another).

drawdowns.[1]

◎ The implications of the above for capital flows and their volatility.

◎ The impact of these developments on market infrastructure (e.g. payments, settlement systems and clearing depositories).

These interactions generate risks that only joined-up surveillance can capture. The global risk map would highlight a range of risks and possible pockets of vulnerability with the potential of leading to new crises.

A **joint team from the three institutions**–taking inputs systematically from various official[2] and non-official sources but remaining independent in its analysis–should be tasked with developing and continually updating the global risk map. **Critically, the process must preserve the independence of the three institutions' own assessments and staff views,** including the appropriate flagging of risks identified by each of them. It must avoid converging on a diluted consensus.[3] While the integrated global risk map would help to synthesize the risks identified by the three institutions, it would also be useful if the joint assessment highlights any differences in perspectives of the three institutions.

---

[1] For example, the shift from active to passive or trend-following investment models; the increased sectoral concentration in major equity indices; and reduced market making liquidity.

[2] In particular, inputs from the FSB Plenary and the IMF's WEO and GFSR. Inputs from the money-center central banks should also be sought.

[3] To overcome institutional arrangements pertaining to confidentiality and disclosure, which currently pose a hurdle to systemic risk monitoring, robust protocols for knowledge and data-sharing need to be developed–with source authorities and the IFIs–on how to handle these concerns.

02 SECURING THE BENEFITS OF INTERCONNECTED FINANCIAL MARKETS: REFORMS FOR GLOBAL FINANCIAL RESILIENCE

Proposal 12a: Incorporate non-official and contrarian views systematically for more robust risk surveillance.

Conventional official wisdom has tended to be behind the curve, particularly in detecting major disruptions in the global financial system. The last crisis was a case in point, where it was the minority view that warned of the coming disruption. Furthermore, given the complexity and decentralization of today's global financial system, a systematic way of tapping market views and intelligence on potential disruptions is required.[1] The surveillance framework in Proposal 12 should seek out such views.

Proposal 13: Build on the IMF-FSB Early Warning Exercise (EWE) to ensure policy follow-up from the global risk map.[2]

The IMF-FSB EWE should provide the home for policy discussion of global risks among Ministers and Central Bank Governors.[3]

---

[1] Opportunities also exist to seek inputs from regional systemic risk boards that have evolved since the GFC.

[2] Since the Annual Meetings of 2009, the IMF and the FSB have collaborated in a biannual EWE. The EWE largely assesses low probability but high impact risks in the global economy and financial system and has been extremely useful in raising awareness around tail risks. Given the type of risks identified, policy recommendations do not always fall within the policy realm of IMFC members. There is also limited continuity in topics over time.

[3] Current collaboration between the IMF and the FSB is based on a Joint Letter between the Managing Director of the IMF and the Chairman of the Financial Stability Forum in November 2008.

Following from the global risk map (developed through Proposal 12), the EWE should bring together a discussion of risk drivers and outcomes, to raise awareness of both major conjunctural risks and tail risks in the global system. Most importantly, it would facilitate discussions about policy directions and concrete actions to mitigate the key risks and vulnerabilities flagged. Where possible, distinction should be made between risks that require national attention and those that warrant coordinated international efforts, including through further collaboration between the IMF, FSB and BIS.

The exercise should retain the EWE's closed-door nature, which allows for sensitive assessments and discussion among principals. This will help avoid the risk of triggering market reactions that become self-reinforcing. Nonetheless, in the interest of transparency and accountability, after an initial period the institutions should assess options for disclosure–for example, around the risks identified and recommendations made. This should be in addition to other inputs to the global risk map that are already published.[1]

The IMF should continue to cooperate closely with other relevant bodies, especially the OECD and the Financial Action Task Force on Money Laundering (FATF), to tackle the challenges to the integrity of

---

[1] As prospective inputs to elements of a Global Risk Map, the IMF currently publishes its GFSR, WEO, ESR, Fiscal Monitor and Article IVs. The CGFS of the BIS publishes various reports on potential sources or stresses in global financial markets, while the BIS itself also hosts public data platforms on global financial flows including by currency. The SCAV of the FSB periodically publishes reports on risks and vulnerabilities in the financial system.

the global financial system. The **threats posed by tax evasion, money-laundering and terrorism financing are ever-present**. Further, they could **interact with cyber-security risks, and innovations that may not be negative in themselves such as new payment platforms and crypto assets**, but together bear close watching and could require tighter global governance in the future.

C. Stitching Together the Fragmented Global Financial Safety Net

Sustaining openness and policies aimed at global growth requires a more predictable global safety net, in which various layers cohere, based on a clear articulation of roles and responsibilities and viable safeguards. Resources should also be adequate and responsive to different stress situations, including systemic global crisis episodes. **We do not currently have this safety net.**

In the last decade, **a multi-layered safety net has evolved** arising from growth of country reserves, bilateral swap agreements (BSAs) and regional financing arrangements (RFAs) (see Chart 2). However, the **current decentralized structure has several key shortcomings:**

◎ **The safety nets are highly uneven in scale and coverage across regions.** About 70 percent of global RFA resources are concentrated in the Euro Area, which has a political underpinning and a common currency that allows the RFA to function quickly and effectively. Other RFAs lack similar underpinnings. There are also large regions which have no access to RFAs, or on any adequate scale.

Chart 2: Evolution of the GFSN

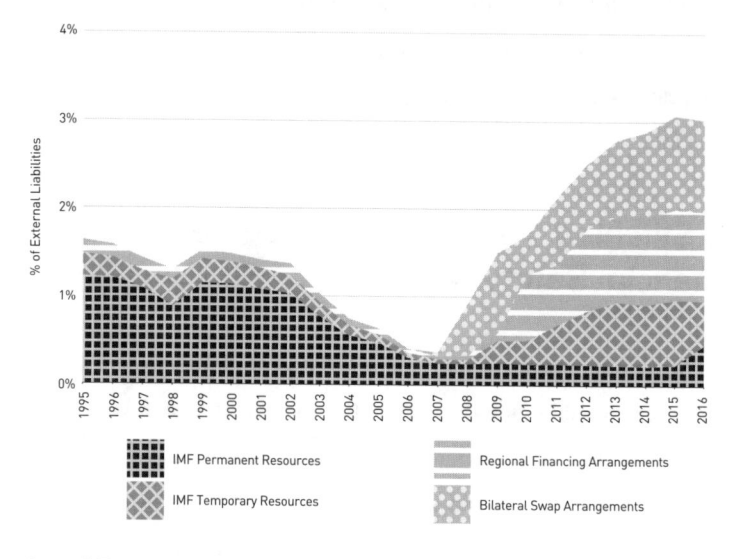

Source: IMF and Bank of England

◎ **Much of the GFSN's growth has comprised of BSAs and RFAs which have not been crisis tested,** and are subject to conditions prevailing in providing countries and regions. The RFAs and BSAs also do not cover several systemically significant countries.[1]

---

[1] The jurisdictions with systemically important financial sectors are: Australia, Austria, Belgium, Brazil, Canada, China, Denmark, Finland, France, Germany, Hong Kong SAR, India, Ireland, Italy, Japan, Korea, Luxembourg, Mexico, Netherlands, Norway, Poland, Russia, Singapore, Spain, Sweden, Switzerland, Turkey, the United Kingdom, and the United States.

02 SECURING THE BENEFITS OF INTERCONNECTED FINANCIAL MARKETS: REFORMS FOR GLOBAL FINANCIAL RESILIENCE

◎ **The system as a whole lacks the necessary coordination** to effectively use its aggregate financial capacity.

It is therefore critical to have a strong and reliable global layer in the GFSN in place before the next crisis.

The IMF provides this key **global layer** in the GFSN. The **IMF's permanent resources (i.e. quotas), supplemented by standing borrowing arrangements (i.e. NAB) should meet the needs of balance of payments crises and contagion episodes in most circumstances** and enable the IMF to perform its role as the lender of last resort.① Quota and NAB resources thus form the first and second "lines of defence" of the IMF.② The IMF also raised bilateral borrowings in the wake of the GFC as a third "line of defence". These combined resources at the IMF equalled 90 percent of total GFSN resources before the GFC and fell to one-third of total GFSN resources in 2016.③ (See Chart 3.) **When the current bilateral borrowings expire, the IMF's resource base would fall short of the needs of the global layer of the GFSN that it provides.**

---

① While respecting existing lending policies including the Exceptional Access Framework.
② The proposed liquidity facility (Proposal 15) would also fall under this category.
③ The IMF's financial resources today are about US$661 billion from quota subscriptions; about US$253 billion from the NAB; and, approximately US$450 billion in bilateral borrowings that expire in 2020.

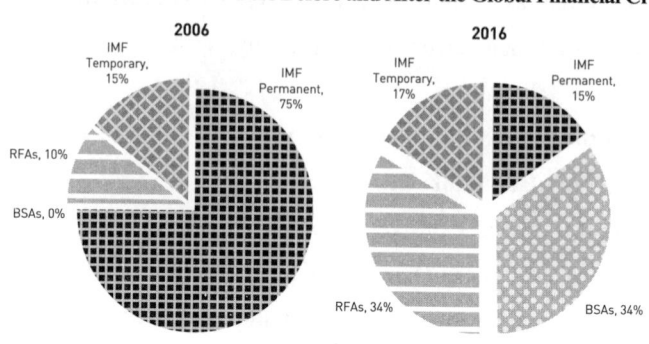

Chart 3: Share of IMF Resources Before and After the Global Financial Crisis

2006
- IMF Temporary, 15%
- IMF Permanent, 75%
- RFAs, 10%
- BSAs, 0%

2016
- IMF Temporary, 17%
- IMF Permanent, 15%
- RFAs, 34%
- BSAs, 34%

Source: IMF and Bank of England

Proposal 14: Stitch together the various layers of the GFSN to achieve scale and predictability.

It is crucial to stitch together the various layers of the safety net well before any major crisis occurs and resources are needed. Effective governance arrangements should encourage **sound country policies, and, under specified circumstances, effect joint use of financial resources. A properly designed system, applied in an even-handed manner, can avoid moral hazard, minimize contagion**[1] **and avoid excessive self-insurance.**

No one design will fit all regions. However, a clear assignment of

---

[1] Coordination during the 2013 IMF program in Cyprus and the engagement of the European Commission and the ESM was deemed exemplary, guided by the 2011 G20 Principles for Cooperation between the IMF and RFAs and building on lessons learnt from preceding European crisis programs. Coordination benefitted from important complementarities such as knowledge for immediate crisis support on one hand and a longer term structural agenda on the other hand, as well as appropriate burden sharing.

02 SECURING THE BENEFITS OF INTERCONNECTED FINANCIAL MARKETS: REFORMS FOR GLOBAL FINANCIAL RESILIENCE

responsibilities between the IMF and each RFA and protocols for joint actions are needed to make the GFSN effective.[1] Work has already begun and should be concluded urgently, respecting key principles as follows:

◎ When macroeconomic adjustments and reforms are necessary, the **GFSN must agree on appropriate ex-post conditionality** and avoid postponing adjustment.
◎ In case of a **temporary liquidity need,** without conditionality, the provisions outlined in Proposal 15 would operate.
◎ **IMF is the most credible and independent party to lead in making these assessments.** It alone conducts macro-financial surveillance at a global level and bilateral level, and operates financing facilities which places it in a unique position to provide required assessments.

Proposal 15: Establish a standing IMF liquidity facility to give countries timely access to temporary support during global liquidity shocks.

It is critical that we build and achieve consensus on a 'standing' global liquidity facility, drawing on IMF permanent resources (see also Chapter II, Section A). Without a reliable liquidity facility, countries will build up excessive reserves, which will hamper global growth. Timely access to such a facility would also strengthen countries' ability

---

[1] This work should build on ongoing cooperation efforts such as the regular dialogue between IMF and RFAs on test runs, exchanges of experiences, and work on the consistency of intervention modalities.

to withstand liquidity shocks and avoid a deeper crisis.

The facility will provide predictable support to, in line with the IMF's normal access policies, a set of countries that have been qualified in advance at their request.[1] In the design of this revolving facility, the IMF needs to ensure that: (i) lending decisions follow a separate process rather than being part of an Article IV discussion, thereby maintaining the integrity of the surveillance process; and (ii) the IMF does not act as a de facto rating agency.[2]

This process would give a broad set of countries with sound policies timely access to temporary liquidity support, without the need for protracted negotiations with the IMF. The ability of a country to do so is critical in dealing with 'IMF stigma'.

Proposal 15a: Use a country's qualification for the IMF's liquidity facility in considering the activation of RFA support.

A stitched together GFSN could include parallel activation of temporary liquidity facilities by the RFAs, which would:

◎ Leverage each other's resources to substantially increase the capacity to support their respective membership.
◎ Involve a regional layer to address 'IMF stigma' concerns, and thereby

---

[1] Assessment of re-qualification will be done annually.
[2] Unlike a rating agency, all countries would not be assessed unilaterally and the assessment process would be kept confidential thereby protecting those countries that either did not qualify or expressed an interest to join.

02 SECURING THE BENEFITS OF INTERCONNECTED FINANCIAL MARKETS: REFORMS FOR GLOBAL FINANCIAL RESILIENCE

encourage countries to access support more promptly.
◎ Promote common operating protocols and hence improve speed of crisis response.

Proposal 16: Enable the IMF to rapidly mobilize additional resources in large and severe global crises.

There is a critical need to plug the gap in the GFSN with regard to future crises of a systemic, 'tail risk' nature. This requires exploring the possible **temporary mechanisms** through which the international community can **rapidly** access a significant amount of liquidity to ensure or restore financial stability.

During the last GFC, around US$500 billion were deployed through the US Federal Reserve's liquidity swaps with selected central banks. These interventions were critical in ensuring the integrity of the global US$ payment system and in calming global markets–although the majority of emerging market economies did not directly benefit from them. Importantly, **such actions cannot be taken as assured in the future**.

Furthermore, in response to a joint call by the IMFC and G20, **a significant group of countries pledged US$450 billion to temporarily augment IMF resources** during the crisis. Participation was not universal. This option of bilateral borrowings for future major crises will require swift mobilization.[1]

---

[1] This temporary financing round was launched in April 2012. Pledges by lending countries were received in June 2012 and the first set of agreements came into effect in October 2012. In August 2016, the bilateral borrowings were extended to end-2019, with the option for a further one-year extension.

There are other solutions that should be explored to enable the IMF to **swiftly mobilize** resources **on the scale required** to ensure global stability in the event of a major, systemic crisis. The illustrative options are described in Annex 5.

However, while these options are feasible in financial terms, they pose governance and policy challenges (as identified in Annex 5), on which there are differing views. A period of **consensus building** within the international community will be required for them to be overcome. Consequently, **the EPG is not making a proposal for immediate endorsement.**[1]

Given the significance of the reforms proposed in this chapter and the key roles of the IMF in effecting them, the **IMFC should be regularly updated** on the status of their implementation and challenges faced.

---

[1] In similar vein, the option of coordinated central bank swap lines has been assessed to be not feasible at this stage, and is not being considered.

03
THE G20 AND THE IFIS: MAKING THE SYSTEM WORK AS A SYSTEM

03 THE G20 AND THE IFIS: MAKING THE SYSTEM WORK AS A SYSTEM

The role of the G20 in the global financial architecture should be reset. It should **focus on developing political consensus on key strategic issues and crisis response.** This requires freeing up space from its current crowded agenda and devolving work to the IFIs.

We need governance to ensure the system works as a system:

- **Implementing the system-wide reorientation in development finance.** A G20-led group, including key non-G20 stakeholders, should steer these shifts over the next three years, before handing the coordinating role to the IFI Heads. These should include achieving complementarity among multiple institutions (multilateral, regional and bilateral) and establishing a clear system of metrics to track impact and value for money.
- **Addressing development challenges early.** A biennial strategic dialogue, building on existing IFI fora, should bring together the IFIs and other key stakeholders to identify future development risks before they create lasting damage, and assess the adequacy of collective responses.
- The governance reforms to foster **global financial resilience** require the IMF to play a key role, in interaction with other institutions that are integral to the international monetary and financial system, and with regular updates to the IMFC.

> Governance reforms within the IFIs themselves should cut back on today's significant overlap between Board and Management responsibilities. They should enable **Boards to focus more on strategic priorities, and empower and hold Management accountable for outcomes.**

Governance of the system of IFIs requires **two significant step-changes–to ensure coherence and synergies in a more diverse and decentralized world, and to achieve a critically needed shift in business models to catalyze private investments and enable greater development impact.**

We are not taking off from a standing start. However, while progress is being made to align initiatives and operations to the new priorities, the weight of legacy business models remains substantial. There has also been an **accumulation of governance in the wrong areas**–resulting in overlapping responsibilities and inefficient decision-making–**taking attention away from governance of strategic issues**. Given the scale and urgency of needs identified in previous chapters, **decisive shifts in governance are needed to drive a system-wide re-orientation.**

There is also a need to reset **the role of the G20 in global financial governance** to make more effective use of its core strengths, avoid duplication of work, and maximize the effectiveness of the system as a whole.

Our proposals pertain to three broad sets of changes:

◎ **The role of the G20** in developing forward-looking thinking and on global financial governance and crisis responses.

03 THE G20 AND THE IFIS: MAKING THE SYSTEM WORK AS A SYSTEM

◎ **Governance of the IFIs as a system,** so that they collectively deliver much more than the sum of their individual contributions.
◎ **Governance within IFIs,** in particular streamlining responsibilities for Executive Boards and Management to ensure effectiveness and outcome-driven oversight.

A. THE ROLE OF THE G20 IN PROVIDING FORWARD-LOOKING STRATEGIC GUIDANCE IN GLOBAL FINANCIAL GOVERNANCE

The **G20 can be a powerful impetus for change,** in particular during crises or imminent crisis situations, with an ability to respond more quickly to major strategic challenges than the individual institutions are often able to. Members also have an equal standing within its consensus-based setting, which gives the G20 added credibility in a multipolar world. The G20 has used these leadership advantages to promote change in several important areas since the global crisis, for example in strengthening financial regulation via the FSB and achieving tax transparency via the OECD.

However, the governance relationship between the G20 and the IFIs is key to effective global financial governance. The G20 does not have universal membership. Unlike the treaty-based organizations, it is also not legally constituted to deliver on decisions. It has to work in coordination with the IFIs and other international organizations to advance many of its aims.

As for the G20 itself, it is widely felt that **the weight of its legacy agenda and the significant expansion of its activities over time have made** it increasingly difficult to focus on strategic issues.

Important steps were taken this year by the Argentine Presidency to gather G20 members' views on the way forward for the Group's agenda. **Our proposals follow in that spirit.**

Proposal 17: The G20 should refocus on a multi-year, strategic agenda, rationalize workstreams, and devolve more work to the IFIs.

Over time, the number of G20 workstreams and the frequency of meetings have grown substantially[1] (see Table 1). In addition, the growing G20 agenda and activities have overlapped with the governance of the IFIs. **The accumulation of initiatives and activities risks crowding out issues that require the G20's strategic guidance**–those where governance hurdles in the system need to be overcome, and where decisive shifts can only be implemented when they are effected across institutions, not just in individual institutions.

The G20 needs to **refocus on strategic global goals while leveraging more on the IFIs and other international organizations**.

In keeping with this objective, **a two-tier system within the G20 could be sufficient for most purposes, comprising Ministerial meetings focused**

---

[1] From 2009, G20 Finance Ministers and Central Bank Governors (FMCBGs) have met four times a year on average. There have been similar increases in other Ministerial meetings: 50 meetings involving G20 working groups and task forces took place in 2016–20 within the Finance Track–compared to a total of three working group meetings in 2009.

03 THE G20 AND THE IFIS: MAKING THE SYSTEM WORK AS A SYSTEM

on strategic challenges and Deputies' meetings to support the former and ensure follow through.

- **Ministerial meetings should refocus on critical strategic issues and emerging threats that require international coordination.** One to two meetings of FMCBGs per year may be adequate in normal times, with further meetings if crisis circumstances require.
- With the tasks of the work streams devolved to IFIs and other competent bodies, **two meetings of Deputies per year should be the norm.**

Much of the work being done in working groups can and should be devolved to the IFIs, individually or jointly, in accordance with their mandates and comparative strengths, together with establishing a process of exchange between the institutions and the G20.

However, from time to time, to drive major new system-wide initiatives, the G20 might need to constitute a Working Group. Such groups should always be time-bound. **The G20 should in such situations have the explicit aim of running the first leg and passing the baton to an existing institution within a three-year period.**

While our proposals are, in keeping with our mandate, focused on global financial governance, we note that they may have relevance to the rest of the G20's work.

Table 1: G20 Meetings Over Time[1]

	1999	2000	2001	2002	2003	2004	2005	2006	2007	2008	2009	2010	2011	2012	2013	2014	2015	2016	2017	2018
Leaders										1	2	2	1	1	1	1	1	1	1	1
Sherpas													5	6	4	4	5	5	5	4
Finance Track																				
FMCBGs	1	1	1	1	2	1	1	1	1	2	4	4	4	3	4	5	2	4	3	5
Deputies					1	2	2	2	1		2	3	1	5	6	3	4	5	5	5
Global Economy/Framework											1			3	4	3	4	2		2
Green /Sustainable Finance											1					2	4	4	4	4
Int. Financial Architecture														4			4	5	5	3
Infrastructure																4	3	3		4
Financial Inclusion															3	2	3	3	2	
Data Gaps																				4
Compact with Africa																			2	1
Sherpa Track																				
Labor /Employment M											1	1	1	1	1	1	1	1	1	1
Foreign M											1	1	1		1			1		1
Agriculture M&D											1	1				1	3		4	3
Trade M											1			1		1				1
Energy																1	1	1		1
Health M																			2	1
Digital M																			1	1
Education M																				1
Development										1		1		4	3	4	3	3	3
Anti-Corruption															3	3	3	3	3	3
Employment															4	4	3	3	4	4
Energy Sustainability/Transitions															2	3	3	3	1	2
Trade & Investment																	3	3		2
Steel Capacities (+M)																		4		3
Digital Economy																		4		2
Sustainability																		3		2
Health																		3		3
Education																				4

---

[1] Estimates of the number of meetings during the early Presidencies (2008-2011) are based on available data.

B. GOVERNANCE OF SYSTEM-WIDE REFORMS

Achieving greater development impact

Governance of the IFIs as a system should be focused on **ensuring coherence and synergies in a more diverse and decentralized world, and on collectively catalyzing private investments, so as to enable greater development impact.**

Proposal 18: A G20-led group, with representation from key non-G20 constituencies and the IFIs, should steer the reorientation of development finance over the next three years before handing the coordinating role to the IFI Heads. This should include building complementarity among all development partners, and a clear system of metrics to track impact and value for money.

An effective forum is required to ensure this major reorientation of the system of development finance. However, there is currently no effective forum with universal membership that has a system-wide remit in development and that can steer the important shifts to ensure coherence and complementarity among the IFIs as well as with other major development partners. The G20, which has a system-wide focus as a result of major countries being represented in the Group, does not have universal membership. The Development Committee (DC), which has universal membership, primarily focuses on one institution.

It will require dedicated steering over three years to move to this new development landscape, building on current initiatives in the IFIs, and to establish the appropriate systems and metrics to ensure continuity of the reforms beyond that period.

A G20-led group of Deputies, with representation from key non-G20 constituencies and the IFIs, reporting periodically to Ministers, is the most effective way to fill this gap over the next three years before handing the coordinating role to the heads of the IFIs. **A G20-led group is best placed to effect coordination among member countries who are stakeholders in multiple institutions: multilateral, regional and bilateral.** In addition, the proposed group should include representation from the RDBs and **major providers of bilateral development finance that are not G20 members**. Consideration should also be given to include the Chair of the International Development Finance Club, which comprises major DFIs.

A key task of this group would be to propose **system-wide objectives, milestones, and associated metrics to evaluate progress** (see Annex 6 for illustration).[1] It should focus on:

◎ Strategic guidance on the **risk appetite** appropriate to IFIs' roles in

---

[1] The July 2018 report by the Joint MDB Task Force on a harmonized framework for additionality is a useful development, in addition to the earlier work of the DFI Working Group on Blended Concessional Finance for Private Sector Projects. Further work needs to be done to establish common indicators to enable evaluation of system-wide progress and comparison between IFIs.

03 THE G20 AND THE IFIS: MAKING THE SYSTEM WORK AS A SYSTEM

achieving development impact.[①]

◎ Stronger **system-wide collaboration**, including through country platforms which leverage on the strengths of all development partners, and convergence around core standards.

◎ The shift in MDB **business models** and mobilization of private finance.

◎ Metrics of **value for money** to ensure that the MDBs, individually and collectively, are achieving the best value for their clients, shareholders and other stakeholders.[②]

Proposal 19: A biennial strategic forum convened by the IMFC and DC[③] should identify development risks before they manifest, and the required collective responses.

We have to **do better in anticipating risks to development before they manifest, spiral across countries and create lasting damage**. There are repeated instances where we have failed to do so in the last few decades.

[①] Particular attention is needed with regard to the IFIs' roles in states with features of fragility. In such an environment, taking on higher risks to kickstart investments and mobilize resources could lead to higher development impact and potential returns over time, as is being attempted by IDA's private sector window, for instance.

[②] The G20 IFA working group has developed a framework for measuring value for money. The value for money concept includes measures of the MDBs' efficiency in achieving their strategic objectives, including their engagement in fragile states.

[③] The International Monetary and Financial Committee (IMFC) and the Development Committee (DC) of the World Bank and IMF.

It is also essential that Finance Ministers be engaged in addressing these risks. A **biennial dialogue on a Global Development Risk Map should be convened jointly by the IMFC and DC** (who together represent 25 constituencies), and include representatives from IFIs, the UN Development System, key civil society and philanthropic players, and the private sector. The Global Development Risk Map[1] should be prepared by a joint secretariat from World Bank and the IMF, in cooperation with the RDBs. The risk map would look at emerging trends and challenges and should also include insights from the system-wide metrics to be developed. The risk map should enable stakeholders to assess the adequacy of responses and the future collective effort required.

Achieving global financial resilience

Chapter II has set out reform proposals on fostering global financial resilience in three interdependent areas, including: (i) getting the benefits of capital flows without risks arising from excessive market volatility; (ii) strengthening risk surveillance for a more complex and interconnected global financial system; and (iii) creating a strong and reliable global financial safety net (GFSN). For ease of reference, the governance imperatives stated in Chapter II are summarized below.

On capital flows. First, **the IMF, World Bank and RDBs** should

---

[1] This should be viewed broadly to include risks to development progress and risks of missed opportunities.

accelerate efforts to help countries develop **deep, resilient and inclusive domestic financial markets**. Second, the IMF's framework of policy guidance should enable countries to move toward openness as a long-term goal, at a pace and sequence that enables them to preserve financial stability, and to manage episodes of excessive volatility. This involves (i) **evolving and extending the IMF's Institutional View** to integrate an assessment of a country's capital flows at risk and macro-financial stability, the cyclical context of 'push' factors from sending countries, and evidence on the effectiveness of various instruments, as a basis for developing policy options for receiving countries; and (ii) the IMF complementing this by developing a **policy framework that enables sending countries to adopt their own policies to meet their domestic objectives while avoiding large adverse spillovers**. The IMF should develop this with inputs from national authorities and the BIS. Third, we must achieve consensus among shareholders to put in place a **standing IMF liquidity facility**.

The IMF's formal mandate, established in an era when capital flows were small, includes only the current account. Over time, as the IMF and international community build up experience with the proposed framework, and once there is strong international acceptance developed around its policy advice on capital flows, the **long term goal should be to bring the IMF's formal mandate up to date to include its role with regard to capital flows.**

On risk surveillance. The IMF, FSB and BIS should integrate their surveillance efforts in a coherent global risk map, while preserving the integrity of the three institutions' perspectives. A joint team from the three institutions should take inputs from various official sources including the money-center central banks, as well as from non-official sources. **The IMF-FSB Early Warning Exercise should provide the home for policy discussions and resulting follow-up.**

On the GFSN. Timely conclusion of IMF quota reviews is necessary to ensure an adequately-resourced global layer of the GFSN.[①] Further, the **IMF and the RFAs** should intensify their work to establish a **clear assignment of responsibilities and protocols for joint actions,** so as to create a stronger and more reliable GFSN. This includes discussions on coherence of ex-post conditionality in adjustment cases, the determination of liquidity needs, and the possible signaling role of an IMF liquidity facility.

Further, in addition to the needed strengthening of its permanent resources, **the IMF should explore temporary mechanisms to swiftly mobilize resources on the scale required to ensure global stability in future crises of a large, systemic nature.**

Given the significance of these three sets of reforms and the key roles of the IMF in effecting them, the **IMFC should be regularly updated** on the status of their implementation and challenges faced.

[①] The International Monetary and Financial Committee (IMFC) has called on the IMF Executive Board to work expeditiously towards the completion of the 15th General Review of Quotas by the Spring Meetings of 2019 and no later than the Annual Meetings of 2019.

C. GOVERNANCE WITHIN IFIs

The governance of IFIs themselves has to be brought up to date. The IFIs should each develop a framework to streamline the roles of the Executive Board and Management to avoid overlaps, and ensure clarity of responsibilities and accountability on the part of each.

Current governance arrangements are tailored to an era of traditional banking operations and need transformation. There are well-established regulatory and supervisory standards with regard to corporate governance within banks. Current IFI governance structures and processes do not accord with these established standards and require transformation.[1]

Key priorities in governance reforms should include:

◎ **Eliminate overlap of responsibilities** between Executive Boards (representing shareholders) and management so as to reduce inefficiency in decision-making.[2]
◎ Focus the agendas of Executive Boards on **governance of strategic issues and country strategies** and away from a disproportionate tilt towards operational decision-making and transactional functions.

Proposal 20: The Executive Board of each IFI should focus on

---

[1] Past studies of IFI governance have also identified these gaps.
[2] An example of an initiative aimed at efficient and effective decision making is the AIIB's new accountability framework, described in its *Paper on the Accountability Framework*.

strategic priorities for the institution and advancing system-wide goals.

The Executive Board should focus on articulating and implementing system-wide policies and standards and setting directions for the institution in line with the agreed goals. The re-orientation of responsibilities in the case of the MDB boards could include determining:

◎ **Risk appetite** appropriate to a shift of business models, and achieving development impact.
◎ **Capital adequacy and liquidity policies.**
◎ **Country strategies.**
◎ **An appropriate risk-based framework** for delegation of operational issues to management (Proposal 21) and compliance policies.

With greater clarity of roles and responsibilities, shareholders should also evaluate the different models of Executive Boards across IFIs based on effectiveness, cost structure and frequency of meetings.

Table 2: IFI Executive Board Budgets

Organization	Size	Membership	Budget (US$ mn)	Frequency of Meetings
IBRD	25	189	88	Twice / week
IMF	24	189	70	Several times / week

03 THE G20 AND THE IFIS: MAKING THE SYSTEM WORK AS A SYSTEM

Continuation Table

Organization	Size	Membership	Budget (US$ mn)	Frequency of Meetings
EBRD	23	69	20	2-3 times / month
ADB	12	67	34	Several times / month
IDB	14	48	23	Once a week
AfDB	20	80	17.5	As required
EIB	29+6*	28	1.5	10 times / year
IFAD	24	176	2.5	3 times / year
AIIB	12	86	2.7	4 times / year (plus 4 virtual meetings)
IsDB	18	57	2.0	5 times / year

* In addition to the 28 members and the European Commission (with voting rights), the EIB's board also comprises 6 permanent experts (without voting rights).

Sources: Stilpon Nestor, 2018, *Board Effectiveness in International Financial Institutions*, AIIB Yearbook of International Law; and IFIs.

Proposal 21: Adopt a practical, risk-based approach to delegate greater responsibility to IFI Management, and hold them accountable for outcomes.

There is significant scope for Boards to delegate greater responsibility to IFI Management, on a practical and risk-based approach. As part of a holistic review, consideration should be given for the IFIs to amend their Articles of Agreement, where necessary, to support this.[1]

The clarity of roles and responsibilities will enable Management to be empowered and held accountable for ensuring that the strategic priorities of the IFIs and the system as a whole are effectively translated into policies, operations and incentives. The major strategic shifts in business models within the IFIs will not be achieved without profound changes in organizational culture. These reforms in policies, operations and incentives have to be **focused on achieving two step changes:**

◎ **Complementarity and synergy amongst IFIs** and other development partners through collectively operating on country platforms.
◎ **Fundamental change in MDB business models** to refocus on policy and institutional capacity in countries, and risk mitigation to catalyze private investment.

Management would have to guide this process of transformation within each institution.

Proposal 22: Ensure diversity and better match the skills available to IFI Boards and Management to the shift in business models and increased complexity of challenges.

---

[1] In the case of MDBs delegation of project approvals could be based on size and whether there are special features of the project that raise broader policy issues. In the case of the IMF, surveillance and lending programs may involve broader considerations that require Board discussion.

03 THE G20 AND THE IFIS: MAKING THE SYSTEM WORK AS A SYSTEM

The Executive Boards should adopt modern corporate governance practices to ensure the IFIs' effectiveness in a more complex environment. This should include:

◎ Defining skills sets relevant for constituencies' own selection of Executive Directors, as well as for the Board's selection of Management.
◎ Complementing this with regular feedback and self-assessment of the Board's effectiveness.
◎ Seeking external input for Board committees requiring specialized knowledge (e.g. in audit and risk assessments and strategies to catalyze private investment) to ensure that appropriate considerations are factored into decision making.

An open, transparent and merit-based process for the selection of IFI Heads is also essential to the sustained legitimacy and effectiveness of the IFIs.

ANNEXES

ANNEXES

Annex 1: Categories of Existing Platform Arrangements

Development partner coordination platforms serve as mechanisms to help governments develop comprehensive public investment projects/programs, prioritize them and match development partners to needs based on their comparative advantages. Successful coordination platforms are usually characterized by strong government ownership, transparency and consultation with participants in the platform. (See Box 1 on the Rwandan example.)

> **Box 1: Rwanda-Development Partner Coordination**
>
> The Government of Rwanda has developed a successful development partner coordination mechanism that has several features of the proposed country platforms. The Government's long-term development goal is to transform Rwanda into a middle-income country, through a series of five-year development strategies. It has a strong emphasis on sustainability and inclusivity. Development partner support is achieved through a coordinating mechanism that embodies several principles of good governance–strong country ownership with coordination by the Minister of Finance; the alignment of partners around a coherent development strategy; mutual accountability of Government

agencies and the development partners; transparency; and a system within Government (including local government) of managing for development results. This coordination mechanism also facilitates an agreed division of labor among the development partners, to reduce transaction costs and ensure engagement in line with comparative advantage. It has **resulted in greater focus by each development partner and continuity in their programs, and scale efficiencies**. To date, it involves largely official development partners and NGOs but the Government is now focusing on incorporating DFIs and the private sector. Doing so will broaden its reach. Convergence among all the development partners around core standards would also enhance development impact and sustainability.

Reconstruction platforms tend to be formed to address specific post-conflict or fragility needs. Two recent examples are: Ukraine reconstruction activity, in the immediate aftermath of the conflict, which was led by the EBRD and the EU with the involvement of the EIB and the IBRD/IFC as well as bilaterals and philanthropies; and the Jordan Response Plan for the Syrian crisis which brings together the main MDBs, bilaterals, UN agencies and NGOs.

Single sector platforms have been successful in bringing together projects for private sector financing alongside official financing. The Colombia 4G program and the associated DFI Financiera de Desarrollo Nacional (FDN) is a successful example, involving an investment program to create a nationwide toll road network through up to 40 different public private partnerships (PPPs) with mostly greenfield infrastructure projects. Indonesia's national slum upgrading program is also instructive (see Box 2). The Brazilian Private Sector Participation Facility, a joint effort of IDB, IFC and BNDES, is another platform designed to enhance private sector participation in infrastructure by helping to structure projects from technical and economic feasibility studies to financial closing. A program/platform for ports in Ukraine was just started by the EBRD and the IFC.

> **Box 2: Indonesia-National Slums Upgrading Program (NSUP)**
>
> The Government of Indonesia has taken a 'platform approach' to the financing of some of its major development programs. This has enabled the Government of Indonesia to bring together financing consortiums of MDBs as well as the government's own program budgets. An example of this approach is the "National Slums Upgrading Program (NSUP)," which is a nation-wide program to improve urban infrastructure and services for 29 million Indonesian slum residents living in 239 cities throughout the country. The NSUP included financing from four MDBs (IBRD, IsDB, AIIB and ADB) and from community and government sources. The World Bank took the lead role in preparing the project and coordinating the financing. Project implementation is being overseen by a common project management unit and the project is applying the same policies and safeguards to all investments financed under the project, regardless of the source. This is an example of how a platform approach can be country-

> driven, attract financing at scale, build government capacity, use a set of common standards and bring together all tiers of government. Early evidence also indicates that it has improved the quality of government expenditures in a critical area for sustainable and inclusive growth. While this approach exclusively involved the Government and the MDBs, it does illustrate some clear advantages of taking a platform approach to development financing.
>
> Source: World Bank staff and EPG secretariat.

Global/regional infrastructure platforms are relatively new initiatives and have embodied aspects of the platform approach for infrastructure finance globally.

◎ The Global Infrastructure Facility (GIF) is a partnership among governments, MDBs, private sector investors, and financiers to support governments in bringing well-prepared and structured projects to the market. It offers four services: infrastructure project prioritization, project preparation support, preparation of transaction documentation, and support through the process of financial closure.

◎ The AfDB is developing the Africa Investment Forum (AIF)–a multi-stakeholder, multi-disciplinary regional platform. The AIF is designed to screen and enhance projects, attract co-investors, reduce intermediation costs, improve the quality of project information and documentation, and increase active and productive engagements

between African governments and the private sector. The objective is to offer access to bankable, de-risked projects within an enabling environment.
- ◎ The Western Balkans Investment Framework (WBIF) is a multi-stakeholder, government-led coordination platform–including beneficiary governments, IFIs, 20 bilateral donors and the European Union (EU)–which supports the socio-economic development of the Western Balkans region.

Annex 2: Building a Large and Diversified Asset Class of Developing Country Infrastructure

There is large scope and a real need to mainstream infrastructure financing/investments into a recognized asset class to catalyze the participation of institutional investors. This can be achieved by developing simple, standardized instruments that allow investors to invest on a portfolio rather than an individual loan/entity basis. Thus far there have been promising but piecemeal efforts to structure investible products for private investment that lack the necessary scale. There are major possibilities for strong multipliers.

To achieve the scale of an asset class and meet vast development needs, **risk exposures have to be standardized and pooled from across the MDB system,** into securitization or fund structures that enable easier investor access. **Non-sovereign loans, infrastructure-related and others, would be a good group of assets with which to start.** In the MDB system alone there are US$200-300 billion of such loans, which offers a critical mass for institutional investors. Including an aggregation of commercial bank loans would lead to much larger asset class (see two paragraphs down).

Individual MDB loans and portfolios of loans can potentially be transferred via a clean sale to private investors, in other words a complete transfer of the loan exposure to the private investor. MDBs are best placed to manage country and construction risk during the early phase of an infrastructure project, and hence should "hold" the loan during this phase. This early phase also coincides with the period when the MDBs add the most value. **Upon completion of construction, the risk of the investment is reduced substantially and can be sold with the MDB retaining no interest in the investment.** Should private investors demand slightly higher returns than what the MDBs price into the loan, a step-up pricing feature can be considered, such that loans have lower pricing during the construction phase but which are subsequently raised at project completion to commercial rates.

Beyond the loans originated by MDBs and bilateral agencies, **the pool can be expanded to include commercial banks' infrastructure loans or debt issued by commercial banks.** This frees up balance sheet space or provides funding for commercial banks to extend new infrastructure loans. The growth of green bonds and green bond funds is another opportunity for MDBs and commercial banks to originate infrastructure loans that responds to the needs of institutional investors.

◎ An example is the IFC-Amundi Green Cornerstone Bond Fund, a US$2 billion initiative aimed at unlocking private funding for climate-related projects. The fund will invest in green bonds from emerging market financial institutions, which on-lend the funding to climate-related projects in emerging markets. Credit enhancement is provided via IFC investing in a junior tranche amounting to 6.25% of the total fund.

MDBs' sovereign loans could be potentially more challenging to pool and redistribute, compared to commercially-priced MDB non-sovereign loans and commercial banks loans. One challenge in pooling and redistributing sovereign loans to private investors is the wedge between MDB loan pricing and commercial loan pricing and the issue of preferred creditor status. While a clean sale of such sovereign loans would not involve a transfer of preferred creditor status, it may have to be done at lower than book value. This problem dissipates over time with better investor risk perception of developing countries and as implementation of the Proposals take effect. Sovereign loans can be pooled for investment at a later stage when commercial pricing and MDB pricing narrows.

In the course of the EPG's consultations, a large body of feedback was solicited on tapping private capital markets and creating an asset class. This feedback can be summarized in the following key considerations for building a successful asset class[1]:

◎ **Communicate clear commitment to build a credible asset class:** Investors will need certainty that the asset class being offered is part of a durable commitment by MDBs to engage with and support market development.

◎ **Standardize loan contracts and criteria:** Standardized loan documentation and disclosures would enable loans from across the MDB system to be packaged together more easily and help attract

---

[1] The feedback affirms a number of points highlighted in the *Roadmap to Infrastructure as an Asset Class* report by the G20 Infrastructure Working Group.

private investment. MDBs will also need to agree on a common underwriting framework for loans to be eligible for investment by private institutional investors, and also address investor expectations of 'permissible investments' and credit enhancements (e.g. guarantees, over-collateralization, liquidity facilities).

◎ **Build a broad database on loan performance:** For developing country infrastructure to become an established asset class, data on the underlying assets must be more readily accessible to build investors' comfort level and familiarity. Greater transparency[1] would also enable MDBs to engage regulators and credit rating agencies in a coordinated fashion, analyze the data to identify key risks that are preventing investments, and develop risk mitigation products to address these risks.

◎ **Start with a small pilot, then scale up:** For a start, two or three MDBs (partnering with private financial institutions) could be tasked to manage a pilot pooled program. Working with the MDBs, the investment community and credit rating agencies, the program manager(s) would decide on the investment vehicle structure, criteria for pooling assets, and the capital structure. In the longer term, pooling assets across institutions for greater diversification benefits should be considered.

---

[1] MDBs can contribute their data in an anonymized fashion to preserve borrower confidentiality.

Annex 3: Preparing for Pandemics and AMR-related Public Health Emergencies

Pandemics and public health emergencies are high-probability, high-risk events the prevention of which are severely underfunded. The annual global cost of pandemics is estimated at US$570 billion, or 0.7% of global GDP. Growing interconnectedness has increased the risk of national or regional events spreading globally quickly.

These threats require global as well as local and national responses to ensure early detection and adequate response facilities at the global level and within countries. This requires global financing that can be directed nimbly and swiftly, as well as stable funding to boost existing health systems in developing economies, especially those experiencing fragility. The nature of the desired response, of course, would depend on the pandemic, but would require global intervention to develop vaccines and treatments using primarily national delivery systems.

The current global architecture of readiness for public health emergencies has recently coalesced, but still is not fully fit for purpose. A succession of pandemics, most recently the outbreak of Ebola, and the specter of Antimicrobial Resistance (AMR) driving dangerous outbreaks have spurred efforts to organize the system and develop fit-for-purpose financing mechanisms (see Figure 1 for an outline of the actors involved):

- The bulwark of the system to protect against pandemics and AMR must be the **development of domestic health systems with the countries taking ownership.** The international community–MDBs, especially the World Bank, bilateral agencies, foundations, and the vertical funds–would need to provide financial and non-financial support.
- **WHO plays the role of guardian of the effort to control pandemics and AMR**, identifying global health emergencies and organizing the immediate response by other UN agencies, vertical funds, official agencies and foundations to provide medicines, other supplies and services.
- The **World Bank leads the effort to organize contingent finance** through insurance financed by bonds and derivatives, a cash window, and future commitments from donor countries for additional coverage.

Building this emerging structure into a durable and fully effective international response to global health emergencies will require strong action within countries and collaboration among countries, IFIs and the UN agencies with the WHO at the center. The first line of defense against global health emergencies is building country health systems with the support of MDB country programs integrated with funding from donors, foundations and the vertical funds. In support of WHO's role as first responders, the IFIs also must invest in data, knowledge and analysis for risk identification and mitigation to help countries build resilience and reform programs.

Recent efforts to establish the new pandemic financing vehicles have led to a viable framework, but the system remains vastly unfunded. There is a need to:

◎ **Scale-up the Pandemic Emergency Facility,** which has proven to be a cost-effective approach, as its resources are inadequate considering potential estimates of a full-scale emergency.
◎ **Enhance existing contingent resources to enable a rapid disbursement of grant resources** in response to a crisis either directly to countries impacted or to international first responders.

Figure 1:
Global Health Architecture: Structure and Relevant Agencies

WHO
Other UN Agencies
UNICEF
WFP

Capacity & Regulatory Support
ECDC
CDC

World Bank

Countries of operations

Research
CEPI
Pharmaceutical companies
Wellcome Trust

Funds & Foundations
Global Fund
Gavi
Gates Foundation

Official Agencies
RDBs
Bilaterals

ANNEXES

Annex 4: Illustrative Institutional Roles for Risk Identification

Note: The roles below reflect the comparative advantages of the IMF, FSB and BIS in the various dimensions of risk identification. They are purely illustrative and not intended to be confining.

	Credit Risk	Market and Liquidity Risk	Country Specific Risk (e.g. Emerging Market)	Macroeconomic Risks
Monetary Conditions	[IMF] Implications of loose/tight monetary policy	[IMF/BIS] Market interest rate deviations from interest rate parity	[IMF] Funding at risk: capital inflows [BIS] Inter-bank (cross-border) flows	[IMF] Adequacy of macro policies (e.g. overheating)
Regulatory Conditions, and Intermediation Environment	[FSB] Adequacy of prudential standards for credit (e.g. capital requirements) [BIS] Resilience of market infrastructure [FSB/BIS] Scope and impact of shadow banking	[FSB] Adequacy of capital and liquidity coverage ratios [BIS] Resilience of market infrastructure [FSB/BIS] Scope and impact of shadow banking	[FSB] Adequacy of buffers [BIS] Inter-bank (cross-border) flows	[IMF/FSB] Overall financial stability e.g. FSAP process

293

Continuation Table

	Credit Risk	Market and Liquidity Risk	Country Specific Risk (e.g. Emerging Market)	Macroeconomic Risks
Financial Conditions	[IMF] Macro-fin: credit cycle in line with economic developments; leverage [BIS] Inter-bank (cross-border) credit exposure	[IMF/BIS] Excess liquidity, willingness and capacity of banks to lend	[IMF] Funding at risk: capital outflows; debt sustainability [BIS] Inter-bank (cross-border) flows	[IMF/BIS] Overall financial stability
Risk Appetite	[IMF/BIS] Asset price developments and investor behavior	[IMF] Willingness of intermediaries to adjust portfolios	[IMF/FSB/BIS] Assessment of investor behavior (safe haven vs search for yield)	[IMF/FSB/BIS] Assessment of investor behavior (safe haven vs search for yield)

ANNEXES

Annex 5: Possible Options for IMF Funding in Large and Severe Global Crises

This Annex sketches out possible temporary mechanisms through which the IMF can rapidly access a significant amount of liquidity to ensure financial stability in the event of a global 'tail risk' event. However, a period of consensus building is needed to overcome the governance and policy challenges described below. The EPG is hence not proposing a solution for endorsement at this stage.

Option 1: On-lending of unused SDRs from member country savings

The IMF membership holds substantial SDRs with the IMF (i.e. positive balances), currently amounting to approximately US$150-200 billion. Positive balances could be activated for IMF program lending purposes during times of heightened stress. Interested surplus countries would temporarily lend SDRs to the IMF or a special purpose vehicle, administered by it, at an appropriate fee and incentive structure.[1] The additional firepower would correspond to around US$200 billion at maximum, possibly supporting programs in smaller to medium-sized

---

[1] Pricing policies could be designed to ensure: (i) interest by surplus countries; (ii) sustainable finances for the IMF (i.e. borrowing below on-lending rates); and (iii) incentive to restore the balances during normal times.

countries (or programs with strong RFA components which the IMF is partnering with). This option could be an additional line of defence and complemented with other options in case of a full-fledged tail risk scenario.

Option 2: Market borrowing by the IMF

Market borrowing, with or without using SDR allocations or existing SDRs as equity, could be operationalized through a cooperative arrangement between the IMF and members to leverage their reserve assets (or issue own SDRs) to constitute a special purpose vehicle that would then issue highly-rated securities on global capital market.[1] This has some parallels with the approach taken by the European Stability Mechanism (ESM)[2] to leverage the capital contributions from Eurozone countries through market borrowing. Applying an illustrative (conservative) leverage ratio of five times for the IMF–the current leverage ratio of the ESM is about six–would yield up to US$1 trillion additional resources from existing dormant SDR balances. Against this backdrop, the IMF's Articles of Agreement allow the IMF to borrow on the market.

Market borrowing by the Fund faces important governance challenges. First, in the case of SDRs being used as equity by a vehicle

---

[1] The proposed mechanism is an adaptation of IMF Staff Position Note 10/06.
[2] One important difference is that the equity for the ESM is provided by fiscal resources, and for the IMF from central bank reserves (including quota resources and SDR allocations).

ANNEXES

that borrows on the market, the preservation of the reserve asset status of the SDRs held by central banks will need to be addressed. Moreover, the regulatory and fiscal treatment of capital contributions by the membership will need to be examined to ascertain permissible use of allocations. An alternative to this mechanism would be for the IMF to use its balance sheet to access the market directly-as allowed by its Articles.[1]

Option 3: Replenishing NAB, and expanding it when needed

Coalitions of the willing have been mobilized in the past and while a repetition in the future is not guaranteed, experience has shown that countries are prepared to come together with additional resources, if needed, to overcome global challenges. There is merit in not phasing out existing arrangements and consider contingency plans for rapid expansions, which should include triggers depending on the severity of systemic crises.

---

[1] Article VIII, Section 1 of the Articles permits the IMF to borrow from private markets. As with other IMF borrowing, such a decision would be taken by the Board and no special majority is required. The consent of the member whose currency is being used in the borrowing operation would also be required.

Annex 6: Illustrative Agenda for the G20-led Group of Deputies

The G20-led Group of Deputies (Proposal 18) should endorse the **strategic directions and priorities for the MDBs as a system**. In the initial stages, the focus would also be on tracking the implementation of the proposed reforms to the system. The **key priorities would include**: (i) **strategic guidance on the risk appetite appropriate to MDBs' roles in achieving development impact;** (ii) ensuring stronger **system-wide collaboration**, including through country platforms which leverage on the strengths of all development partners, and convergence around core standards; and (iii) **tracking the shift in business models, and mobilization of private finance** through system-wide initiatives.

Decision-making and accountability will be enhanced by developing and refining a system of common metrics amongst MDBs for (i) the planning, monitoring and execution of projects; and (ii) sound risk management. It will require establishing common principles and indicators upon which **efficiency and effectiveness** of the MDBs should be assessed enabling:

◎ A better **measurement and tracking of key outcomes and results**, including **value for money**.
◎ Comparisons across the MDBs while taking into account their roles in different areas–including geography, knowledge creation as well

as over the project and development cycle.
◎ Establishing a common statistical base.

The **Group should endorse the core development standards** underpinning country platforms and leverage on the shareholders represented in the Group to promote convergence to those standards across MDBs and bilateral development finance agencies.

Risk management practices will have to develop significantly for MDBs to embrace the proposals in this Report. The Group should **establish a framework to be used by the individual MDBs to specify the risk appetite acceptable to shareholders and the development impact expected, and the trade-off between the two.** Implementing this common risk management framework will enable the MDBs to:

◎ Make decisions to take **higher risk for higher development return**, within an overall risk envelope.
◎ **Implement system-wide risk pooling and diversification**, including insurance, aimed at mobilizing much higher levels of private capital.
◎ **Collectively seek guidance from the Basel Committee** and engage credit rating agencies on capital and liquidity requirements, taking into account the MDBs' unique characteristics and default experience.

ABBREVIATIONS

ADB	Asian Development Bank
ADF	African Development Fund
AEs	Advanced Economies
AfDB	African Development Bank
AIF	Africa Investment Forum
AIIB	Asian Infrastructure Investment Bank
AMR	Antimicrobial resistance
AU	African Union
BIS	Bank for International Settlements
BMGF	Bill and Melinda Gates Foundation
BNDES	Brazilian National Bank for Economic and Social Development
BRAC	Building Resources Across Communities
BRICS CRA	BRICS Contingent Reserve Arrangement
BSAs	Bilateral Swap Arrangements
CDC	Center for Disease Control and Prevention
CEPI	Coalition for Epidemic Preparedness Innovations
CGFS	Committee on the Global Financial System
DC	Development Committee
DFIs	Development Financial Institutions
EBRD	European Bank for Reconstruction and Development

ECDC	European Center for Disease Prevention and Control
EIB	European Investment Bank
EMs	Emerging Markets
ESM	European Stability Mechanism
ESR	External Sector Report
ETFs	Exchange Traded Funds
EU	European Union
EWE	Early Warning Exercise
FDI	Foreign Direct Investment
FDN	Financiera de Desarrollo Nacional
FSAP	Financial Sector Assessment Program
FSB	Financial Stability Board
G20	Group of Twenty
GEMs	Global Emerging Markets Risk Database
GFC	Global Financial Crisis
GFSN	Global Financial Safety Net
GFSR	Global Financial Stability Report
GIF	Global Infrastructure Facility
HIPC	Heavily Indebted Poor Countries
IDB	Inter-American Development Bank
IAIS	International Association of Insurance Supervisors
IBRD	International Bank for Reconstruction and Development
IDA	International Development Association
IDFC	International Development Finance Club
IFAD	International Fund for Agricultural Development
IFC	International Finance Corporation

ABBREVIATIONS

IFFEd	International Finance Facility for Education
IFIs	International Financial Institutions
IMF	International Monetary Fund
IMFC	International Monetary and Financial Committee
IMFS	International Monetary and Financial System
IOSCO	International Organization of Securities Commissions
IsDB	Islamic Development Bank
JASPERS	Joint Assistance to Support Projects in European Regions
MDBs	Multilateral Development Banks
MIGA	Multilateral Investment Guarantee Agency
NAB	New Arrangements to Borrow
NDB	New Development Bank
NGOs	Non-Governmental Organizations
NSUP	Indonesia National Slums Upgrading Program
OECD	Organisation for Economic Co-operation and Development
PPPs	Public-Private Partnerships
R&D	Research and Development
RDBs	Regional Development Banks
RFAs	Regional Financing Arrangements
SCAV	Standing Committee on Assessment of Vulnerabilities
SDGs	Sustainable Development Goals
SDRs	Special Drawing Rights
SEWA	Self Employed Women's Association
TCFD	Task Force on Climate-related Financial Disclosures
UN	United Nations

UNICEF	United Nations Children's Emergency Fund
WBG	World Bank Group
WEO	World Economic Outlook
WFP	World Food Programme
WHO	World Health Organization

ABOUT THE G20 EMINENT PERSONS GROUP ON GLOBAL FINANCIAL GOVERNANCE

The Group was formally established by the G20 Finance Ministers and Central Bank Governors in April 2017. Its mandate was to recommend reforms to the global financial architecture and governance of the system of international financial institutions so as to promote economic stability and sustainable growth in a new global era; and to discuss how the G20 could better provide continued leadership and support for these goals. (See terms of reference.)

MEMBERS

Tharman Shanmugaratnam (Chair)-Deputy Prime Minister, Singapore; Chairman, Monetary Authority of Singapore; Chairman of the Group of Thirty; former Chairman of the International Monetary and Financial Committee; former Minister for Finance, Singapore

Sufian Ahmed-Advisor to the Prime Minister of Ethiopia; former Minister for Finance and Economic Development, Ethiopia; former Vice-Chair of the Intergovernmental Group of Twenty-Four on International Monetary Affairs and Development

Ali Babacan-Former Deputy Prime Minister for Economic and Financial Affairs; former Foreign Affairs Minister and former Treasury

Minister, Turkey

Marek Belka-Former Chairman of the Development Committee; former Prime Minister, Poland; former President of the National Bank of Poland

Jacob A. Frenkel-Chairman of JP Morgan Chase International; Chairman of the Board of Trustees of the Group of Thirty; former Governor of the Bank of Israel; former Chairman of the IDB; former Economic Counsellor and Director of Research of the IMF

Otmar Issing-President of the Center for Financial Studies, Goethe University; former member of the Executive Board and Chief Economist of the European Central Bank

Takatoshi Ito-Professor of International and Public Affairs at Columbia University; former Deputy Vice-Minister of Finance for International Affairs, Japan

Nora Lustig-Samuel Z. Stone Professor of Latin American Economics and Director of the Commitment to Equity Institute at Tulane University; President Emeritus of the Latin American and Caribbean Economic Association; former Senior Advisor on Poverty of the IDB

Ngozi Okonjo-Iweala-Chairperson of the Board of Gavi; former Coordinating Minister for the Economy and Minister for Finance, Nigeria; former Managing Director of the World Bank

Raghuram G. Rajan-Katherine Dusak Miller Distinguished Service Professor of Finance at Booth School of Business, University of Chicago; former Governor of the Reserve Bank of India; former Economic Counsellor and Director of Research of the IMF

ABOUT THE G20 EMINENT PERSONS GROUP ON GLOBAL FINANCIAL GOVERNANCE

Fabrizio Saccomanni-Chairman of the Board of Directors of UniCredit; former Minister for Economy and Finance, Italy; former Director General of the Bank of Italy

Lord Nicholas Stern-IG Patel Professor of Economics and Government at the London School of Economics and Political Science; former Chief Economist and Senior Vice-President of the World Bank; former Chief Economist of the EBRD

John B. Taylor-Mary and Robert Raymond Professor of Economics at Stanford University and George P. Shultz Senior Fellow at Stanford University's Hoover Institution; former Under Secretary of the Treasury, US

Jean-Claude Trichet-Chairman of the European Group of the Trilateral Commission; Chairman of the Board of the Bruegel Institute; former President of the European Central Bank

Andrés Velasco-Dean of the School of Public Policy at the London School of Economics and Political Science; former Sumitomo Professor of International Finance, Harvard Kennedy School; former Minister for Finance, Chile

Zhu Min-President of the National Institute of Financial Research at Tsinghua University; former Deputy Managing Director of the IMF

SECRETARIAT

Siddharth Tiwari (Executive Secretary)-Distinguished Visiting Fellow at Lee Kuan Yew School of Public Policy; former Director of the Strategy, Policy and Review Department of the IMF

Erik Berglöf-Director of the Institute of Global Affairs at the

London School of Economics and Political Science; former Chief Economist of the EBRD

David Marston-Former Chief Risk Officer of the IMF

R. Kyle Peters-Former Senior Vice-President of Operations of the World Bank

The Secretariat was ably assisted by Christina Kolerus, and received organizational support from the Monetary Authority of Singapore and the Lee Kuan Yew School of Public Policy.

TERMS OF REFERENCE
G20 EMINENT PERSONS GROUP ON GLOBAL FINANCIAL GOVERNANCE

- ◎ The G20 Eminent Persons Group on Global Financial Governance (the Group) was formally established by G20 Finance Ministers and Central Bank Governors on 21 April 2017.
- ◎ The Group comprises eminent persons with deep knowledge and experience in the area of the global financial architecture and governance.
- ◎ The Group will be chaired by Tharman Shanmugaratnam, Deputy Prime Minister of Singapore. Its members will contribute in their personal capacities. Collectively, their experiences reflect a broad diversity, geographically and of different stages of economic development.
- ◎ The work of the group will be centered around the following tasks:
    - ◆ to review current and possible future challenges and opportunities facing the international financial and monetary systems, and the current state of the global financial architecture and governance;
    - ◆ to consider, having regard to relevant past reviews, the optimal role of the international financial institutions (IFIs) comprising the IMF, the WBG, and other multilateral development banks, including how these IFIs interact and coordinate with one

another, with the G20, and with their respective memberships; their capacity to catalyze private capital flows and domestic resources; and corporate governance and accountability structures, to ensure efficiency, effectiveness and transparency in addressing the challenges identified;

◆ to recommend practical reforms to improve the functioning of the global financial architecture and governance so as to promote economic stability and sustainable growth; and to discuss how the G20 could better provide continued leadership and support for these goals.

◎ The Group's work will not duplicate existing efforts in the G20 and the IFIs related to Shareholding Reviews and the IMF General Review of Quotas.

◎ The Group will provide its findings and recommendations to G20 Finance Ministers and Central Bank Governors for their deliberation. Decisions on any proposals concerning the IFIs would have to be made by their respective governing bodies.

◎ The Group will provide an outline of its work to G20 Finance Ministers and Central Bank Governors at the IMF/WBG Annual Meetings 2017. A progress update will be provided by the IMF/WBG Spring Meetings 2018. The mandate of the Group will be fulfilled with the delivery of final recommendations by the time of the IMF/WBG Annual Meetings 2018.

LIST OF CONTRIBUTIONS

The Group received valuable feedback from national authorities from a broad range of developing and advanced countries.

The Group also benefited from consultations with the following institutions:
- African Development Bank
- Asian Development Bank
- Asian Infrastructure Investment Bank
- Bank for International Settlements
- European Bank for Reconstruction and Development
- European Investment Bank
- European Stability Mechanism
- Inter-American Development Bank
- International Development Finance Club
- International Monetary Fund
- Islamic Development Bank
- New Development Bank
- Organisation for Economic Cooperation and Development
- United Nations Development System
- World Bank Group

We are grateful for the views and written contributions from the following individuals with extensive experience as national and international policy-makers, thought leaders, and private sector and civil society leaders:

- Timothy Adams (Institute of International Finance)
- Montek Singh Ahluwalia
- Masood Ahmed (Center for Global Development)
- Marc Andreessen (Andreessen Horowitz)
- Susan Athey (Ripple)
- Abhijit Banerjee (Massachusetts Institute of Technology)
- Tim Besley (London School of Economics and Political Science)
- Amar Bhattacharya (Brookings Institution)
- Nancy Birdsall (Center for Global Development)
- Gordon Brown (UN Special Envoy for Global Education)
- Sharan Burrow (International Trade Union Confederation)
- Mike Callaghan (Australian Aged Care Financing Authority)
- Nikhil da Victoria Lobo (Swiss Re)
- Jacques de Larosière
- Thierry Déau (Meridiam Infrastructure)
- Rafael del Pino (Ferrovial)
- Victor Dzau (US National Academy of Medicine)
- Mohammed El-Erian (Allianz)
- Jeremy Farrar (Wellcome Trust)
- Daniel Gros (Centre for European Policy Studies)
- Jerome Haegeli (Swiss Re)
- Chris Heathcote (Global Infrastructure Hub)
- Yiping Huang (Beijing University)

LIST OF CONTRIBUTIONS

- Bimal Jalan
- Harold James (Princeton University)
- Donald Kaberuka (Special Envoy of the African Union for Sustainable Financing)
- Ravi Kanbur (Cornell University)
- Devesh Kapoor
- Takatoshi Kato
- Masahiro Kawai (University of Tokyo)
- Vijay Kelkar
- Homi Kharas (Brookings Institution)
- Caio Koch-Weser (European Climate Foundation)
- Horst Köhler
- Aleksei Kudrin (Saint Petersburg State University)
- Jean-Pierre Landau (Sciences Po)
- Nancy Lee (Center for Global Development)
- Jean Lemierre (BNP Paribas)
- Fei-Fei Li (Google)
- John Lipsky (Johns Hopkins University)
- Susan Lund (McKinsey Global Institute)
- Mark Machin (Canada Pension Plan Investment Board)
- Richard Manning (Oxford University)
- Pratap Bhanu Mehta (Ashoka University)
- Rakesh Mohan (Yale University)
- David Mulford (Hoover Institution)
- Xavier Musca (Amundi)
- Adebayo Ogunlesi (Global Infrastructure Partners)

- Guillermo Ortiz (BTG Pactual Casa de Bolsa Mexico)
- Henk Ovink (Dutch Special Envoy for International Water Affairs)
- Jean Pisani-Ferry (Sciences Po)
- Mark Plant (Center for Global Development)
- Annalisa Prizzon (Overseas Development Institute)
- Hélène Rey (London Business School)
- Mark Suzman (Gates Foundation)
- Adam Posen (Peterson Institute of International Economics)
- Bob Prince (Bridgewater Associates)
- Alex Rampell (Andreessen Horowitz)
- Michael Sabia (Caisse de Depot et Placement du Quebec)
- Stephen Schwarzman (Blackstone)
- Anish Shah (Mahindra Group)
- Lucy Shapiro (Stanford University School of Medicine)
- Naoyuki Shinohara (University of Tokyo)
- George Shultz (Hoover Institution)
- Arvind Subramanian (Harvard University)
- Shigemitsu Sugisaki (Goldman Sachs Japan)
- Davide Taliente (Oliver Wyman)
- Arvind Virmani
- David Wehner (Facebook)
- Mark Wiseman (BlackRock)

The Group also had valuable engagement with the following additional civil society representatives at a roundtable hosted by the Center for Global Development:

LIST OF CONTRIBUTIONS

- Motoko Aizawa (Institute for Human Rights and Business)
- Nancy Alexander (Heinrich Böll Foundation)
- Aron Betru (Milken Institute)
- Lindsay Coates (InterAction)
- Sara Harcourt (ONE)
- Andres Knobel (C20 International Financial Architecture)
- Paul O'Brien (Oxfam)
- Stephanie Segal (Centre for Strategic and International Studies)
- Elizabeth Summers (Bank Information Centre)
- Marc Uzan (Reinventing Bretton Woods Committee)
- Luiz Vieira (Bretton Woods Project)